John C. Calhoun - Opportunist

JOHN C. CALHOUN IN THE EYES OF HIS CONTEMPORARIES

JOHN QUINCY ADAMS (1820's)

"He is above all sectional and factious prejudices more than any other statesman of this Union with whom I have ever acted."

ANDREW JACKSON (1830's)

"What must a moral world or community think of a man so perversely prone to secret lying as John C. Calhoun is proven to be?"

BEVERLY TUCKER (1840's)

"How he might manage the affairs of a great nation I do not know, but he is certainly the most unskillful leader of a party that ever wielded a truncheon."

JAMES H. HAMMOND (1850's)

"Pre-eminent as he was intellectually above all the men of this age as I believe, he was so wanting in the managing of men, was so unyielding and unpersuasive, that he could never consolidate sufficient power to accomplish anything great, of himself and in due season ... and jealousy of him — his towering genius and uncompromising temper, has had much effect in preventing the South from uniting to resist evil."

JAMES PARTON (1860)

"I can not reconcile some of his important actions with the usual theory that he was a pure, but mistaken man. I can not resist the conclusion that it was a mania for the presidency (which has led so many promising spirits to their damnation) that inspired all his later efforts."

VARINA HOWELL (MRS. JEFFERSON) DAVIS (1890's)

"No dignity could be more supreme than Mr. Calhoun's. . . . He always appealed to me rather as a moral and mental abstraction than a politician, and it was impossible, knowing him well, to associate him with mere personal ambition. His theories and his sense of duty alone dominated him."

JOHN C. CALHOUN

"If I am judged by my acts, I trust I shall be found as firm a friend of the Union as any man in it. . . . If I shall have any place in the memory of posterity it will be in consequence of my deep attachment to it."

John C. Calhoun-Opportunist

A REAPPRAISAL

GERALD M. CAPERS

University of Florida Press
Gainesville - 1960

TO

RALPH HENRY GABRIEL

A University of Florida Press Book

Copyright 1960 by the Board of Commissioners
of State Institutions of Florida
Library of Congress Catalogue Card No. 60-15788
Printed by The Record Press, St. Augustine, Florida

ABOUT THE AUTHOR

Gerald M. Capers was educated at Southwestern College (A.B., 1930) and at Yale University (Ph.D., 1936). After teaching four years at Yale, he became head of the history department of Newcomb College, Tulane University, where he is now Professor of History. A frequent contributor to scholarly journals, Dr. Capers is the author of *Biography of a River Town: Memphis, Its Heroic Age*, and a biography of Stephen A. Douglas, as well as co-author of *Our Fair City*. He has also been the recipient of fellowships from the Guggenheim Foundation and the American Council of Learned Societies.

Preface

I HAVE CHOSEN to call this work a reappraisal to emphasize its intended limitations. The definitive biography of Calhoun would require a number of volumes on the history of the United States from 1800 to 1850, in which he took such a prominent part. Surely this is the main reason why for so long no adequate biography of the South Carolinian existed; in fact, until Charles M. Wiltse completed his three-volume study in 1950, no academic historian of note except Gaillard Hunt even attempted one. It is significant, however, that Frederick Jackson Turner at the time of his death was toying with the idea, his last work having convinced him of the importance of Calhoun's political tactics in the Age of Jackson.

My work on Calhoun has been in progress since 1940, but it was severely interrupted for three years by the war. The first draft was completed in 1948, before the publication of Margaret Coit's *John C. Calhoun: American Portrait* and when only the first of Wiltse's volumes had appeared. Normally, propriety would restrain me from commenting on these two biographies, but I think I should state my reasons for presenting another Calhoun study.

Wiltse's biography is most thorough, but it seems to me that its irrational bias in favor of Calhoun and the South more than offsets its value. To echo the judgment of the reviewer in the *Mississippi Valley Historical Review*: "All in all, as Arthur Schlesinger's *Jackson* votes for Franklin D. Roosevelt and the New Deal, so Wiltse's *Calhoun* votes, though much more quietly, for a coalition of the Dixiecrats and the American Liberty League." Miss Coit, a sympathetic biographer of the psychographic school, reveals at times an intuitive insight into Calhoun's personality, but she has manufactured far more color than the facts warrant. It is obvious that she has written down, often in disregard of historical fact and perspective, to the level of the readers of the *Ladies' Home Journal* — a

v

magazine which she cites as a source. In general I would say, since new books on Jackson and Clay continue to appear, that there is ample room for another interpretation of their great Carolina rival.

Calhoun is by far the most difficult subject of the three. Because of the complexity of his personality as well as of his ideas, and because he so long ago became the symbol of the Lost Cause, he has rarely been approached as a human being. This I have attempted to do, since I believe, like Miss Coit, that the biographer's primary function is to explain what makes his subject "tick." Yet no man can be removed from his own historical environment, which in Calhoun's case is about as involved as his personality. The "Cast-Iron Man" did not understand himself, nor was he generally understood by his contemporaries. I am quite conscious of the hypothetical nature of my interpretation; for that reason I have let him speak for himself as much as possible so that the reader will have a basis for his own conclusions.

The first draft of my manuscript was carefully read by my former colleague Wendell Stephenson, and I am another member of the host of authors who are under obligation to him for his able editorial criticism. In deference to the canons I have included notes, but I have attempted my own procedural compromise. Citations are printed at the end of the book; but notes of an explanatory nature and those particularly relevant to the text are inserted at the bottom of the pertinent pages. For the sake of the general reader certain events well known to mature students of American history are thus briefly summarized. I assure the latter that no affront to their knowledge is intended.

Contents

Contents

CHAPTER ONE

A Backwoods Farmer Goes to Yale

PROBABLY the single point of agreement between Timothy Dwight, President of Yale, and Thomas Jefferson, President of the United States, was that the election of the Virginian as President in 1800 constituted a "revolution." Firm believer in the aristocratic principles of the Federalist party, Dwight had fought throughout the last decade of the eighteenth century to prevent the triumph in the United States of the obnoxious Republicans, whose ideology in his eyes would produce a replica of the anarchy in which the French Jacobins were striving to engulf Europe. Jefferson's election, he was convinced, was a victory for atheism over religion and portended the inevitable destruction of contemporary American society. Despite the fact that none of Dwight's dire predictions came to pass during Jefferson's two administrations, the Yale president continued in the classroom to preach high Federalism and to attack the vicious doctrine of the sovereignty of the people.

Upon one such occasion in 1804 a tall senior from the Carolina back country, John Caldwell Calhoun, boldly defended the odious principle of popular sovereignty. A heated discussion followed between professor and student, and though neither retreated from his position, the doctor had the last word. "Young man," said Dwight, "your talents are of a high order and might justify you for any station, but I deeply regret that you do not love sound principles better than sophistry — you seem to possess a most unfortunate bias for error."*

Forty years later, long after both Dwight and Federalism were dead and the sovereignty of the people was canonized into the national political philosophy, the former Yale senior held high hopes of receiving the Democratic nomination for President. For twenty years Calhoun had been on the verge of being nominated and now it seemed success was in his grasp. But once again blocking his path was his old rival, former President Martin Van Buren, who twelve years before had displaced him in the affections of Andrew Jackson and the party.

To encourage the Carolinian's nomination, there appeared in 1843 an anonymous but highly eulogistic biography of him which, it was revealed after his death, was largely his own composition and in essence a political autobiography.† Its purpose was not merely to convince the nation that Calhoun's course in his previous thirty-five years of public life had in every instance been motivated by a pure and high-minded statesmanship, but also to portray him as the conspicuous and consistent champion of democracy and the rights of the people. At a time when the Whigs had at last captured the presidency by the simple device of putting forward as their candidate the old Indian fighter General William Henry Harrison — who supposedly was born in a log cabin and drank hard cider — such an appeal for the vote of the common man was a political essential.

Consequently in the autobiography the Dwight incident was cleverly retouched to make Calhoun appear the democratic knight in shining armor: "The doctor was an ardent Federalist, and Mr. Calhoun was one of the very few, in a class of more than seventy, who had the firmness to avow and maintain the opinions of the Republican Party, and, among others, that the people were the only legitimate source of political power. Dr. Dwight entertained a different opinion.... A discussion ensued between them, which exhausted the time allotted for the recitation, and in which the pupil

*This account appeared in a newspaper clipping enclosed in a letter from J. L. Petigru to H. S. Legaré, Dec. 17, 1836. It is so much closer to what Dwight might have been expected to say in 1804 that in my opinion the version in the autobiography (quoted below) is obviously an interpolation designed to suggest that Calhoun's fitness for the presidency was recognized by a prominent opponent even in his college days.

†For a detailed discussion of this point see the Appendix.

maintained his opinions with such vigor of argument and success as to elicit from his distinguished teacher the declaration, in speaking of him to a friend, that 'the young man had talent enough to be President of the United States,' which he accompanied by a prediction that he would one day attain that station."[1]

*   *   *

While the French and the English were fighting on three continents in the mid-eighteenth century for the mastery of the colonial world, the Cherokees in February, 1760, attacked the little settlement of Long Canes in the Carolina piedmont, just as its inhabitants were preparing to retreat for safety to Augusta, Georgia. According to the *South Carolina Gazette*, Patrick Calhoun, a survivor who had brought the news to Charleston, "had since been at the Place where the Action happened, in order to bury the Dead, and found only 20 of their Bodies, most inhumanly butchered.... He believes all the fighting men would return and fortify the Long Canes settlement, were part of the Rangers so stationed as to give them some Assistance and Protection."[2]

Pat Calhoun, Scots-Irishman, had arrived as a lad in America more than thirty years before in company with his parents, uncles, and brothers. His story was the typical saga of the frontier. Soon the little immigrant group moved to western Pennsylvania, where Patrick began his long fight with the Indians. Then the pioneer family retreated to southwestern Virginia, whence Braddock's defeat forced them farther south to Long Canes Creek in the northwestern corner of South Carolina. Four years later, when the French and Indian War followed them to the southern frontier, another retreat became necessary. But this time the Calhouns were too slow, and in the Long Canes massacre Patrick's mother, his uncle, and two of his nieces were lost. Until the Cherokees were finally subdued in 1764, the son took his vengeance upon them as an officer in a local company of "Rangers." Of Scots-Irish ancestry and exposed for half a century to all the dangers of the American wilderness, Patrick became, like most of those who survived, a stout, two-fisted backwoodsman.[3]

But peace came not to Long Canes with the passing of the Indian menace. Anarchy arose as settlement increased. The nearest court was over two hundred miles away in Charleston, and the planter-controlled legislature turned a deaf ear to all upcountry petitions for judges, representation, or even the right of suffrage. Thereupon the Long Canes men resorted to an often-to-be-repeated frontier device: they set up their own government, the "Regulation," based not upon legality but upon necessity and natural rights. When those who felt the heavy hand of the Regulation fought back, the governor arrested its leaders to avoid the bloodshed which threatened. But the legislature in 1769 established the demanded formal government by organizing the District of Ninety-Six, including Long Canes.

A brief interlude of quiet so begun ended with the outbreak of the Revolution. Regulators became Whigs and their opponents Tories. The various nationalities of Carolina upcountry settlers magnified enmities of long standing and civil war began. After Charleston fell in 1780, the British occupied Ninety-Six. Nathaniel Greene's counterattack failed to dislodge them, and when the American Colonies finally forced England to recognize their independence, the district contained fourteen hundred war widows and orphans. Hardly had the community begun to enjoy the fruits of victory when a final enemy appeared and conquered. The lowcountry "Federalist" planters, whom it hated as it had hated Indian and Tory, fastened upon the piedmont the shackles of the federal constitution of 1787.

Patrick Calhoun, leader of men that he was, took part in each of these great events. He served in both provincial congresses in South Carolina at the beginning of the Revolution, and then returned to Long Canes for the duration of the war to defend his home against Tories, Indians, and British. He opposed the adoption of the Constitution because "it permitted people other than those of South Carolina to tax the people of South Carolina, and thus allowed taxation without representation, which was a violation of the fundamental principle of the revolutionary struggle." In his political philosophy he echoed Jefferson. His son recalled that he "maintained that government to be best which allowed the largest amount of individual liberty compatible with social order and tranquility, and insisted that the improvements in political science would be found to consist in throwing off many restraints then imposed by law, and deemed necessary to organized society."[4]

Calhoun could fight not only with fist and gun, but with words, a talent fully recognized by his neighbors. In 1769 he became, by election from Prince William Parish, the first upcountry representative in the South Carolina Assembly, and in that capacity he continued to serve until his death three decades later. As a man of affluence, he was appointed justice of the peace and later judge of the Abbeville county court. Just prior to his death he was elevated to the state senate in recognition of his long and active career of public service.

When the Calhouns settled at Long Canes in 1756, it numbered only twenty inhabitants. Only recently ceded by the Cherokees, the region was so wild that buffalo were still plentiful. Despite vicissitudes, the settlement grew rapidly by migration from both the back country to the north and the Carolina seaboard. With its growth the fortunes of Patrick kept pace. Trusting the Scriptures as he trusted the might of his good right arm, he took literally the biblical command to become fruitful and multiply. He was a surveyor by profession, and he made six purchases of land between 1763 and 1768. By 1790 he owned thirty-one slaves; only three residents of the South Carolina piedmont owned more. Before the outbreak of the Revolution he married his second or perhaps his third wife, Martha Caldwell, who bore him four sons and a daughter. He built the first frame house in his neighborhood, an eight-room, two-story affair. A rich man for his region, he was commonly addressed as "Mister" or "Esquire" in a day when those titles implied high social position. Evidently he held on to his property as well as he did to his scalp.

"He was a friend to virtue and piety," read the obituary of this patriarch of Long Canes in a Charleston newspaper, "and a foe to vice in every form."[5] Such a trite and colorless characterization did injustice to Patrick Calhoun. It should rather have been recalled that he had led his neighbors, armed with rifles, down to within twenty-three miles of Charleston to exercise a right of suffrage; that he appeared in a Virginia court as his own attorney to recover a tract of land in litigation; that in a fight with an Indian chief he had drawn his opponent's fire by holding his hat up on a stick and, when the red man's ammunition was exhausted, had shot him; that in a discussion in the legislature on a bill to offer a reward for wolf pelts, he had remarked he would much rather "gie a poond for a lawyer's scalp."

It was the irony of fate that a large portion of Patrick's estate was spent after his death to train his third son, John Caldwell, for the legal profession.

*   *   *

John C. Calhoun

John Caldwell Calhoun was born at Abbeville (Long Canes) on March 17, 1782. Since he was almost fourteen when his father died, he was undoubtedly influenced by Patrick's character and opinions. Indeed, though John was different in temperament from his two-fisted sire, their ultimate views upon government were identical — their *summum bonum* was the largest amount of individual liberty possible under the restrictions necessary to ensure social order.

The comfortable means of the family could not offset a certain cultural poverty inevitable in a backwoods community. Of formal schooling there was little, but Martha Calhoun, a strong-minded woman, taught her offspring the rudiments of the three *R*'s and much more of life. Possibly because he gave evidence of precocity, his parents sent John in the winter of 1795 to the nearby school of his brother-in-law, the Reverend Moses Waddel, in Appling, Georgia. Hardly had the lad begun his studies when both his father and Mrs. Waddel died, and the school was discontinued. But he remained in Appling, and since Waddel was absent most of the time attending to his ecclesiastical duties, the boy was left for fourteen weeks almost entirely alone.

In his house Waddel had a small circulating library, austere in selection as would be expected of a Presbyterian divine. Books being a rarity in the upcountry, the lonely lad, in the absence of normal distractions, attacked them with adolescent enthusiasm. History particularly appealed to him, he stated in the autobiography, so he consumed "Rollins' *Ancient History*, Robertson's *Charles V*, his *South America*, and Voltaire's *Charles XII*. After dispatching these, he turned with like eagerness to Cook's *Voyages* (the large edition), a small volume of Essays by Brown and Locke on the *Understanding*, which he read as far as the chapter on Infinity."[6] Such assiduity undermined his health. He lost weight, his eyes became affected, and when his mother learned of his condition she promptly summoned him home.

For the next five years John assisted his mother in the management of their farm. As his two older brothers had gone into business, one in Augusta and the other in Charleston, he became the male head of the house and naturally assumed more and more domestic responsibilities. In view of its size and its large number of slaves, the Calhoun estate might well be considered a plantation. Such an experience, under the tutelage of a frugal and efficient mother, produced in the youngster an early maturity in worldly wisdom. The more specialized organization of the tidewater plantations had not penetrated the piedmont area, which as yet was unfettered by a rigid social hierarchy. On his plantation-farm the upcountry owner was his own overseer and often worked behind the plow with his slaves. "We worked in the field," said Sawney, Calhoun's Negro and boyhood hunting companion, "and many's the times in the brilin' sun me and Marse John has plowed together."[7]

During these years John spent much time in hunting, fishing, and other country sports, which bred in him a love of the land that he always retained. The neighborliness of rural life must have developed in him, in spite of his reticence, a sociability and an interest in people. The strenuous exercise of work and recreation gave him a sturdy physique which was to stand him in good stead in the busy years ahead. Probably his brilliance was recognized by his fellows, as well as the capacity for leadership which he, like his father before him, possessed to a high degree.* Otherwise, in view of his four years' absence in New England, he would hardly have been later elected by his piedmont neighbors to public office.

Doubtless it was at this time that he became aware of his superior ability, and the good opinion of his community could not fail to please a young man of eighteen and to stir his ambition. He must also have realized the conspicuous lack of intellectual stimulus in his environment, a serious consideration to one of his avid intelligence. Books were few at Abbeville, and any chance copy of a newspaper was treasured — there is still preserved a copy of the *South Carolina Gazette* for May 10, 1798, worn by much handling and copiously pencil-marked by young Calhoun. More immediate matters than these, however, determined his plans for his future. He had a farm and a mother to care for, and he lacked the funds necessary for the professional training which at times he may have secretly desired. Without serious regrets and making a virtue of necessity, he settled upon the career of a planter, since so many aspects of the bucolic life attracted him.

Quite naturally the young farmer acquired many of the conventional beliefs and prejudices of his community. Reared as he was

---

*Starke states that according to Calhoun's brother-in-law James Edward Calhoun, "by and by a feeling manifested itself among the people in remarks that John C. Calhoun ought to be educated."

in a strict Presbyterian home where the Bible was accepted literally, his character always bore the dent of this early evangelical influence. Though in later years he became a deist who refused to join any particular sect, he never succeeded in throwing off his backwoods puritanism in his attitude towards human conduct. He devoutly believed in work and duty; a South Carolina gentleman and a politician, he never drank, gambled, or joked. Throughout his life he lacked a "sense of the ludicrous," as an ardent admirer observed. Charleston he regarded in his young manhood as a debauched Babylon, a place "which in everything was so extremely corrupt." The theater seemed to him so indecent that shortly after his marriage he refused to accompany his bride and a group of friends to a Charleston performance.[8]

Stirred by the momentous events of the Napoleonic era in Europe and America, he developed a strong antipathy for the English and for tidewater Federalists, as did his upcountry neighbors at Abbeville. He heartily espoused the agricultural imperialism of the Republican party, which pointed to Florida and Louisiana. Four years of schooling in the East were only to intensify these views. His spirited advocacy of this popular cause was to elevate him in less than a decade of public life to the state legislature, Congress, and the cabinet.

*　　　　*　　　　*

The series of events which were to set him on the road to an unforeseen destiny began for Calhoun in the very year in which Jefferson unhorsed the Federalists and became President of the United States. In that year James Calhoun returned from distant Charleston to spend the summer in Abbeville, and at once he began strongly to urge his younger brother to acquire a good education and to pursue one of the learned professions. John replied that he was "not averse to the course advised," but that obtaining the consent of his mother and his lack of the necessary financial means were serious obstacles. "His property was small and his resolution fixed: he would rather be a planter than a half-informed physician or lawyer."

Then, with the relentless logic which would characterize many of his later actions, he made his brother a bold and by no means unselfish proposition. If James "could so manage his property as to keep him in funds for seven years of study preparatory to entering his profession" and if their mother should freely consent to the arrangement, he was ready to begin his education the next week. Accordingly William, the oldest brother, was summoned from Augusta, a family conference was held, and the extreme terms of John Caldwell were accepted.[9]

Immediately he entered, for the second time in his life, the academy of his brother-in-law, Moses Waddel, who had married again and had resumed teaching in Georgia. Later moved to Willington in Abbeville County, South Carolina, Waddel's school became famous throughout the South as the Willington Academy, including among its graduates such leaders as Hugh S. Legaré, James L. Petigru, William H. Crawford, Augustus B. Longstreet, and George McDuffie. Life at the academy was patterned somewhat after that of the Spartan barracks. Students lived in log cabins and subsisted on the simple diet of cornbread and bacon; rose at dawn to the sound of a horn and began the day with group prayer; read at night by the light of pine torches and studied in the forest except in severe weather. The curriculum was as plain as the two-room log schoolhouse where students, because of the lack of chairs, had to recite standing. It consisted of Latin, mathematics, moral philosophy, and drill in rhetoric at the weekly debating club. So thorough was this training that within two years Calhoun was qualified to enter the junior class at Yale.

A farmer of twenty from the backwoods, even one sophisticated enough to select an eastern school for purposes of professional training and social prestige and possessed of sufficient intelligence to enter the junior class in college after two years of formal schooling,* might be expected to experience inevitable handicaps. Not so Calhoun; on the contrary his career, according to his own account, resembled that of a Horatio Alger hero. Upon being asked years later by Colonel W. Pinkney Starke as to when he first became aware of his superiority to ordinary men, he replied with more honesty than modesty: "I went to Yale College fresh from the backwoods. My opportunities for learning had been very limited. I had a high opinion of the New England system of education.

---

*Calhoun's training had actually been more thorough than that of most of his classmates, many of whom lacked formal schooling and had instead been tutored by the local minister. In view of this advantage, there was nothing unusual in his entering as an upperclassman, nor was he older than the average of the group.

My first recitation was in mathematics, and we had been told to fetch our slates into the classroom. On taking our seats the professor proceeded to propound certain arithmetical questions to us. I found no difficulty in working out the first, and on looking about me was surprised to find the others busy with their slates. The professor, noticing my movement, asked me if I had got the answer and I handed him my slate. The answer proved to be correct. The same thing occurred every time. On returning to my apartment I felt gratified."[10]

In a New England incensed by the recent victory of the "atheist" Jefferson and driven by his purchase of Louisiana to serious contemplation of forming a separate northern confederacy, an ardent Republican from the piedmont was regarded somewhat as were the carpetbaggers of the 1860's in the South — particularly in that orthodox *sanctum sanctorum* of Timothy Dwight, Yale College. Despite this hostility, according to his own account Calhoun gained greater distinction from the expression of his political philosophy than from his earlier display of mathematical knowledge. While at Yale he was elected to Phi Beta Kappa.

*   *   *

These years in New Haven revealed and developed the two qualities of Calhoun's personality which were to drive him on incessantly for half a century — genius and ambition. Only an individual possessing intelligence and industry of the highest order, as well as a mighty will and a rare fixity of purpose, could so lift himself by his bootstraps. A country boy begins school at nineteen, forces his middle-class family to give him the best education possible, decides to attend a distant eastern college, and after four years of schooling graduates with distinction in a selected group of the nation's youth. Is it any wonder that such rapidity and degree of success produced in him an overweening self-confidence which he never lost? Irresistible logic and earnest, unswerving industry served him so well here at the outset of his career that he never sought other weapons. Upon them alone he afterwards relied, both in speaking and writing, rather than upon grace of style or appeal to human foibles; in this he was the antithesis of his future rivals, Clay and Webster. He sought to overpower all obstacles by the sheer force of cold, impelling reason.

The ambition and natural egoism which accompany genius were

conspicuous in him at this time and later. Indeed they were evident in his determination not to be a half-baked lawyer or doctor, in his desire for the best education possible in the nation, in his choice of New England schools. The sweet plaudits he won in college and his own realization of what he had accomplished spurred him on to greater things. On the other hand, the emotions of a sensitive young man moving from the world of Abbeville to the world of Yale should not be forgotten. His Carolina confreres at New Haven were sons of wealthy tidewater grandees, probably not always cordial to an upcountry farmer; and Federalist gentlemen of New England may have been inclined occasionally to sneer at or to patronize a backwoods Republican grind. Certainly, because of the bitterness of political feeling, he mingled little in society later at Litchfield, and this was probably also true at Yale.

At any rate it will become evident that his endeavors in the years immediately following graduation were directed as much towards social position, perhaps unconsciously so, as towards professional distinction. He may already have been aware of the relation of both to politics as a career, for he told his fellows that he studied so hard "in order that he might acquit himself creditably when he should become a member of Congress." He had no doubt, he added, as to his "ability to reach Congress within three years."[11]

Once again fate smiled on him. A serious illness prevented his delivering an oration at the graduation exercises in 1804 on the "Qualifications Necessary to Constitute a Perfect Statesman," but it brought him an invitation from Mrs. Floride Calhoun, Carolina low-country heiress and widow of his first cousin, the late Senator John Ewing Colhoun (*sic*),* to convalesce at her summer place in Newport.[12] He did so, and her ensuing role as patroness, confidante, and finally mother-in-law to her country cousin was to prove vital to his destiny.

*Sometime after her husband's death, Mrs. Calhoun apparently changed her name from Colhoun to Calhoun. Since both mother and daughter had the same name, even before Calhoun married the latter, the mother is referred to in this work as "Mrs. Calhoun" and the daughter as "Floride."

CHAPTER TWO

John C. Calhoun Becomes a Gentleman

NEWPORT is quite a pleasant place," wrote Calhoun to his cousin Alexander Noble, "but it has rather an old appearance which gives it a somewhat melancholy aspect. I have found no part of New England more agreeable than the island of Rhode Island.... But as to the civil situation of this State and its manners, customs, moral and religious character, it seems much inferior, so far as my information extends, to every other part of New England."[1]

Despite its moral drawbacks, Newport in the company of rich relatives has often been attractive to Yale men and to South Carolinians. Mrs. Calhoun seemed captivated by her newly discovered cousin, whom she had not found time to meet until he had graduated from a prominent eastern college. She insisted that he accompany her and her three small children on a week's visit to Boston and later on their return by sea to Charleston. No young man of twenty-three, however serious-minded, could remain unimpressed by such acceptance for the first time in his life by the social elite, and the visit was the beginning of a warm and intimate friendship between John and his hostess.*

Arriving in Charleston in November, he spent the winter reading Blackstone in the office of William Henry De Saussure, Mrs.

---

*Assuming that Mrs. Calhoun was sixteen when she married John Ewing Calhoun in 1786, she was only twelve years older than her future son-in-law.

Calhoun's attorney and a future chancellor of South Carolina.[2] The tutelage of this leading lawyer of the state, which gave Calhoun inestimable prestige and assured his success in legal practice, was obviously due to the influence of Mrs. Calhoun. Undoubtedly it was planned by them in advance. On his journey north the following year Calhoun stopped at Princeton to see De Saussure's son and wrote the judge full details as to the youngster's progress in college.[3]

Calhoun's mother had died while he was at Yale, and apparently his brother James was managing the family estate. Following the custom of Yale men, as many ambitious, well-to-do Carolinians were to do later, he decided to continue his professional studies at the Litchfield Law School in Connecticut. Consequently in the spring of 1805 the little village of Abbeville, where the young lawyer had returned for a visit, was honored by the arrival of Mrs. Calhoun's coach, drawn by four gray horses and driven by an English coachman in full livery, to carry its illustrious son to Newport in style.

According to legend, John persuaded Mrs. Calhoun on this trip to make a detour by Charlottesville, Virginia, where President Jefferson was then enjoying a brief visit at his home. Calhoun called on the President who insisted that he stay overnight, and it was rumored that the conversation between them lasted until midnight. The following day Mr. Jefferson, in conversing with the widow, gratified her greatly by his complimentary remarks about her protégé. The story is probably spurious, since it is likely that Jefferson was in Washington at the time, but it is typical of the numerous apocryphal anecdotes which sprang up later about Calhoun's early career.*

After a brief stay in Newport, Calhoun reached Litchfield in the latter part of July, 1805. Here for more than a year he applied himself to an assiduous study of law. His residence in this little town in the hills of western Connecticut, the birthplace of Harriet Beecher Stowe, contributed to his dislike for Federalism and for

---

*The incident illustrates the difficulty in separating fact from fancy as to the early life of a famous man. Starke uncritically accepts the story, told by Calhoun's brother-in-law James who at the time was seven years old, at face value. Wiltse rejects it, however, on the basis of seemingly valid evidence and certainly of logic. Miss Coit, with her penchant for anything that smacks of the sensational and colorful, argues somewhat unconvincingly for its authenticity, and makes much of it.

his chosen profession, but it proved an ideal place for concentration upon "the dry and solitary journey through the exterior fields of law." That it was the home of Miss Sarah Pierce's famous Young Ladies' Seminary is not mentioned in any of his letters, and the only pleasure of the flesh in which Calhoun seems to have indulged was sleighing. His single friend was his roommate and fellow Carolinian, John M. Felder, with whom he had graduated from Yale.[4]

"I take little amusement," he gloomily wrote Mrs. Calhoun, "and live a very studious life. This place is so much agitated by party feelings, that both Mr. Felder and myself find it prudent to form few connections in town.... This is rather a solitary place; and, unless, it is now and then a southerner from college, we rarely see anyone from our end of the Union.... We both console ourselves, that in a few years we shall acquire a pretty thorough knowledge of our profession; and then our time shall be more at our own disposals. Perhaps this is but a pleasant dream; as every succeeding year comes loaded with its own peculiar cares and business."[5] Little wonder that he sought escape from his loneliness in communion by letter with Mrs. Calhoun, and that at the end of his exile he fell in love with her daughter. In a few years he deserted law, associated as it was with the unpleasant year at Litchfield, for the more congenial life of a southern planter.

*   *   *

The Litchfield Law School, one of a very few in the nation at the time, consisted of one small building, two instructors, and about forty students. It conferred a diploma upon candidates after the satisfactory completion of fourteen to eighteen months' work, and its high reputation resulted from the ability of its faculty — Judge Tapping Reeve and his assistant, James Gould. Students attended lectures, studied cases from English reports, and held moot courts once a week. The major emphasis of the curriculum was upon Blackstone and the common law, but the chief benefit derived came rather from training in moot court sessions and exposure to Gould's method of lucid analysis. It was here that Calhoun developed the art of extemporaneous speaking,[6] later so useful to him in Congress, and it may have been from Gould that he acquired the logical method which was to make him cogent in debate.

Reeve at this time was a staunch advocate of the secession of New England, and Gould, son-in-law of Uriah Tracy, another prominent New England irreconcilable, probably concurred in this view. Such a conviction was bound to have colored their teaching of constitutional law and American government. This open disunion sentiment in high places, from Dwight of Yale and Reeve of Litchfield, must have whetted Calhoun's already ardent Republicanism, smarting as he was from the social ostracism forced upon him in New Haven and Litchfield. Certainly it made him apprehensive of the future of the republic.

He had been struck, he wrote years later, with "the working of the odious party machinery" of the caucus system in New England at this time, and was convinced that "in the end it would supersede the authority of law and the Constitution."[7] As much as any other factor, his emotional reaction to these conditions in Connecticut from 1802 to 1806 made him the strong nationalist which he was soon to prove himself in Congress and in Monroe's cabinet. Though a generation later he was to advocate nullification himself, the state-rights doctrine of Reeve was repugnant to him in 1805 and for the next twenty years. Exposure to the doctrine could, however, have made an impression which would influence his more mature view.

Frustrated socially and intellectually as he was in this environment, disliking as he did New England, Yale, Litchfield, and his teachers, it was only natural that he should develop an antipathy for law — though with Scots-Irish stubborness he persisted in the course he had started. "You do me an injustice," he wrote his friend Andrew Pickens, "in supposing your letters intrude on my studious disposition; I am not so much in love with law as to feel indifferent to my friends. Many things I study for the love of study, but not so with law. I can never consider it but as a task which my situation forces on me. I therefore, often lay it aside for the more delicious theme of the muses, or interesting pages of history; and always throw it away with joy to hear from my Carolina correspondents. But, I confess, from my aversion to law, I draw a motive to industry. It must be done, and the sooner the better is often my logic."[8]

There was a deeper reason for this dislike, however, than mere dissatisfaction with his environment. Gould taught his students that Blackstone and the common law were the perfection of human reason. Such scholasticism failed to stimulate the inquiring mind of Calhoun. What challenged his hungry intelligence was not rules for litigation over property rights, but the great experiment of the United States in government unfolding before his eyes. He was a student of society, of *contemporary* society; the past interested him only to the extent that it explained the present and the future. Moreover, his interest was not detached. Ambition, intelligence, and emotion — as events were to prove — all impelled him towards participation in the government as a leader rather than towards the passive observation of the scholar.

In his letters from Litchfield, therefore, the only references to law were disparaging. In the politics of Europe and particularly of South Carolina, however, he seemed quite absorbed, and apparently he carried on considerable correspondence with friends in his native state with the purpose of keeping in touch with developments there in his absence. "It is high time," he wrote in regard to some unidentifiable conflict between Carolina factions, "for those selfish usurpers on publick opinion to be painted in their true light. For my part, I never could think with complacency of some upstarts in that part of the State.... They have had their day; [the eyes] of the people will be opened."[9]

*　　　　*　　　　*

The mutual affection that sprang up in this period of his life between Calhoun and his widowed cousin — which was shortly to result in his attainment of financial competence and his admission into Carolina tidewater society — cannot be lightly dismissed as mere accident or the natural result of his loneliness in New England. No young man just graduated from college, even the more dull-witted, needs to be convinced of the relation between proper social connections and personal success. Ambitious as he was, denied social recognition both in Carolina society and in college, old for his years in knowledge of the ways of men, and determined upon success, Calhoun could hardly have failed to realize the potentialities of the patronage of the low-country heiress.

It need not be inferred that his regard for her was forced, nor that he at once in Machiavellian fashion planned to marry her twelve-year-old daughter for her social position. Yet it is perfectly obvious, both from his letters and from convincing circumstantial evidence, that he ardently cultivated a rich woman older than himself and far beneath him in intelligence. She was his cousin and he was indebted to her; he was fond of her and such an association had definite advantages; the role of benefactress and the affection of a brilliant young man gratified her ego. It was not the first time and by no means the last that Calhoun would use his friends. Such conduct was quite in keeping with his character. He had maneuvered his family into providing him with the best education, unhesitatingly accepting the sacrifice it entailed on their part. From the beginning he had carefully planned and industriously executed the steps which led to the goal he had set for himself. Family legend has it that he was romantically attached to Mrs. Calhoun; if so, it is understandable that a young man of twenty, starved for affection, might so regard a widowed relative older than himself, but not too old.

The intimacy between them was well established when he entered Litchfield, as might be expected from his long visit in Newport the previous autumn, their journey south together by boat, and the return trip in the Calhoun coach to Newport in the summer of 1805. In his many letters from law school he was increasingly solicitous of her health and that of her children, to whom he always sent his love. He advised her as to the schooling of her boys and chided her when she often failed to answer his frequent epistles. Soon she began to address him as "dear son," and in an early letter he thanked her "for your affectionate mode of address; which, I assure you, is much more agreeable to my feeling than any other. Your whole actions in kindness and affection have been to me, like a mother's tenderness."[10]

Calhoun frequently mentioned religion in these early letters. "I receive with gratitude your friendly advice and anxious solicitude for my welfare on the all important subject of religion. ...Be assured that whatever you may say on this head will be kindly received." "Tell James [her youngest son]," he wrote in another letter, "I wish to hear him read in the bible [sic] very much; and that I hope he will learn from it to be a good boy."[11] He commented on rumors of a rivival of religion in Charleston. Repeatedly he condemned the immorality of that city, and he spoke in complimentary terms of a sermon in Litchfield by a Newport minister — probably Mrs. Calhoun's pastor. Yet the rare use of the word "God" is noticeable throughout this correspondence, in his references to deity he employed instead such phrases as "author of good," "good providence," "heaven," etc.*

*From the use of these and other abstractions, such as "He who governs all things," it is apparent that even at this early age Calhoun was a deist. Later in his career in Washington he attended the Unitarian Church, but he

17

But he refused an invitation to live with the Calhouns in Newport and to continue his studies there, as he felt he could not afford
to miss the lectures, and his cousin was unable to visit him in Litchfield. In July, 1806, when his brother James was unable to supply
him with the usual funds, he appealed to her for a loan of two
hundred dollars. The customary vacation in August he spent with
her in Newport and seemed quite impressed with the many friends
to whom she proudly introduced him. Although he had received
his diploma from Litchfield, he returned after the vacation to attend
some important lectures for a few weeks. Upon their completion
in mid-autumn he proceeded to Carolina—by stage to Philadelphia
and thence on horseback to Charleston. Before commencing the
actual practice of law he resumed his study in Charleston for six
months in De Saussure's office.

*   *   *

After seeing the Calhouns in Charleston in the spring, John returned to Abbeville in June upon completion of his study with
De Saussure, continuing his training in the office of George Bowie,
a relative and eminent attorney. Shortly he was admitted to the
bar after examination by the state supreme court, and he began
practice. The pages of patriotic local historians, as with other
national heroes, attest to his early prowess. "His reputation was
extraordinary for so young a man," wrote John B. O'Neall, South
Carolina's legal historian. "He was conceded, as early as 1809, to
be the most promising young lawyer in the upper country. Chancellor Bowie . . . says: 'with the members of the bar as well as the
people, he stood very high in his profession. Perhaps no lawyer in
the state ever acquired so high a reputation from his first appearance
at the bar as he did.'" Starke even asserts that he made sufficient
income within three years to retire and become a planter.[12]

Properly discounting such fables, one cannot doubt that Calhoun,
brilliant, industrious, with his Litchfield training and the prestige
of De Saussure's tutelage, enjoyed almost instant success. Despite
this fact he disliked the practice of law even more than he had the
study of it. He found it too confining and unstimulating. "It is

never became a formal convert to any denomination. His direct use of the
word "God" in these early letters occurs only three times, in each instance
in an epistle to his fiancée. The word appeared in the phrases "bliss that
God has permitted," "God preserve you," and "blessing of God."

perhaps one of the most disagreeable circumstances in our profession," he complained to Mrs. Calhoun, "that we cannot neglect its pursuit, without being Guilty at the same time of imprudence and a breach of confidence, reposed in us by our clients. I feel myself now and while I continue at the practice of law almost as a slave chained down to a particular place and course of life. I have been very successful on the circuit in obtaining business; and doubt not in a short time to have as much as I can conveniently attend to; however, I still feel a strong aversion to the law; and am determined to forsake it as soon as I can make a decent independence; for I am not ambitious of great wealth."[13]

Obviously, then, during these years he determined to give up law as soon as possible for the life of a Carolina country gentleman. The income from his practice coupled with the increase in value of the land inherited from his father would enable him eventually to set himself up comfortably as a planter. Such a life, indeed, had been his early intention. "I have been looking out for some weeks past," he wrote his future mother-in-law in 1810, "for a place to purchase so as to establish myself permanently for life. I was desirous of purchasing on the Savannah River near my relatives, but I find only one place for sale there and that at a price nearly double its value. At present I have a place near my brother Patrick. It is a valuable one and as pleasant as any in that part of the state."[14]

In 1808 occurred two events which convinced him of the desirability of such a course and hastened its realization. In that year he was elected to the legislature from the Abbeville district, and it was probably on a visit to Mrs. Calhoun's estate at Bonneau Ferry in the same year that he fell in love with and determined to marry her sixteen-year-old daughter Floride. When this marriage shortly occurred, it gave him social position in the tidewater and a temporary financial independence which permitted him to retire from the odious law. His election as legislator, in addition, opened a political career which might lead to higher office in the nation. The role of planter-statesman was the supreme ideal of ante-bellum southern society. Certainly it was the accepted goal of most ambitious youngsters — and Calhoun attained that happy station before he was thirty. Well might he rejoice: "This swells the cup of bliss to the full. I, in every event of my life, seem to myself more fortunate than I deserve. How shall I be sufficiently grateful?"[15]

*　　　　*　　　　*

In the spring of 1809, when Mrs. Calhoun and her family visited relatives in the back country in response to his insistent invitation, the pressure of his practice prevented his finding an opportunity to speak to her of his affection for Floride and his desire to marry her. Apparently he made a hurried trip down to Bonneau Ferry in June to obtain the mother's permission to woo her daughter. Failing to receive an immediate consent, he continued to press his suit by letter. "It will be useless for me," he wrote shortly, "to conceal from you my increased anxiety on that subject [marriage]. The more I reflect on it, the more indissolubly does my happiness seem to be connected with that event. If, I should be disappointed by any adverse circumstance, which heaven forbid, it will be by far the most unlucky incident in my life.... P. S. Do make no delay in writing to me. I expect to hear from you by the time you receive this."[16]

In her reply Mrs. Calhoun gave him her permission to make known his affection to Floride, but he was unable to do so, unless he proposed by letter, until the following winter when they returned briefly to Carolina. Even then Floride did not give him an immediate answer, but finally consented on her next visit in late spring. Thereupon Judge De Saussure was called in by Mrs. Calhoun as the final arbiter, and in January, 1811, the marriage took place at Bonneau Ferry amid great celebration. In regard to Floride's property, the groom objected firmly to a marriage settlement on the grounds that it would imply a lack of confidence in him as a husband, and apparently he was given full control as he insisted. The extreme uncertainty and secrecy of the courtship can only partially be explained by the youth of the bride. It was certainly rumored long in advance that a marriage was in the offing.[17] Perhaps Mrs. Calhoun, rather than her daughter, selected John as the most promising suitor.

With his stern and reticent temperament it was difficult for Calhoun to be the romantic lover. No more eloquent proof of this fact could be offered than his attempt at a poem to his ladylove, each line of which began with "whereas."[18] But Floride's brother James Edward indignantly reported to his mother that he saw Calhoun slyly kissing his sister when the three of them were out riding in a carriage. The single letter from him to his intended bride which has been preserved, though it indicates deep emotion on his part, is oppressively stilted even for a day of conventional formality. Actually he wooed the mother, not the daughter. "In this, the true criterion of friendship," he wrote his future mother-in-law, "you have exceed[ed] all my friends.... Never shall I be able to make you suitable return.... Let me add, without the least imputation of flattery, that, to be so nearly related to yourself, is a fruitful source of happiness. I know not why, from my first acquaintance with you at Newport, I have loved you as a mother.... Such is the warmth of my affection, which, I feel towards you, that I can scarcely refrain from addressing you by the endearing epithet of mother. I hope that the time now will not be long, when I may with propriety use it."[19]

There can be no doubt of the genuine quality of his love, once he decided to yield to his emotion — even the "cast-iron" man could not have controlled his passion after it was unloosed. In regard to his personality it is noteworthy that the intensity of his emotional disturbance surprised him. "This language does not correspond with my former opinion upon this subject," he confessed. "I formerly thought that it would be impossible for me to be strongly agitated in an affair of this kind; but that opinion now to me seems wholly unfounded, since, as it were in the very commencement, it can produce such effects."[20]

In this instance, however, it is a significant revelation of his character that he chose to yield to the pull of his emotions while they were yet under control, and that he selected the particular woman whom he did for his wife. Capable of and believer in Calvinistic self-restraint that he was, he certainly would have attempted to inhibit his emotions had his reason counseled such action. An ambitious but humorless cynic, he would hardly have permitted himself to become enamored of a nobody, much less would he have married one. In his decision to marry Floride, he was at least unconsciously influenced by the obvious effect of her property and social position, as well as her personality, upon the career he had planned for himself. To argue otherwise is to belittle his cold intelligence and to ignore completely his conduct earlier and later in life. In this, as in all the major steps in a long and hectic career, he followed a policy dictated by enlightened self-interest.

According to a persistent legend, now disproved, Calhoun was one of a dozen men alleged to have been the father of Abraham Lincoln. This canard arose from a Carolina story that during his early career on the back-country circuit he had an affair with a barmaid named Nancy Hanks (possibly a relative of Lincoln's mother). No record exists of his participation in the brawling, gambling, and drinking then common on the circuit, but it is at least possible that even so self-righteous and puritanical a man as he had one overt affair of the heart prior to his marriage at the late age of twenty-nine. The dubious evidence for the story rests upon a statement made many years later at a drunken party by his cousin Armistead Burt that Calhoun "looked back on his youth with regret for one mistake."[21] If he jilted a barmaid for a lady, it was entirely in keeping with his character.

*   *   *

In the month of June, 1807, when Calhoun was just beginning his practice of law at Abbeville, the attack of the *Leopard* upon the *Chesapeake* united the majority of Americans in support of an immediate declaration of war upon England — a policy which Jefferson rejected in favor of his unromantic "peaceable coercion." Upon receipt of the news of this outrage, the farmers of Abbeville, like their Republican brethren up and down the back country, called a public meeting of protest. The committee on arrangements selected Calhoun to harangue them and to present to them a series of resolutions. So completely did he espouse their jingoistic nationalism that in the next election he was sent by the community to represent them in the legislature. Continuing his nationalistic utterances as legislator, he was in 1810 one of the many War Hawks elevated to Congress by disgusted patriots throughout the Union. Obviously he had decided upon politics as a career in his college days. His election was, therefore, the result of deliberate intent and effort on his part. "Much of his success," stated his autobiography thirty-three years later in regard to his brilliant performance in his first Congress, "is to be attributed to his early and wise determination not to *come forward* until he had laid the foundation in a solid education, and fully prepared himself to act his part in life."[22]

The choice of law as a career in that age, particularly in the South, was usually indicative of political aspirations. His schooling in the East, which gave him prestige in the low country, his return to Abbeville where he was a prominent local son, and his immediate identification with the rising war sentiment may well have been deliberate steps in a carefully laid plan towards the goal of public office. His defense of the sovereignty of the people in his argument at Yale with Dwight indicated both a staunch Republicanism and a probable desire for definite connection with the Republican party. His aversion to law, which strengthened his resolve to enter politics, may have been due in large part to an impatience to commence a political career — an impatience exaggerated by his growing realization that a national crisis was at hand which offered rapid political fortune to the courageous neophyte who would lead his people against the enemy. If it was his plan at this time to become the spokesman in Congress not merely of the piedmont but of the entire state of South Carolina — in view of the competition for that role which he was soon to face from William Lowndes and Langdon Cheves — then his marriage into a low-country family was a master stroke.

During the two sessions of the legislature in which he sat, Calhoun "originated and carried through several measures which proved in practice to be salutary."[23] It is likely that he was influential in the selection of his benefactor De Saussure, in spite of that gentleman's strong Federalism, as chancellor of the state. Actually his only important act was a clever speech in regard to party nomination for the presidential election of 1812, by means of which he assumed the leadership of the Carolina Republican War Hawks, thus insuring his nomination and election to the next Congress.

Though this speech occurred in party caucus, it brought him great popularity in the legislature and throughout the state.* He boldly attacked the unpopular "restrictive system" of Jefferson and Madison, and declared that war with England was inevitable. Under the circumstances the primary consideration of all patriots should be the unity of the Republican party. For that reason he opposed the renomination of the New Yorker George Clinton for the vice-presidency, since he would become the leader of the antiwar Republicans and thus split the party. Instead he proposed John Langdon of New Hampshire for that office. By this public declaration for a policy of war Calhoun not only immediately gained a large following in South Carolina, but when George Clinton's nephew De Witt was nominated three years later by antiwar Republicans to

---

*The only record of this speech is the summary in the autobiography. Undoubtedly it was far more jingoistic and emotional than the summary infers.

oppose Madison, he also acquired a reputation for political sagacity which impressed his constituents and enhanced his standing in the party.[24]

In 1810 he was "nominated" as the Republican candidate for Congress from the Abbeville-Laurens-Newberry district, though undoubtedly he was actually selected by the party caucus. It seems that his cousin Joseph Calhoun, who was then serving as representative for the district, "retired" in his favor. Against his antiwar Federalist opponent, General John A. Elmore, he made a spirited canvass, and his success was apparent long before the election.[25]

In the year's interim between his election and the opening of the new Congress, Calhoun disposed of his remaining legal cases and discontinued practice. Shortly after their wedding the young couple made their home at "Bath," a plantation which the groom had bought near the original family settlement on the ridge between the Savannah and Little rivers. Part of the time they spent in Columbia and Charleston, but the young husband was even then too busy or too uninclined towards pleasure to join his wife in much social activity. In October, 1811, immediately after the birth of their first child, he left his bride of nine months and journeyed to Washington to begin his national duties.[26] The particular circumstances of his departure were symbolic and prophetic; thereafter the private life of John Calhoun was always subordinated to his public life.

CHAPTER THREE

"Young Hercules Who Carried the War on His Shoulders"

CALHOUN arrived in the nation's capital in a time of crisis. This fortuitous circumstance enabled him early to display his inherent qualities of leadership and, in fact, to develop them. The outcome of this crisis and Calhoun's own role in it naturally influenced his future career in politics, but more than that, they determined his philosophy of government and his ideas on national policy for many years to come.

Strictly speaking, the crisis was not new or sudden; it had only deepened. It had begun a score of years before when revolution in France and the general war in Europe to which it led had placed the Washington administration in a diplomatic dilemma, the seriousness of which neither Washington nor his cabinet underrated. "Sure am I," wrote the President to Gouveneur Morris in 1795 to explain his acceptance of the unpopular Jay Treaty, "if this country is preserved in tranquility twenty years longer, it may bid defiance in a just cause to any power whatever; such in that time will be its population, wealth, and resources."[1] Agreeing with this fundamental logic, Washington's successors Adams and Jefferson also chose peace in several crises when insults or violations of American rights as a neutral produced a strong public demand for war against England or France.

25

Madison, too, attempted to preserve American "isolation." Yet at the end of his first term the young western War Hawks, elected like Calhoun to Congress in 1810 because they called for war with England, forced the second Republican President into hostilities which he hoped and definitely planned to prevent. In fact, the young Republicans accomplished their objective, in spite of opposition from the Federalists and the Old Guard of their own party, within half a year after the new Congress assembled for the first time in the winter of 1811-12.

Like early World War I a century later, the hostilities between France and the European coalition brought increasing prosperity to all classes and sections in the United States, interrupted only by Jefferson's Embargo of 1807. Agricultural goods rose sharply both in price and quantity in response to an abnormal demand abroad, and the American merchant marine took over much of the carrying trade between France and her colonies. The various nations of Europe were prevented by their preoccupation with war from blocking American westward expansion. Both England and Spain evacuated their troops from the trans-Appalachian West, and in 1803 Napoleon sold the vast expanse of Louisiana to the young republic for fear of losing it to England. Continuing good times, in contrast to the depression of the earlier Confederation period, increased the attachment of citizens to the Constitution and the Union. For the same reason many Federalists became Republicans after their party lost power in 1800, particularly when it became evident that Jefferson would not radically alter their established domestic policies. American participation in the war could — and did — end this prosperity, which the violation of neutral rights had hardly checked.

The situation which caused Madison to fail was largely inherited from his predecessor and was aggravated by the Federalists who favored peace at any price. The first Republican President and his party had been pro-French before the dictatorship of Napoleon. Actually Jefferson was isolationist in a deeper sense than Washington, for unlike the pro-British Federalists he would play the belligerents off against each other, though he would also avoid war at almost any cost. When he learned of Napoleon's secret acquisition of Louisiana in 1801, he considered an alliance with England, but the sale of the territory to the United States ended his dilemma. When the British frigate *Leopard* in 1807 fired on the American

Chesapeake in an effort to recapture alleged deserters, he resisted the strong public demand for war.

Realizing, however, that the practice of "impressment," or increasing violation of neutral rights by either of the belligerents, might force us into war, he induced Congress to pass an embargo on all trade with Europe. Here he was trying his pet weapon of economic retaliation to insure American rights and thus to prevent some martial incident, assuming that our agricultural exports were more vital to Europe than her exports to us. The resulting depression revived the Federalists — who now cast Jefferson's earlier state-rights doctrine back at him — and drove the northern wing of his own party into opposition. Within fifteen months Congress repealed the embargo, substituting for it nonintercourse with France and England. Then in 1810 the Macon Bill Number Two removed all restrictions, offering to restore them against either belligerent if the other would cease its violation of rights which Americans claimed as neutrals. Outraged at this abject retreat, the public in the election of that and the following year retired half the membership of Congress.

The new congressmen came mostly from the West, where a powerful Indian confederacy had recently been formed under Tecumseh to check American expansion. Open fighting broke out between the Indians and Governor William Henry Harrison's militia in the battle of Tippecanoe in the fall of 1811. Westerners had already concluded that an alliance existed between English Canada and the redmen, and to a lesser extent between the southwestern tribes and the Spanish in Florida. Actually both England and Spain had followed a conscious policy of using the Indians as a buffer to check American migration westward. Since the two European powers were allies in the struggle against Napoleon, which at this point was requiring their full energies, western War Hawks openly demanded war on England for the conquest of Canada and Florida. They justified their demands as a proper defensive measure, since they were convinced that intrigue and military supplies from the neighboring European colonies had produced Tecumseh's power. But westerners also wanted the new areas for economic reasons; Lewis and Clark had reported that Louisiana was a desert, and frontiersmen regarded the prairies of the Old Northwest as unfit for cultivation. Thus the region which owned no ships and produced few sailors found in the violation of neutral rights a convenient pretext to get eastern votes for a war which they desired for their own sectional advantage. With England preoccupied in Europe the moment was opportune, but the westerners had no doubt that they could conquer her, as their fathers had, in the face of any odds.[2]

The War Hawks were but one of the three main groups in the new Congress. The small Federalist minority vehemently opposed a declaration of war for sectional reasons. Despite all violations of neutral rights, profits from the legal and illegal trade in which shipowners indulged were high even after losses were subtracted. England in the Federalists' opinion was the only hope of civilization against French anarchy. The northern wing of the Republican party generally opposed war because its members regarded war as suicidal. How could their small agricultural republic hope to defeat the wealthiest nation in the world with its diversified economy and its big navy, particularly if by defeating Napoleon England should become free to turn her full power on the United States? Those Federalists who placed the interests of the nation above those of their party — some die-hards would sink the ship of state if they could thereby discredit their Republican rivals — agreed with this conclusion. The presidential election of 1812, held in the fall following the declaration of war in June, left no doubt that these two groups would have succeeded in avoiding hostilities but for western belligerency. The seaboard sections divided their votes evenly between Madison and his antiwar Republican opponent De Witt Clinton, whom the Federalists supported. The West voted solidly for the re-election of Madison and for continuation of the war, obtaining the necessary southern support by the prospect of the conquest of Florida and the retention of a southerner in the White House.[3]

*　　　　　*　　　　　*

The young South Carolinian who arrived in Washington in the fall of 1811 to fulfill his destiny was physically one of the most striking figures ever to appear in Congress. Well over six feet in height, gaunt and wiry of frame, he bore a remarkable likeness to his future enemy, Andrew Jackson, whom he also resembled in the stubborness of his Scots-Irish character. It was the brilliant eyes, however, which marked the man — eyes so burning and in his last years so haunting that contemporaries seldom noticed other physical features. So attracted were men by their luminous quality that there was a general disagreement among his friends as to their color. Their effect was best described by Harriet Martineau when she referred to Calhoun as "the cast-iron man who looks as if he had never been born, and never could be extinguished."[4]

"He has seen nothing of the world," wrote one of his early biographers in describing the new congressman in 1811. "The young man's life has been narrow."[5] No statement could be farther from the truth, but it was quite in keeping with the reputation for complete innocence and purity of motives with which Calhoun and his personal supporters later sought to clothe the Carolina statesman in the eyes of the public of his day.

As a matter of fact, there were probably few men in the government who had seen as much of, or who knew as much about, the United States of 1811 as did he. He had lived in the Carolina piedmont and in Charleston, in New Haven, and in Litchfield; he had visited Boston, Newport, New York, and Philadelphia. His frequent travel up and down the length of the land, by ship, by coach, and on horseback, had made him as cosmopolitan as an American could be without crossing the Atlantic, and undoubtedly he knew his contemporary United States as a whole better than did President Madison, Nicholas Biddle, or James Fenimore Cooper. Furthermore, his advent into national affairs was no accident; rather it was the result of years of careful planning and hard work.[6] By his own admission he had delayed seeking office until he had fully prepared himself for the role, so he had certainly familiarized himself with the intimate details of customary procedure in Washington.

At least it is undeniable that the most cunning politician could not have proceeded more directly towards his goal. Having distinguished himself in his own state and in the South as a leader of the New Republicans, when Calhoun reached Washington he took quarters in the strongest war "mess," i.e., boarding house, which included Speaker Henry Clay, Felix Grundy of Tennessee, and his fellow South Carolinians, William Lowndes and Langdon Cheves.[7] Within a month Clay appointed him to the second place on the Committee on Foreign Relations, the most important committee of the House in that session. Shortly he became its chairman, and he introduced the bill calling for a declaration of war. During the war years, though other able men competed with him for the position, he became the outstanding majority leader on the

floor. Within six years of his entrance into Congress he was elevated to the cabinet, and in another six years he was one of
several candidates for the presidency.

Calhoun at once impressed his mess with his ability. Clay selected
him as a henchman, assigning to him the difficult task of checking
the veteran John Randolph; and his Carolina colleague Lowndes
wrote confidentially: "I like him already better than any member
of our mess."[8] The new congressman took his job quite seriously;
evidently he realized that his moment had arrived. "Our society
is delightful," he informed his mother-in-law. "This place is quite
gay, during the season; but I do not participate in it much myself.
You know I never had much inclination to such enjoyment. I am
invited to a ball to the French minister's on Monday next; and to
dine with him on Christmas day; but for political reasons have
declined his invitation."[9]

It was more than a mere rationalization for agricultural imperialism when the War Hawks spoke of national honor, for Clay, Calhoun, and their colleagues spoke without effort the language of a
new United States. Children of their own age, America's Silver
Age which was then beginning, they expressed a faith common
among their constituents. They were the first generation of Americans who had never been English, who did not remember the
Revolution, and who knew almost nothing about Europe. Having
conquered a wilderness with their own hands, they had little doubt
that they could similarly conquer England and France if the
necessity arose.

It was necessary to their self-respect, and in keeping with their
self-confidence, to avenge any insult to their nation's honor, regardless of the amount of damage arising from the insult. The cautious
policy of Jefferson and Madison, however sound it may have been
on rational grounds, seemed to them disgusting and treasonable.
Clay and his friends, wrote the British minister, "always talked to
me of war as of a duel [necessary to a young nation as to a young
man] to prevent his being bullied and elbowed." When over, it
"would probably leave them both better friends than they had ever
before been."[10] Given the state of mind in 1812, war was necessary
to the national ego. Though none of its specific objectives was
realized in the Treaty of Ghent, its miraculous outcome did restore
national self-respect and confidence in the government.

Many War Hawks wanted war against Napoleon as well as

against England. Indeed, what prevented triangular war was its physical impossibility, not its inexpediency. A nation without a navy could not attack Napoleon bottled up in Europe, but England could be attacked in Canada on this side of the Atlantic, and indirectly in the Mississippi Valley by war on the Indians. Once we had answered "the insolence of British cannon . . . we can then speak to the hushed batteries of French aggression," stated Clay. But for the moment, "the one we can strike, the other we cannot reach."[11]

Calhoun expressed the credo of this new nationalism in his first important speech.* His committee had reported, urging preparation for war, and Randolph had answered by calling the War Hawks plunderers motivated by "agrarian cupidity." If the country was unprepared, replied Calhoun,

> let us remedy the evil as soon as possible. . . . But it may be, and I believe was said, that the nation will not pay taxes, because the rights violated are not worth defending or that the defense will cost more than the profits. Sir, I here enter my most solemn protest against this low and "calculating avarice" entering this hall of legislation. It is fit only for shops and counting-houses, and ought not to disgrace the seat of sovereignty by its squalid and vile appearance. Whenever it touches a sovereign power, the nation is ruined. . . . I only know of one principle to make a nation great, to produce in this country not the form but real spirit of union, and that is to protect every citizen in the lawful pursuit of his business. He will then feel that he is backed by his Government; that its arm is his arm; and will rejoice in its increased strength and prosperity. Protection and patriotism are reciprocal. This is the road that all great nations have trod. Sir, I am not versed in this calculating policy; and will not, therefore, pretend to estimate in dollars and cents the value of national independence, or national affection. . . . The honor of a nation is its life. Deliberately to abandon it, is to commit an act of political suicide.[12]

*　　　*　　　*

*Calhoun's first speech was on a bill for the new apportionment of membership in the House. Since the Senate and the House had passed different bills, he argued that the Constitution made the House the sole judge of the qualifications of its members. As to the actual ratio for the apportionment, however, he urged that national interests, not those of particular states, should determine the decision.

Coercive legislation had been attempted by the United States because the European war had reached a state of attrition; England's naval blockade and her Orders in Council had been answered by the Continental System of France. Upon the passage of the Macon Bill, Napoleon formally announced that he would repeal his decrees if the United States would compel England to respect her neutral rights also. In 1811, therefore, Madison reinstituted nonintercourse with England. Though Napoleon did not carry out his bargain, as the English kept insisting, the American President refused to admit that he had been duped. Instead he increased the pressure for the withdrawal of the Orders in Council by appearing to yield to the War Hawks of his own party.

As soon as Congress assembled, Speaker Clay (who had recently shifted from the Senate to the House) marshaled his forces to drive Madison into an active belligerency, for which they suspected he was lukewarm. The Speaker put his henchmen in the chairmanships and in the majority on all important committees. Taking literally the advice in the presidential message to put the republic "into an armor and an attitude demanded by the crisis," the Foreign Relations Committee introduced specific resolutions for that purpose. By narrow margins bills were passed increasing the size of the army, raising taxes, and authorizing loans, but their most important measure for a larger navy was rejected. Nevertheless, at the end of March the War Hawks demanded that Madison agree to a declaration of war, and he compromised by approving a ninety-day embargo. When the *National Intelligencer,* the administration paper, came out dramatically for war in mid-April, Old Guard Senator William B. Giles complained that the reins had been "given into the hands of boys."[13]

This step, which signified that Madison for various party reasons had accepted the War Hawks instead of the Old Guard as the majority wing of the Republicans, did not at the time commit him definitely to war. Rather it was a clever move consistent with his policy of playing for time and of keeping actual control in his own hands. Caught in a dilemma, since it was becoming increasingly apparent that France had not, as he officially insisted she had, repealed her decrees, the President chose the alternative of desperately increasing pressure on England. Using poker tactics, by seeming to yield to the War Hawks on all questions he was merely raising the bet. Actually he had ninety days for negotiation, in which time much could happen. If England did not yield as he expected he could always back down, with the aid of Old Guards and Federalists, by blocking a declaration or modifying it into a privateer war like that against France in 1798.

The President opposed war because he knew the country was unprepared, in spite of War Hawk legislation. Regulars could not be found for the army, neither officers nor equipment were available, the war and navy departments were notoriously inefficient, and a strong minority opposed belligerent action. Madison erred, so events proved, in thinking he could rely upon this minority as a last resort, but it was true, as Calhoun was "sorry to say [that the] greatest impediment" to the War Hawks was the President himself. It was not his active opposition, but that "he reluctantly gives up the system of peace."[14]

Fate defeated the President's strategy, though if he could have temporized a month longer the repeal of the Orders in Council would have prevented war. On May 22 the overdue *Hornet* arrived with a note, dated April 10, which stated that England would never withdraw her orders until she had absolute proof that France had withdrawn her decrees, and that she could make no exception in regard to the United States alone among neutrals. In spite of rumors of repeal, the British minister repeated this uncompromising stand on May 23, June 10, and as late as June 14. Under these circumstances Madison, renominated by his party in May, was forced to send a war message to the House, which in secret session passed it on June 4 by a vote of 79 to 49.

The President was counting on the Senate to defeat the measure. The Old Guard first introduced amendments to issue letters of marque and reprisal against France also, but they were barely defeated, 17 to 15 and 18 to 14. Another amendment proposed that war be limited merely to letters of marque and reprisal against Great Britain, but it too was narrowly rejected. After a week of debate the Senate was equally divided on the war bill, 16 to 16. The whole cabinet, according to William Lowndes, was in favor of this amendment and "a considerable effort was made [by] the Executive to prevent a declaration of war ... to substitute something else and less." But the War Hawks were ready for such a move. "We determined to adjourn, go home, doing nothing — or have a War in common form."[15]

At this impasse the Old Guard finally surrendered and passed the war bill, 19 to 13. What had happened was clear. Through their superior organization the War Hawks, exerting constant pressure on the Federalists, the Old Guard, and the President, eked out a victory by the narrowest margin. Had it been known that Parliament had repealed the obnoxious Orders in Council on the very day the Senate reluctantly voted for war, James Madison would have handsomely won his diplomatic poker game.

*   *   *

The War Hawks' victory was so clearly the result of close cooperation between half a dozen men that it is impossible to arrive at an exact estimate as to how the credit should be divided. Clay the quarterback called the signals, but his teammates freely gave him advice in the huddles. Calhoun, Lowndes, Cheves, Grundy, and others all took their turn at carrying the ball, leading the interference, and tackling the opposition when it was on offense.

As to Calhoun himself, it was his role in the later war sessions of Congress which caused Pennsylvanian Alexander J. Dallas enthusiastically to single him out as the "young Hercules who carried the war on his shoulders."[16] In the earlier session which declared war, only Clay contributed more to the outcome than he, and not even Clay profited more in popularity as consequence. Though a newcomer, Calhoun acted as chairman of the Foreign Affairs Committee during the prolonged absence of Porter, the regular chairman. Together with the Speaker he overcame Randolph's obstructionism which before had gone uncurbed. Towards the end of the long struggle in May, when the spirits and energy of some were faltering, he whipped up their enthusiasm with the confident assertion that "in four weeks from the time that a declaration of war is heard on our frontier, the whole of Upper and a part of Lower Canada will be in our possession."[17] When the final vote on war was about to be taken in the House, it was to Calhoun that Madison sent a request for delay until a new communication could be considered. Finally, it was he who presented the war resolution in June, and though he was not its author "the presentation ... immediately gave him a national reputation."*

The major significance of these events is not merely that they led to a war which gained no territory for the United States and not a single diplomatic concession as to the freedom of the seas, but

*Secretary of State James Monroe wrote the resolution.

also that they reversed early Jeffersonianism and accelerated the transition to a strange new Republicanism. Jefferson had laid down fundamental principles in 1800: a frugal, simple, and unobtrusive government, strict construction of the Constitution, state rights, a quiet not a rampant patriotism, peace, no army, no navy, no taxes, no debt. Each of these the War Hawks specifically, and in many instances deliberately, violated. They raised an army, they raised taxes, they created a navy. Their endeavor was frankly to make the nation great by war; they cherished expansion and hailed the military victories of the Revolution. In the debates on the volunteer bill they unhesitatingly cast off strict construction. It was the sovereign power of Congress, argued Clay and Cheves, despite an implied constitutional prohibition, to employ the militia on foreign soil if the objectives of war demanded it. Yet many of these were the identical Federalist measures which the Republicans had heatedly condemned in 1798.

Here Calhoun found his role. Not only did he actively support all these measures, but he welded the arguments advanced for their enactment into a single piece and so became the supreme advocate for the new Republicanism. Lacking the oratorical ability of Clay, unable and temperamentally disinclined to sway greatly the emotions of his audience, he turned, as it was only natural that he should, to close logic and to what had the appearance of cold reason to justify the program which both of them considered desirable. Clay and Calhoun from the outset of their careers were cooking the brew of nineteenth-century "planned-economy" eventually to be known as the American System. In their defense it should be noted that Jefferson had scuttled much of his original program during his presidency, evoking Randolph's accusation that he was only "spelling Federalism backwards."

Clay was popularly given more credit by posterity for their handiwork, but contemporaries gave the Carolinian due recognition. "Clay, Cheves, Lowndes, and Calhoun," wrote William Reed, "... confessedly the best informed and most liberal men of their party ... have regardless of the wishes of and consequences upon the administration uniformly declared themselves for War ... *for a general and effective system.*"[18]* A decade later, when Cheves and Lowndes had passed from the national stage, John Quincy Adams (who in his own way had arrived at the same conclusion as Calhoun

*Italics added.

and Clay) also paid his tribute to the Carolinian as "a man of fair and candid mind, of honorable principles, of clear and quick understanding, of cool self-possession, of enlarged philosophical views, and of ardent patriotism. He is above all sectional and factious prejudices more than any other statesman of this Union with whom I have ever acted."[19]

Calhoun had succinctly stated the basis of his philosophy of nationalism in his speech on the report of the Foreign Affairs Committee in 1811. Shortly after the declaration of war, he amplified his reasoning in a speech for the repeal of all nonimportation measures previously enacted by the administration. He did not censure the motives which led to the passage of the restrictive legislation, but he objected to the method

> because it does not suit the genius of our people, or that of the Government, or the geographical character of our country. We are a people essentially active. I may say we are preeminently so. Distance and difficulties are less to us than any people on earth. Our schemes and prospects extend everywhere, and to everything. No passive system can suit such a people, in action superior to all others; in patience and endurance inferior to many. ... I would prefer a single victory over the enemy by sea or land to all the good we shall ever derive from the continuation of the non-importation act. I know not that it would produce an equal pressure on the enemy; but I am certain of what is of greater consequence, it would be accompanied with more salutary effects on ourselves. The memory of a Saratoga or a Eutaw is immortal. It is there you will find the country's boast and pride; the inexhaustible source of great and heroic actions.[20]

Three years ahead lay the Battle of New Orleans and the Era of Good Feeling.

* * *

In the three sessions of Congress which met during the hostilities into which the young Republicans had thrust the nation, Calhoun labored like a Hercules to defend the war and, what was infinitely more difficult, Madison's conduct of it. No longer an insurgent but a supporter of the administration, he met a solid phalanx of enemies, now including antiwar Republicans in addition to Federalists. Randolph failed of re-election in 1812, but his place was ably filled by Daniel Webster of New Hampshire and Thomas Grosvenor of New York, with each of whom the Carolinian broke lances. The increasing opposition from opponents of the war both in and out of Congress, coupled with a general public attitude of "business as usual," eventually proved too much for the War Republicans. Only a peace, as sudden as it was fortuitous, prevented an admission of ignominious congressional bankruptcy early in 1815.

The war, Calhoun reiterated, had been undertaken "to curb belligerent injustice." After the repeal of the Orders in Council, it was "continued from no project of ambition, or desire of conquest; but from a cause far more sacred — the liberty of our sailors and their redemption from slavery.... War ought to continue until its rational object — a permanent and secure peace — is obtained." Peace in 1813, which the Federalists advocated on the basis of the withdrawal of the Orders in Council, would without a settlement of the impressment issue "leave the root that must necessarily shoot up in future animosity and hostilities."[21]

The opposition in Congress incessantly charged that the war was an offensive one, to which for that reason the minority had a constitutional and moral right to refuse its support. War, answered Calhoun, was offensive or defensive not by the mode of carrying it on, which was an immaterial circumstance, but by the motive and cause which led to it. The invasion of Canada, therefore, was an offensive method designed to accomplish a defensive purpose — the security of the country.

The "cry of French influence, that baseless fiction" he dismissed with ridicule. "We united with France? We have the same cause? No; her object is dominion and her impulse ambition. Ours is the protection of the liberty of our sailors. But say our opponents, we are contending with the same country. What then? Must we submit to be outlawed by England, in order that she may not be by France? ... Must we enter the European struggle not as an equal, consulting our peculiar interest, but be dragged into it as the low dependent, the slave of England?"[22]

Calhoun placed the blame for American failures in the war squarely upon his congressional opponents. Yet not even after the defeat of Napoleon, with England free to direct all her energy against the United States, did he yield to despair. "Our enemy never presented a more imposing exterior. His fortune is at the flood. But I am admonished ... that such prosperity is the most fickle of human conditions.... The great cause will not be yielded. No; never! never! ... The future is audibly pronounced by the splendid victories over the Guerrier, Java, and Macedonian.... The charm of British naval invincibility is broken."[23]

Nor did he despair when news arrived of the severe terms which had been presented to Gallatin's peace commission. War-weary England, fearful alike of enemies and allies on the continent who must of necessity oppose her commercial policies, would compromise her conflict with the United States if the republic would continue to increase the pressure upon her:

> But suppose, instead of vigorous and prompt preparation, we consume our time in debate here, and permit our affairs to go in the consequent slow and feeble way — where is the man so blind as to believe that England will limit her views by her present demands, extravagant as they are? We are already told that she will proportion her future demands to the relative situation of the two countries. She neither expected or desired peace on the terms which were offered. Her bosom is repossessed with the ambition and projects that inspired her in the year seventy-six. It is the war of the Revolution revived; we are again struggling for our liberty and independence.[24]

* * *

The major attack upon the administration after the declaration of war came in the form of a resolution introduced by Webster in June, 1813, calling upon the executive to inform the House exactly when the government had first learned of the repeal of the Berlin and Milan decrees. The obvious insinuation was that Madison had withheld this information from the British to prevent their repealing the Orders in Council until the War Hawks had won Congress over to a war declaration. In the long, heated debate that followed, Calhoun failed to induce the House to soften the tone of the resolution, for which he himself finally voted. When Monroe's reply repudiating Webster's insinuations was referred to Calhoun's Foreign Relations Committee, he likewise was unable to persuade the House to adopt a resolution approving it. But the defenders of the administration had fairly exonerated Madison from duplicity, though it was clear he had been duped by Napoleon.

In the course of this debate Calhoun used strong language which involved him in a bitter quarrel with Grosvenor of New York, with whom he had previously clashed over the right of the Speaker to exclude a certain stenographer. It seems that a duel between them was actually arranged, but was prevented at the last minute through the intervention of Francis Scott Key.[25] For several years the two did not speak to each other, though they became reconciled in 1816. No incident so well illustrates the postwar popularity of Calhoun as the fact that Grosvenor, his former personal and political enemy, should have publicly commended him in Congress for "the judicious, independent, and national course which he [Calhoun] has pursued in this House for the last two years.... Let the honorable gentleman continue with the same manly independence, aloof from party views and local prejudices, to pursue the great interests of his country, and fulfill the high destiny for which it is manifest he was born."[26]

Though Calhoun was tireless in his constant defense of the war and Madison's program, he did oppose the administration on three matters: a question of the forfeiture of certain merchant bonds early in the war, nonimportation, and the bank bill of 1814. This independent action did not require the courage which the autobiography suggests, nor did it injure his party standing, since many prominent Republicans, notably Lowndes and Cheves, took similar stands. The issue of merchant bonds arose because American merchants in England, ignorant of the declaration of war by Congress, shipped to this country over twenty million dollars' worth of goods upon repeal of the Orders in Council. These were seized by customs officials upon their arrival, since they were sent in technical, if not deliberate, violation of the nonimportation act which with the outbreak of war continued to operate.

Gallatin, Secretary of the Treasury, proposed that the goods be sold on the market, but that the government should take for itself all the excess profits they would bring because of the high prices resulting from nonintercourse and war, in addition to the duties of five million dollars assessed on them under the existing tariff; and that the owners retain merely the cost of the goods. Calhoun argued that this matter was exclusively in the province of the legislature, not the executive (Gallatin), and that Congress should reject the proposal. "If the merchants are innocent, they are welcome to their good fortune; if guilty, I scorn to participate in its [*sic*] profits. I will never consent to make our penal code the basis of our Ways and Means, or to establish a partnership between the Treasury and the violators of the Nonimportation Law."[27]

Calhoun's attitude in this instance was undoubtedly influenced by his opposition to nonimportation and the restrictive system as a weapon against England. It will be recalled that in June, 1812, shortly after the declaration of war, he had spoken strongly in favor of a bill to repeal nonimportation. At that time repeal was barely defeated, 61 to 58, and in July, 1813, when Madison sent the House a secret message requesting an immediate embargo — actually designed to punish New England for its refusal to support the administration — once again he voted in the minority against it. In its place he proposed free commerce but high duties. The pressure upon England would be equally as great, he argued, for no more goods would be imported than were actually being smuggled in under nonintercourse. The government would obtain badly needed revenue and would not alienate a large section of the Union by attempting to restrain the commercial activity of its citizens.

> You cannot safely confront premeditated insult and injury with commercial restriction alone. . . . It sinks the nation in its own estimation; it counts for nothing which is ultimately connected with our best hopes — the union of these States. Our Union cannot safely stand on the cold calculation of interest alone. It is too weak to withstand political convulsions. We cannot without hazard neglect that which makes man love to be a member of an extensive community — the love of greatness, the consciousness of strength. So long as an American is a proud name, we are safe; but the day we are ashamed of it, the Union is more than half destroyed.[28]

*   *   *

This was not only high nationalism and enlightened statesmanship — it was realistic political strategy. The administration shrank from burdening its supporters, to say nothing of its numerous and vehement opponents, with high direct taxes to meet the increasing costs of war. Calhoun's plan would provide a source of revenue other than severe direct taxes, which it was to his personal interest as well as to that of every other politician to keep as low as possible. The autobiography states that he opposed nonimportation also because he foresaw that it would encourage manufactures which would have to be protected by a postwar tariff. This must be dismissed as an ex post facto invention of 1843, for in 1814 he was definitely in favor of "a moderate but permanent protection." He did point out at the time that to continue the current nonimportation system merely to protect manufactures, when the war already gave them so much protection (the equivalent of a 50 per cent duty), would be dangerous instead of beneficial to them.[29]

The most serious matter upon which Calhoun broke with the administration was its proposal for a new United States bank, which the House heatedly debated from November, 1814, until peace was announced the following February. With the government facing the prospect of running fifty million dollars in the red during the next year, Alexander Dallas, a Philadelphia lawyer who became Secretary of the Treasury at this critical point, offered a bank bill. Calhoun fought it because he "saw, at once, that the effect of the arrangement would be, that the Government would borrow back its own credit, and pay six per cent per annum for what they [*sic*] had already paid eight or nine."[30]

Though this was a subject new to him, he took the lead in defeating the Dallas plan and substituting one of his own, which in turn was eventually rejected. Half a dozen different bills were introduced during the four months of debate — all, for one reason or another, without success — and the news of the Treaty of Ghent found Calhoun still fighting against a bank which did not suit him. Never in his life was he so abused, he observed later, because of his opposition to this measure preferred by the administration and the banking interests.[31] Yet it should be emphasized that he was in favor of what he regarded as the proper kind of national bank.

The complete paralysis of the majority party in the face of national bankruptcy so unnerved him that once in the course of the long debate he broke down. He walked across the floor of the House to Daniel Webster, and telling him that he would rely on his assistance in preparing a new bill, burst into tears.[32]

Despite occasional opposition to his party Calhoun took much care to build political fences and keep them in repair. He was a party man — probably the administration's most trusted congressional leader after Clay went to Europe on the peace commission. To retain his independence without harm to his party standing, he devised an ingenious practice. When he opposed his party, as on the bank bill, he saw to it that his speeches were not published in the record.[33] Though he refused to surrender to the administration on the bank, and in spite of his long, outspoken opposition to nonimportation, he did vote for an embargo which Madison strongly recommended in December, 1813 (the bill passed by the House the previous July having been defeated in the Senate). "At the earnest entreaties of friends," confesses the autobiography, "and to prevent division in the party when their union was so necessary to the success of war, he gave it a reluctant vote."[34]

When the report of Napoleon's defeat in the battle of Leipzig was shortly received, Madison at once realized the necessity of commencing peace negotiations, and four months later he had to recommend the repeal of his embargo. To Calhoun fell the delicate task of defending this apparent inconsistency, for all of the arguments he advanced for repeal could have equally been used against its passage in December. Though he might well have gloated over his personal triumph and have refused to come to the rescue of the President, he accepted the job of saving the face of the administration. "There are few specimens of parliamentary tact," observed one of Webster's biographers, "on the records of any deliberative assembly, more ingenious than the speech of Mr. Calhoun in favor of repealing the Embargo of December, 1813."[35] Madison and the party were in his debt, and they knew they could rely on him in a crisis.

*   *   *

In view of the rivals within his own party and from his own state, most of whom possessed seniority over him both in age and length of service, Calhoun assiduously conducted himself with the proper humility. In 1812 during his first session in Congress he had acted as chairman of the Committee on Foreign Relations and was therefore the logical appointee for that post in the second session. To avoid embarrassment to Clay, since Lowndes, Cheves, and David R. Williams* from South Carolina all had received important positions, he proposed that the chairmanship of his committee be given to John Smilie, a veteran from Pennsylvania. Smilie refused and Calhoun was unanimously elected chairman by the committee, an office which he held until the last war session when his arrival was delayed by illness. Upon Clay's appointment to the peace commission Calhoun was solicited to become a candidate for the speaker-

*Appointed by Clay as chairman of the House Military Affairs Committee.

ship, but he steadfastly refused to run against his fellow Carolinian Cheves, who was elected.[36]

In his speeches he was also careful to display a studied deference for the House. "Time is precious," he concluded one of them, "and he felt that he owed an apology for having consumed so much of it as he had done."[37] This was bread well cast upon the waters, for his star was even then in the ascendant. The fortuitous Peace of Ghent, by enthroning his party, ensured his fortunes.

Calhoun's immense popularity in the postwar era with his colleagues and the public resulted directly from his identification with the spirit of nationalism, of which he was an outstanding champion. The spirit was conspicuous in every speech and action of his public career during the war years. The union of the states was his primary objective. Union rested upon patriotism, and in turn patriotism was dependent upon the degree of security, both domestic and foreign, which the government provided for its citizens. Unlike many southerners who feared the political predominance which Canada would give the Northwest, he urged its acquisition both on the grounds of military strategy and as an end in itself.

To cement the Union he would protect the interests of all groups — merchants, manufacturers, and seamen no less than farmers. In the matter of merchants' bonds he opposed Gallatin's scheme in 1812, thus defending the merchants from an unjust act of confiscation by the government. He fought to end impressment because it violated the rights of seamen. To the manufactures which sprang up as a consequence of the restrictive policy and war he would extend a proper protection from European competition; though "he, as a grower of produce, should certainly feel an interest in opposing it as it was in the interest of the planter to let commerce run in any channel it might wear for itself."[38]

Not merely did he refuse to place the economic welfare of the planter before that of the whole nation, but he actually apologized for his section's support of slavery. "It covers me with confusion to name it here," he confessed in regard to the compromise in the Constitution permitting the slave trade to continue until 1808. "I feel ashamed of such a tolerance, and take a large part of the disgrace, as I represent a part of the Union by whose influence it might be supposed to have been introduced."[39] Thus the praise of him by John Quincy Adams, cited above, accurately expressed the contemporary estimate of this young Calhoun forgotten by posterity.

CHAPTER FOUR

Calhoun: Hamiltonian Nationalist

IT IS indicative of Calhoun's personality that both as a bridegroom and a young husband, no less than as an elder statesman, he completely subordinated his domestic to his political life. In this the motives of duty and ambition were mixed, but few men would permit preoccupation with the nation's business to result in their sustained absence during the pregnancies of their young wife and the early infancy of their children. In order to attend his first Congress in 1811, he left behind him his week-old son, Andrew. When his wife gave birth to the next two children — Floride in January, 1814, and Anna Maria in April, 1817 — their congressman sire was on both occasions absent in Washington.[1]

Domestic customs change over the span of a century, but human nature does not. Since Calhoun was forced to attend to many of the ordinary functions of husband and father by letters, through them is presented an intimate revelation of his character. These letters reveal an emotional restraint which was one of his conspicuous characteristics. As a husband he was ever paternal, and as a father he displayed the fond detachment of a grandparent.

"I left Floride and our little son," he wrote to his mother-in-law in December, 1811, "at so critical a period that I almost felt alarm at hearing from home for fear that all was not well. I feared that her anxiety of mind at my leaving her might injure her health."

Yet this fear did not delay his departure. "By Dr. Casey's letter of yesterday," he informed his wife upon the birth of their second child in 1814, "I had the pleasure to hear of your safe delivery of a daughter; and that you had comparatively easy times.... You may imagine the relief and joy it afforded me to hear not only of your safety, but the addition to our family. For both of your safety, I have all the fond wishes of a parent and an husband."[2]

In the same vein was his reaction to the death of this daughter a year later. "It is in vain that I tell her [his wife]," he wrote his mother-in-law, "it is the lot of humanity; that almost all parents have suffered equal calamity; that Providence may have intended it in kindness to her and ourselves, as no one can say what, had she lived, would have been her condition, whither [*sic*] it would have been happy or miserable; and above all we have the consolation to know that she is far more happy than she could be here with us."[3]

Soon after his marriage he abdicated in favor of Mrs. Calhoun. Not until his elevation to the cabinet in 1817, when he brought his family to the capital, did he live with them except in periods when Congress was not in session. During the intervening six years he attended to the duty of procreation, but other connubial responsibilities and decisions he surrendered most of the time to his mother-in-law, who doubtless was more than willing to wear the pants in the family. Occasionally he offered advice, but he continued to write her more often than his wife, and he undoubtedly realized and appreciated the value of her service to him. "Floride's letter to me mentions the fine health of Andrew and his disposition to feed. I think it would be advisable for her to wean him as soon as possible. *You however will be the best judge.*"[4*] At no time did he permit his marriage to interfere with his career.

Even the time he spent in South Carolina was devoted more to political affairs than domestic. So popular was his activity in Congress with his constituents that he was re-elected without opposition in 1812 and 1814, and two former congressmen in his district refused to run against him. "You can meet Randolph in debate," said one of them, General William Butler, to his young rival, "I cannot." Despite this success at the polls, he was constantly criticized and ridiculed by the Federalist *Courier* of Charleston; yet by 1816 even it recognized that he was the majority leader in Congress. "We consider it of deep import," commented the *Courier*

*Italics added.

in February, 1816, on an excerpt from his speech on the revenue bill which it had printed, "as indicating the secret purpose, or at least the expectations, of the cabinet and its party."[5]

In the same year the careers of most congressmen in the nation were put in jeopardy as the result of a bill passed by the Fourteenth Congress raising a member's wages to an annual salary of $1,500. Consequently in the fall elections most of them were defeated by an irate public. Calhoun had voted for the bill "because he thought the present pay very inadequate to the dignity of the station, and far short of the time, labor, and sacrifice required."[6] When he returned to Carolina in April he found sentiment so hostile that three candidates were opposing him in the coming election, two of whom were the predecessors who had retired in his favor.

He was advised to apologize for his vote and to cast himself on the mercy of his constituents, but instead he staunchly defended his support of the measure in a public meeting called for that purpose and was easily re-elected in the fall. When the next session of the House repealed the earlier bill, he was one of twenty-seven who refused to retreat and voted nay. Evidently he had already won the same degree of confidence in his native piedmont that he was to enjoy in the whole state after 1832; and it was probably no exaggeration when he told John Q. Adams in 1820 that he was "the most popular man in his district."[7]

*　　　　*　　　　*

"Calhoun is in favor of elevating, cherishing and increasing all the institutions of government," wrote Senator Elijah H. Mills of Massachusetts in 1823, "and of a vigorous and energetic administration of it."[8] Had the senator needed evidence, the records of the first postwar Congress would have been sufficient. Chairman of the Committee on Currency, Calhoun presented the bill chartering the Second Bank of the United States. As chairman also of a special committee on internal improvements, he introduced the Bonus Bill of 1817. At a crucial moment in the debate on the tariff he was called away from his work on the bank report to speak for the endangered bill.

During the war the New York *Evening Post* had called him the "leader of what is called the Administration party in the House."[9] Like Hamilton in the 1790's, Calhoun in 1816 directed the enactment by Congress of a broad nationalistic program. The two programs were similar in spirit no less than in detail. If Jefferson had spelled Hamilton's Federalism backwards, Calhoun did not take the trouble to use any camouflage; he spelled it forward and defended its principles no less boldly than had Hamilton. Clay later claimed paternity of the new offspring and gave it a name — the American System — but equally the father of the new Federalism was John C. Calhoun. His speeches on these several measures rank in clarity and influence with Hamilton's Report on Manufactures; taken collectively, they succinctly express the philosophy of nationalism in the Era of Good Feeling. Since they reveal the political axioms of the first half of his public life, they are essential to an understanding of his political thought and of his career — particularly since he himself later became the chief critic of the national power he had done so much to establish.*

Though they never admitted it publicly, no one knew better than the War Hawks how close the republic had come to military defeat and disunion. They had accomplished none of their objectives except the defeat of the Indians, but the war had convinced them that certain national weaknesses might prove fatal if the Treaty of Ghent should turn out to be only a truce. Calhoun alluded to this danger early in 1816 in his speech against a reduction in direct taxes. The nation was at a crossroads:

> There are in the affairs of nations, not less than those of individuals, moments, on the proper use of which depend their fame, duration, and prosperity. Such I conceive to be the present situation of this country.... The broad question was now before this House, whether this government should act on an enlarged policy; whether it should avail itself of the experience of the last war; whether it would be benefitted by the mass of knowledge acquired within the few last years; or whether we should go on in the old imbecile mode, contributing by our measures nothing to the honor, nothing to the reputation of the country.[10]

In the history of nations he noted two extremes of policy: one in which power was too weak and the other in which it was so strong that it resulted in military violence. Both in his opinion should be equally avoided, but he regarded weakness in governmental power

---

*For that reason I am quoting verbatim several long excerpts from his speeches, rather than paraphrasing.

as the more fatal. Only Rome and France had collapsed through military violence, but numerous states had "sunk into insignificance through imbecility and apathy, [a danger] to which the people of this country are peculiarly liable."

Spain and England, he continued, were the only two countries with whom the United States might become involved in war. Spain was too weak to constitute a menace, but war with England was a constant danger. Future relations between England and America could not be amicable, he was convinced, for England was the most formidable power in the world with the strongest navy. The United States, growing so rapidly and developing economically along the same lines as Great Britain, was certain to challenge her commercial supremacy and political prestige. Judging by the history of Europe in recent centuries, the older nation was certain to take steps to curb this growth and to defeat this challenge.

> I am sure that future wars with England are not only possible, but, I will say more, they are highly probable — nay, that they will certainly take place.... You will have to encourage British jealousy and hostility in every shape; not immediately manifested by open force of violence, perhaps, but by indirect attempts to check your growth and prosperity. As far as she can, she will disgrace everything connected with you. Her reviewers, paragraphists, and travellers will assail you and your institutions.[11]

*   *   *

It was in this atmosphere, then, that what came to be called the "American System" was conceived. In the opinion of Calhoun and his fellow Republicans, Congress must act speedily to put the nation in a state of preparedness for an almost certain war with England. The first step was the construction of a big navy, the cheapest and best defense as well as an effective weapon against an island whose life depended upon commerce. Yet the army should by no means be reduced, since England could attack us through Canada. The ineffective militia system should be completely revamped, recruiting abolished, and the government should resort openly to the draft for its soldiers. Recognizing the relation between military display and nationalism, the Carolinian advocated a military academy in every large state. National bankruptcy, in his opinion, had contributed most to military failure, but the vast distances and the lack of transportation also were major factors.

As a solution to the problem Calhoun ardently proposed two measures: the encouragement of American industry by a tariff and the construction of an adequate network of roads and canals. Both would increase the speed of mobilizing man power and resources. Purely apart from the greater military effectiveness which would result, these measures would produce greater national wealth and a fuller economy in times of peace and of war. Since a government had to collect higher taxes and borrow money to meet the costs of war, the functioning of a full economy during wartime was essential. Should the United States turn to manufacturing instead of concentrating merely on commerce, the enemy could not as easily reduce its wealth or its production. And the farmer, relying upon a home instead of mainly a foreign market, would continue to receive his peacetime income. Prosperity would prevent the rise of a paralyzing sectionalism.

National defense, however, required more than a navy and army. Military effectiveness, Calhoun recognized, was directly dependent upon the total economy of the nation, and upon this subject he directed the full power of his intellect. In numerous speeches he argued cogently that the total economy of the United States should be consciously revolutionized by action of the federal government to create a state of national self-sufficiency. He based his proposals upon the major premise that, though a British invasion by sea could be repelled by a larger navy, in a war with England the United States could not prevent the enemy from cutting off trade with the rest of the world. Such a development had two fatal consequences: it would deprive us of military necessities which normally we imported, but which in wartime were essential to victory; and it would produce a severe depression which would destroy patriotism and bankrupt the government. The depression early in the late hostilities, he well knew, had led to a lack of enthusiasm for the war, to bitter censure of the government, and to the outright opposition of New England.

The proper functioning of the economy in wartime would obviously require the protection of the coastwise trade, the primary defensive purpose of the navy. Expensive fortifications must be constructed, no matter what the cost, on all vulnerable points along the coastline, such as the Chesapeake Bay and the mouth of the Mississippi. Though an increase in manufacturing would cause some decline in the transoceanic merchant marine, seamen for the navy could be just as well trained in coastwise traffic.

A big navy, army, and economy would require a big federal government, but Calhoun did not shrink from such a consequence. On this point he was clear and specific. In a new country there was sufficient room for the action of states and private enterprise, but because of interstate jealousies and the cost of the projects the federal government must assume the leadership and the main responsibility for the general good:

> To legislate for our country requires not only the most enlarged views, but a species of self-devotion not exacted in any other. In a country so extensive, and so various in its interests, what is necessary for the common good may apparently be opposed to the interests of particular sections. It must be submitted to as a condition of our greatness. But were we a small republic; were we confined to the ten miles square, the selfish instincts of our nature might, in most cases, be relied on in the management of public affairs.[12]

High taxes were not a valid reason for the rejection of his defense program. The people, he believed, were basically intelligent and virtuous and would support any measures which they were convinced were necessary and wise. It was the duty of enlightened congressional leaders to win the confidence of the public for the broad program he and his colleagues were advocating, and to convince them that his opponents were lulling them into a state of false security:

> We are charged by Providence, not only with the happiness of this great rising people, but, in a considerable degree, with that of the human race. We have a government of a new order, perfectly distinct from all others which have preceded it — a government founded on the rights of man; resting, not on authority, not on prejudice, not on superstition, but reason. If it shall succeed, as fondly hoped by its founders, it will be the commencement of a new era in human affairs. All civilized governments must, in the course of time, conform to its principles. Thus circumstanced, can you hesitate what course to choose? The road that wisdom indicates leads, it is true, up the steep, but leads also to security and lasting glory. No nation that wants the fortitude to tread it, ought ever to aspire to greatness.[13]

Calhoun's grandiose governmental program and philosophy of government was natural enough in a young politico with his particular experience, and in accord with the climate of opinion which the war produced. His justification of his program on the grounds of its salubrious domestic consequences was, without doubt, in part wishful thinking and rationalization. Yet in 1816, as in the later crises of 1832 and 1850, his solution for sectionalism was the passage of federal legislation which would offer the disaffected region a greater degree of security.

When he urged an "enlarged policy" upon Congress, he did not for a moment consciously place union and liberty second to military security. His program, he believed, would contribute to all three ends. If he placed more emphasis on the matter of national defense, it was because he regarded it at that stage of the nation's career as the more immediate danger, and because he believed (vividly recalling the dark days of 1814) that upon it depended the continuance of union and liberty.

It is significant that his language at this time was identical with that used by Webster fourteen years later in the great debate with Hayne against Calhoun's own doctrine of nullification:

> In his opinion the liberty and union of this country were inseperably united. That as the destruction of the latter would most certainly involve the former, so its maintenance will, with equal certainty, preserve it. He did not speak lightly. He had often and long revolved it in his mind, and he had critically examined into the causes that destroyed the liberty of other states. There are none that apply to us, or apply with a force to alarm. The basis of our republic is too broad, and its structure too strong, to be shaken by them. Its extension and organization will be found to afford effectual security against their operation; but let it be deeply impressed on the heart of this House and country, that while they guard against the old [by hesitating to pass his program] they exposed us to a new and terrible danger, Disunion. This single word comprehended almost the sum of our political dangers; and against it we ought to be perpetually guarded.[14]

Typical of his seemingly dispassionate consideration of the domestic consequences of his program was his concluding argument for the tariff, which preceded the above quotation. The dependence on the part of laborers he admitted to be an evil. But this disadvantage of the rise of manufacturing was more than offset, in his opinion, by certain other results which would follow. It would produce an interest as distinctly American as agriculture, and one more advantageous than commerce. It would bind the country together by increasing regional interdependence and intercourse, and hasten the construction of a transportation net essential to national strength.[15]

Calhoun's pet project at this time was clearly that of internal improvements. In his speech on the Bonus Bill he attributed our freedom from the problems which confronted the small republics of antiquity to the happy division of powers in the Constitution between the national and state governments and to our vast area. But the extent of the national domain was not an unmixed good: "Let it be forever kept in mind, that it exposes us to the greatest of all calamities — next to the loss of liberty — and even to that in its consequences — disunion. We are greatly, and rapidly — I was about to say fearfully growing. This is our pride and our danger; our weakness and our strength."[16]

*　　　*　　　*

The postwar Congress took action on the three main issues that were to plague the nation and Calhoun during his long political career, the tariff, the bank, and internal improvements. His role, both in committee and in debate, was prominent. Because of his later shift his exact position in each of them, here at the outset of his career, should be carefully examined. In the opinion of the administration, apparently the most pressing problem was the disordered state of the currency. During the war all banks south of New England had discontinued specie payment, and as a result most of the nation was flooded with increasing quantities of state bank notes which naturally circulated at a great discount. The import trade, consequently, became concentrated in the Chesapeake Bay region where the discount was greatest, and the government was paid duties — its major source of revenue — in this depreciated paper. Some step to correct this situation was imperative, and it was decided by those in power that a new national bank would be the most appropriate means of forcing upon the state banks resumption of specie payment, thus bringing bank notes up to par.

Because of his prominence in the debates on the bank issue during the war, Calhoun was named chairman of the Committee on National Currency. In January, 1816, he introduced the bill chartering the Second Bank of the United States. He confined his remarks, in his speech supporting it, to the argument that such a bank was the most practical means of rehabilitating the currency. The Constitution, he said, gave Congress the sole power of regulating the currency. As a result of the war, the volume of money was controlled instead by the several hundred state banks which had sprung up. These banks were motivated solely by a desire for profit, which had led them to issue notes without any regard for sound banking principles. They were able to reduce their note issues and resume specie payment, but would not do so unless forced. The states were unable to apply this pressure, but the federal government could and should apply it. The proper device was a national bank which in various ways would compel state banks to redeem their notes or fail.

Calhoun had worked out all the details in conference with Secretary of the Treasury Dallas, but Madison himself in his presidential message had suggested a bank as a possible method of solving the currency difficulty. Randolph and Webster, as earlier, led an opposition which almost succeeded, but finally in March the House passed the measure by the narrow margin of 80 to 71. "I might say with truth," stated its author two decades later, "that the bank owes as much to me as to any other individual in the country; and I might even add that, had it not been for my efforts, it would not have been chartered."[17]

The second key measure of the Young Republicans, introduced and debated almost simultaneously with the bank, was the tariff. Though Calhoun was not a member of the committee which framed the bill, he was certainly consulted in regard to it. When there seemed to be some doubt as to its passage, he was hastily called in to speak in its behalf and he gave it his full and spirited support. In view of his later attitude it should be emphasized that he was definitely in favor of a protective tariff — to the moderate extent that the measure of 1816 was protective — and that in his speech he used all the arguments of later protectionists. Speaking on the Force Bill in 1833, he admitted that the tariff of 1816 introduced the protective principle, but "it escaped my observation, which I can account for only on the ground that the principle was then new, and my attention was engaged by another important subject."[18] The later statement was false and cannot be reconciled with his speech of 1816, although undoubtedly at the earlier date he did not foresee all the consequences of protection. Once again Webster and Randolph led the opposition, the latter taking the stand which Calhoun was to revert to, when he asked "on whom do your import duties bear? ... On poor men, and on slaveholders." Eventually the bill passed easily by a vote of 85 to 54.

Encouraged by their success on the bank, the tariff, and their appropriations for the army and navy, the administration leaders in the House decided to attempt legislation on internal improvements — a subject on which they apparently knew they would experience the greatest opposition. Madison recommended such action in his messages to both sessions of the Fourteenth Congress, but not until most of the Young Republicans' program had been enacted did Calhoun consider the moment opportune for the attempt. Accordingly, in December, 1816, he moved that a committee be appointed to consider the expediency of setting aside the bonus of a million and a half dollars paid by the Second Bank of the United States as a fund for internal improvements. A committee was appointed with him as chairman, and shortly he introduced a bill incorporating his earlier motion. Obviously the wording of the bill — to set aside a fund for internal improvements — was a political ruse to avoid the inevitable question of constitutionality. Of course, once it was passed it would be used as a precedent when a specific bill came up to appropriate funds to build a particular road in a certain state.

His arguments for internal improvements have already been presented, and his constitutional justification for them will be considered below. Though the bill did not call for the building of a single road, he did not hesitate to outline the location of the national roads he considered necessary. The main artery should be a road from Maine to Louisiana. The Great Lakes must be connected with the Hudson, and all of the major ports on the Atlantic, from Boston to Savannah, must be given access to the interior valley. Communication between New Orleans and its valley hinterland must be improved. After numerous amendments were added, the measure passed in February, 1817, by a vote of 86 to 84. Through the South as a whole opposed it, two thirds of the South Carolinians supported it.

Shortly before the session closed in March, Calhoun paid the President his farewell visit and was astounded to be informed that Madison intended to veto the hard-won bill. All last-minute attempts to dissuade him failed and he vetoed it, refuting specifically the Carolinian's constitutional arguments, on the ground that the power was not among those enumerated and it could not be derived from any of the general expressions. Probably Madison had always intended that the subject be approached by amendment, but if so he should have informed Calhoun specifically of his wishes. On the other hand, the President was an Old Guard Republican, and this may have been a Jeffersonian qualm of conscience asserting itself as his last official act. Undoubtedly he thought that the Young Republicans had overreached themselves, and his action in this matter cannot be regarded otherwise than as a personal rebuke to Calhoun. Possibly he may have been jealous of his young lieutenant who had gratuitously taken the helm from him, and he may have deliberately contrived to put him in his place.

*   *   *

A statesman who believed that the federal government had the power to draft citizens into the army, to charter a national bank, and to build national roads where it willed necessarily placed a broad construction upon the Constitution. In his interpretation of the basic law Calhoun was in complete accord in 1816 with Hamilton and Marshall. It is almost unbelievable that the outstanding strict constructionist in all American history could have written in 1823 that "the Supreme Court of the Union performs the highest functions under our system. It is the mediator between *sovereigns*, the State and General Governments, and the actual line, which separates their authority, must be drawn by this high tribunal."[19]* Nor was this all. "Sir, I have a clear conviction," he told the son of Alexander Hamilton during the presidential campaign of 1824, "after much reflection and an entire knowledge and familiarity with the history of our country and the working of our Government that his [the elder Hamilton's] policy as developed by the measures of Washington's administration, is only the true policy for this country."[20]

In this period of his life Calhoun considered the Constitution only when it was used as an objection to some measure which he advocated. Thus it was on this very Bonus Bill of 1817 which Madison vetoed that he expounded in detail his interpretation of that document:

*Italics added.

I am no advocate for refined arguments on the constitution, the instrument was not intended as a thesis for the logician to exercise his ingenuity on. It ought to be construed with plain, good sense; and what can be more expressed than the constitution on this very point [internal improvements]? The first power delegated to Congress, is comprised in these words: "To lay and collect taxes, duties, imposts, and excises, to pay the debts, and provide for the common defense and general welfare of the United States; but all duties, imposts, and excises, shall be uniform throughout the United States." First, the power is given to lay taxes; next, the objects are enumerated to which the money accruing from the exercise of this power, may be applied — viz., to pay the debts, provide for the defense, and promote the general welfare; and last, the rule for laying the taxes is prescribed — to wit, that all duties, imposts, and excises, shall be uniform. If the framers had intended to limit the use of the money to the powers afterwards enumerated and defined, nothing could have been more easy than to have expressed it plainly.[21]

Even were the Constitution silent, he argued, the application of funds need not be confined to the enumerated powers, and he could see no logical reason why the national government should be so restricted. He cited numerous concrete instances in which funds had already been appropriated without any reference to the enumerated powers: the Louisiana Purchase, money donated by Congress to refugees from Santo Domingo, and funds for the construction of the Cumberland Road. He admitted that our government was based on positive principles stated in the Constitution, not on precedent. "I do not deny the position," he concluded, "but I have introduced these instances to prove the uniform sense of Congress and the country (for they have not been objected to) as to our powers; and surely they furnish better evidence of the true interpretation of the constitution than the most refined and subtle arguments." This was a most convenient position for an ambitious statesman — there was nothing in the Constitution to prevent the power of the federal government from growing like Jack's beanstalk.

It is not surprising that Madison, formerly an orthodox Jeffersonian, should have clashed with such a Hamiltonian as the young Calhoun. But perhaps the best critic of the legislation of the Era of Good Feeling was the Carolinian himself; never did an apostle recant his early faith more completely. In his famous *Discourse on the Constitution and Government of the United States*, written shortly before his death, he condemned the whole nationalistic program which he had taken the lead in formulating and enacting. At that later date he regarded the national bank, for the rechartering of which he had been almost singly responsible, as one of the chief evils of the period. Jefferson, he pointed out, "took strong positions against it and laid the foundations for its final overthrow," and the Democratic party was "entitled to the credit of putting down the Bank of the U.S."[22] The bank, in his opinion, was merely one manifestation of the gradual usurpation of power by the federal government which resulted from the centralizing influences of the War of 1812 that drove the nation so far away from its original Republican system.

Yet in 1837 he "admitted that when a young man, and at his entrance upon political life, he had been inclined to that interpretation of the constitution which favored a latitude of powers, but experience, observation, and reflection had wrought a great change in his views; and, above all, the transcendent argument of Mr. Madison himself, in his celebrated resolutions of 1798, had done more than all other things to convince him of his error."[23]

*   *   *

Calhoun's extreme nationalism in the first half of his career — which was both a sentiment and a policy on his part — cannot be denied. Regardless of the position he later came to occupy, in 1816 such nationalism was highly natural in view of the age in which he lived and the circumstances of his life prior to 1828. To begin with, he was a son of the piedmont, which throughout the country was generally more patriotic than the tidewater. This attachment to the Union was intensified by his residence in, and travel through, different sections of the nation. Many Americans were becoming increasingly nationalistic before Jefferson left office. By 1815, as a result of events preceding and during the war, such sentiment was both rampant and predominant outside of New England. In sharing this sentiment with his fellow citizens Calhoun was but a child of his own age, and his attitude was as natural as a Southerner's hatred for Yankees during Reconstruction or an American's hatred for the "Huns" in 1918.

When an individual who personally acquiesced so strongly in

this national passion happened to be a leader of the party in power, at a period which he regarded as an emergency in the evolution of the nation, a broad nationalistic governmental policy was the logical and inevitable result. In this Calhoun differed not at all from the other Young Republicans, Clay, Lowndes, Cheves, Porter, and their colleagues. It is almost impossible to overestimate the influence of his experience in Congress during the war upon his thinking.

He had seen the government impotent when the enemy was marching on Washington; despite the herculean efforts of himself and his colleagues the administration had been unable to get men for the army or money for the martial effort. The various — and to him inexcusable — weaknesses in a nation fundamentally so strong impressed and embarrassed him. His emotional and his intellectual reaction to his experience during the years of the war, when the responsibility of government had been heavy on his shoulders, were one and the same. Never again, could he prevent it, would disaster and disunion be so imminent. Certain as he was of a future war with England, and aware of the natural and self-contented apathy of the public after the Peace of Ghent and the Battle of New Orleans, he regarded all considerations as secondary to the immediate necessity of national self-sufficiency so essential to security.

Nor should it be overlooked that his was the party in power, permanently so it seemed in 1816. Already high in Republican councils, surely he may have envisioned himself as President within a decade. He had plans for the nation, he must have the power to carry them out. As long as he was at the helm, he had no fear that such power would be abused. Power was essential to security, to the preservation of union and of liberty. Few statesmen in office, certainly not Jefferson, Madison, and Monroe, have consistently resisted a broad construction of the Constitution. Furthermore, the advocacy of nationalism was politically advantageous to an aspirant to the presidency. An antiwar Federalist in 1816 had difficulty in getting votes even in New England, but a statesman who was all things to all sections — like Calhoun — might, at the crucial moment in an election, receive invaluable votes far from his own state.

In view of his later reversal it should be emphasized that the Carolinian, in his high Federalism of the postwar era, was a political pragmatist. It was this which made him an eminent statesman. Despite his reputation as a logician, actually he worked from his conclusions, often intuitively reached, back to constitutional and economic premises. His arguments, however impressive, were frequently not his original reasons for his particular stand. He began with an actual situation facing the nation, which called for action; he ended with the Constitution, which he cut to fit the pattern. His objective — other than personal ambition — was that security without which there could be neither union or liberty. To that end a tariff, bank, roads, navy, and army were but incidental means, and the risks which each of those measures involved were far outweighed by the desirability of the end to which they contributed.

He was in favor of a protective tariff in 1816 because certain industries essential to national security were infant. It is true that he did not commit himself to a tariff as a permanent subsidy to a special economic group: "Laying the claims of manufacturers entirely out of view, on general principles, without regard to their interests, a certain encouragement should be extended, at least, to our woolen and cotton manufactures."[24] Years later he argued that he was no bank man per se; the bank was a device necessary in 1816 to increase the value of government revenue and to augment the prosperity of the nation so that it could pay the costs of war: "In supporting the bank of 1816, I openly declared that, as a question *de novo*, I would be decidedly against the bank, and would be the last to give it my support. I also stated that, in supporting the bank then, I yielded to the necessity of the case, growing out of the existing and long established connection between the Government and the banking system."[25] During the years of his cooperation with the Whigs against Andrew Jackson, he favored a recharter of the bank on the same grounds of expediency.

In his speeches during the war and postwar years Calhoun frequently condemned sectional particularism, and there can be no doubt that he was honestly national in his outlook. From this fact, however, it should not be implied that the program he advocated in Washington was detrimental to the interests of his state, or that it was generally so regarded at that time in South Carolina. A majority of her representatives even voted for the first postwar tariff, partly because it was not evident in 1816 that manufactures would shun that region any more than another. A state with a commercial metropolis of the importance of Charleston had good reason to appreciate sound banking, and roads and canals would give it western markets no less than they would New York.

Nor was there any particular menace to South Carolina from the increase in federal power. The Republican party was dominated by the South and the West. It was New England, as the constant opposition of Webster to the Republican program proved, which had to fear a government in the hands of a coalition from rival sections. And what state had so many, or such able, sons in Washington as Calhoun, Lowndes, Cheves, and Williams? In furthering, as he thought, the interests of the nation, John Calhoun could not be accused in 1816 of neglecting South Carolina.

CHAPTER FIVE

Mr. Monroe's Secretary of War

FOR the sake of harmony in his administration, President Monroe
in 1817 sought to avoid partisanship in his cabinet appointments.
Since his was the only national party (this was the Era of Good
Feeling) nonpartisanship required a fair disposition of positions
among the several sections and neutrality between Henry Clay
and William Crawford, the known aspirants for the succession.
Both Monroe and Madison had acceded to the presidency from the
state department, and that post was generally regarded as the step-
ping stone to the highest office.

Thus the new President accomplished a dual purpose by selecting
as Secretary of State the New Englander, John Quincy Adams,
who for the time being kept his aspirations for the presidency to
himself. Crawford was retained in the treasury, but Clay rejected
the offer of the war department. Piqued at the presidential failure
to name him to the leading cabinet post, he spent most of the next
eight years in the House attacking the policy of the administration
on all counts. After Clay's refusal and Jackson's indication of dis-
interest, Monroe in succession offered the post to Governor Isaac
Shelby of Kentucky and William Lowndes, both of whom also
refused. Finally with some reluctance he offered it on October 10,
1817, to Calhoun, who after three weeks' delay accepted.

The assertion of some of the Carolinian's biographers that he was Monroe's first choice, and that these offers were tendered for political reasons with the certainly that they would be rejected, is unsupported by any conclusive evidence. Certainly his prominence made him eligible, and he had not only worked closely with Monroe during the war but had also given him active support against Crawford in the heated caucus of 1816.[1] Yet the President undoubtedly hesitated to include him in his cabinet, possibly because such a choice would result in three southerners and no westerner in that body, or possibly because he, like Madison, feared the consequence of the Carolinian's ambition and positive views upon the harmony of the official family.

There is less doubt about Calhoun's motive in his acceptance. As he stated in his autobiography, it was a general impression that his peculiar abilities lay in the field of thought rather than action. Against the advice of Lowndes and other personal friends, he accepted the post primarily to dispel the doubt that his executive talents were any less brilliant than his legislative.[2] While to a greater degree than any contemporary statesman he regarded preparedness for the third war with England as the most essential of national policies, he must have equally considered the cabinet offer in its relation to his future candidacy for the presidency. At that time no President had been elected whose administrative ability had not been satisfactorily demonstrated. The department of war, equal in importance at the moment to that of state, was in utter chaos, and one who could bring even a semblance of order out of such confusion would be recognized immediately as an executive of first rank. Assuming that the high tide of nationalism would continue, the leader who would conceive and execute a forceful program of national defense could count among his political assets an emotional as well as a rational appeal to the electorate.

Calhoun's hesitation indicated a realization on his part that the decision was crucial and inevitably somewhat of a gamble because of the unpredictability of the future. The very elements of the situation which made so great the rewards of a successful administration of the post increased the odds against that success. The bitter personal attacks to which he was subjected when he did attempt to carry out a vigorous defense program, the endless congressional investigations of his policy and his department, and the animosity which soon developed between himself and his colleagues, notably Clay and Crawford, may have caused him later to regret that he ever accepted. As a matter of fact, his fatal break with Jackson a dozen years later came about because of the use which Van Buren was able to make of Calhoun's censure, in the privacy of the cabinet, of the General's seizure of Pensacola in 1818 in violation of war department orders. Yet his decision to ignore the advice of the dispassionate Lowndes and to accept the challenging post was entirely in character. It was in keeping with an excessive and almost rash self-confidence as yet unchecked by any significant failure.

*   *   *

The war department at that time had under its jurisdiction not merely the army and coastal fortifications, but also Indian affairs, pensions, and land warrants. Supply was in the hands of private contractors, and there were $40,000,000 of unsettled accounts when Calhoun took over his new duties. The army, including the engineers, had a paper strength of 12,000, but actually only 8,000 men were in service. There was no unity of command. Generals Jacob Brown and Andrew Jackson, who commanded respectively the northern and southern departments, held coordinate power and were responsible, through the war secretary, only to the President. Construction of the fortifications urged by Calhoun the year before in Congress had not been started, and a confused Indian policy was already under attack from both settlers and fur traders.

After several years of intelligent planning and hard work, Calhoun as Secretary could boast of a department that was a model of efficiency. Such improvement could not have been achieved without the able assistance of high-ranking officers in the service, of Major Christopher Van Deventer (his chief clerk), and of Tennessee Senator John Williams, chairman of the Military Affairs Committee. A surgeon general and a judge advocate general were added to the newly organized General Staff, each member of which headed a particular bureau. The supply services, previously independent, were reorganized by instituting a system of direct purchase by the commissary general. Regulations were drawn up clarifying the chain of command, the issuance of orders, and the interrelation between staff and line. The Military Academy was modernized and given new life. Expense of operating the army was reduced, claimed the autobiography, from an annual cost per man of $451 to $287, a gross saving of $1,300,000 a year. Only three millions of accounts remained unsettled when the Secretary turned over the department to his successor in 1825.[3]

The excellence of this performance was recognized both by contemporaries and posterity. Lowndes wrote from England in 1819 that British War Minister Palmerston was far less able in that capacity than Calhoun. "The order and harmony, regularity and promptitude, punctuality and responsibility, introduced by Mr. Calhoun in every branch of the service," commented the somewhat wordy Niles in his *Weekly Register*, "has never been rivaled, and perhaps, cannot be excelled." Professor William E. Dodd has called the Carolinian the best Secretary of War until Jefferson Davis took over the department in the 1850's.[4] But the surest evidence of the national reputation Calhoun was gaining from his efforts is the fact that Crawford, correctly regarding him a potential rival as Monroe's successor, used the dominant influence his cabinet position gave him in Congress to block the defense program and to attempt to convict the Secretary of War before the public of dishonesty and militarism.

Calhoun's outstanding accomplishment of departmental efficiency, however, cannot hide the rejection by Congress of the major defense measures which he proposed. This defeat he took bitterly at the time, for he felt it exposed the Republic to serious dangers, and he appealed in vain to the public over the heads of congressmen to save his program. The obvious physical threat to national security, he argued, came from the British, the Spanish, and the Indians. The nation was exceedingly vulnerable, as the late war had revealed, in the extent of coastline and of western land frontier.

The solution he proposed was, first, the construction of strong forts at strategic points on the Great Lakes and along the major bays of the Atlantic and Gulf coasts. For speedy movement of troops a series of parallel east-west and north-south roads and waterways should be constructed in the interior without delay. Since the uncivilized Indians of the trans-Mississippi Northwest were the immediate menace to settlers pushing ever farther westward in greater numbers, new military posts must be established along the upper Missouri. On this frontier the bulk of the army would be stationed, leaving the navy and the small garrisons in the coastal forts to repel any British attack from the sea. Considering the vast extent of the nation and the small size of the standing army concentrated far away in the West, an adequate transportation net was just as essential for military purposes as the forts at the mouth of the Chesapeake, at Mobile Bay, and at the water approaches to New Orleans.

Calhoun thought the third war with England would break out in the West as a result of her efforts, working through the Indians from Canada and Oregon, to block American expansion towards the Pacific. The Indian policy of the government, therefore, was the essence of external as well as internal security. The proposal in his exhaustive report to Congress in 1818 was realistic and yet humanitarian. The settlers must be protected from the Indians and the Indians protected from the settlers. An attempt should be made to induce the semicivilized tribes east of the Mississippi, who except for the Seminoles on the southern border presented no military menace, to migrate to new lands in the "Great American Desert" across the river. These new lands the government must solemly promise not to take from them at any future date. Trade with the Indians would be carried on by government factors and private traders, licensed and rigorously controlled by the government.

Those who could not be induced to migrate must be encouraged to complete their assimilation of the culture of the white race, and when this process was completed under the direction of government factors, the Indians should receive full rights of citizenship. Private traders must pay a license of from one to five hundred dollars, and their accounts and activities must be frequently inspected by the government. The wild aborigines of the Northwest, still seminomadic, for the time being must be guarded from foreign intrigue and prevented by force from attacking settlers. In that area the government would retain the monopoly of the fur trade, and after a thirty-year transition period the civilizing treatment would also be applied to these western Indians.[5]

At first it seemed that Calhoun's broad policy would be adopted. Monroe strongly backed the fortifications on the Atlantic coast, careful plans were drawn up, and construction was begun. Congress voted the necessary appropriations and in 1819, despite opposition from the fur interests, accepted the recommendations of the Report on Indian Affairs as far as extending the factory system. But when the full impact of the Panic of 1819 hit the nation, the Crawford forces launched a campaign for strict governmental economy. Defense appropriations were cut and cut again. Rejecting the Secretary's request for $1,500,000 for fortifications in 1820, Congress voted only $800,000 for that purpose, and in 1821 only $202,000. In 1819 it reduced the army from 12,000 to 6,000 men. When Calhoun proposed as a compromise that the reduction be accomplished by releasing half of the enlisted men of the line companies, leaving the staff and the officers undiminished, even this was rejected. As a result he was forced into the politically embarrassing task of dismissing and demoting numerous officers from the top as well as the bottom of the military hierarchy. As a final blow, after he became openly a presidential candidate at the end of 1821, his appointments under the army reorganization act were rejected by the Senate on a technicality; and his whole Indian program, including the factory system, was abolished with little opposition in either house.

It is easy to explain the causes for the defeat of the War Secretary's "enlarged" program. Calhoun had characteristically let his imagination run away with him; he was never one who found difficulty in justifying his pet projects in terms of national interest and high logic. The menace of Spain was removed by her agreement to cede Florida in 1819 (finally ratified in 1821), and by the successful rebellion of her South and Central American colonies. Canning's flattering proposal to Ambassador Rush in 1822 for joint Anglo-American protection of the new Latin American republics made it clear that England would permit neither the Quadruple Alliance nor any single nation on the European continent to interfere by force in the Western Hemisphere. Czar Alexander of Russia even invited the United States to become a member of the Holy Alliance.

As for the menace of England herself, there was clear evidence by 1821 that her new policy towards her former colonies was conciliatory rather than belligerent. Prime Minister Castlereagh had exhibited a consistent intent to win American friendship. By mutual agreement the Great Lakes were demilitarized in the Rush-Bagot Convention of 1817, by which England risked far more than the young nation across the Atlantic that had so recently entertained imperialistic designs on Canada. The questions of the Newfoundland fisheries and the northern boundary were compromised, and by the Convention of 1818 Oregon was jointly occupied. Most significant of all, Castlereagh had not pressed the protest of Jackson's high-handed execution of Ambrister and Arbuthnot in Florida, when according to Rush war would have resulted "had the ministry but held up a finger."

But domestic developments alone would have killed the expensive defensive program. Postwar nationalism, more emotional than rational in origin, was certain soon to subside under the impact of the increasing sectional divergences of the period. In this regard as in others, the political consequences of the Panic of 1819 were far-reaching. After the direct taxes passed as a war measure had been discontinued, revenue from tariff duties and the sale of public lands were the sole source of income for the federal government, which was still attempting to discharge a heavy war debt. The onset of depression reduced both types of income drastically, and Crawford as head of the treasury demanded the financial retrenchment necessary to balance the budget. What more logical object for such retrenchment was there than the grandiose and costly projects of the war department? In time of depression governmental economy has a cogent appeal to the voter, of which William Crawford was well aware.

Furthermore, an Indian policy centered on government competition with and control of private traders was bound to meet the resistance of the nation's wealthiest citizen, John Jacob Astor. Nor was it an accident that the attack in Congress on Calhoun's policy was capably led by Senator Thomas Hart Benton of Missouri, a state whose metropolis was St. Louis, fur capital of America. Citizens of the West, everywhere covetous of the rich lands still occupied by redmen, simply wanted the Indians removed by fair means or foul. Had the War Secretary been more of a careful observer of his fellowmen and less of a self-deluded dialectician, he would have known that his potential, and later his actual, political rivalry with Crawford and Clay would dictate their concerted opposition to his program in Congress, where each of them had more influence than he.

*   *   *

Monroe's administrations are remembered for their association with the Missouri Compromise and the Monroe Doctrine. Actually, over the entire period of his eight years in office, Americans were even more concerned with the acquisition of Florida, the tariff, internal improvements, western land, and the proposals of the major economic interests of the country by which they expected to gain relief from the depression. The price of government land was reduced in 1820 to $1.25 per acre. The minimum amount of purchase was lowered to 80 acres, and a system of relief was set up for purchasers under the old credit system who were in arrears on their payments. The tariff of 1820, designed for the similar relief of manufacturers, after passing the House was defeated by one vote in the Senate. The bill of 1824 succeeded by the close margin of 107 to 102 and 25 to 21. Like Madison, Monroe insisted upon a constitutional amendment before he would accept a bill for internal improvements. Tired of delay, several impatient states began necessary projects at their own expense. The President vetoed the Cumberland tolls bill of 1822, but yielded somewhat on the point two years later by signing a bill appropriating funds for a general survey of roads and canals important for military and commercial purposes.

With a stronger cabinet than any previous executive, Monroe consulted it on every important step and usually followed its members' recommendations. At its frequent meetings the departmental reports of the various members and even presidential messages were discussed and criticized. In the first term Adams and Calhoun inclined to agree on issues, usually in opposition to Crawford, though the entrance of all three into the presidential race by 1822 disrupted cabinet harmony. During the period of their unity Adams had the highest praise for his Carolina colleague, whose talents were particularly suited to the more intellectual discussions of such a small group. "Calhoun thinks for himself independently of all the rest," wrote the Secretary of State, "with sound judgment, quick discrimination, and keen observation. He supports his opinions, too, with powerful eloquence."[6]

The first crisis which the cabinet faced was the international difficulty with England and Spain in which Jackson placed the nation by his seizure of Pensacola and his execution of the Englishmen Ambrister and Arbuthnot for inciting the Indians. The cabinet had already voted for a showdown with the Seminoles who had for months been terrorizing the southern border, retreating into Spanish Florida after each raid for safety. War department orders issued to General Gaines, soon inherited by Jackson, directed the southern army to cross the border and destroy them "unless they should shelter themselves under a Spanish fort. In the last event, you will immediately notify this Department."[7]

It was this latter provision to which Jackson objected in a letter sent over the head of the new Secretary directly to Monroe, in which he proposed the capture of all East Florida. This could be done without compromising the administration if the President would secretly so indicate through the Tennessee congressman, John Rhea. Jackson later claimed he received such an indication, though Monroe denied it.[8] In his usual fashion the General quickly defeated the Indians, and in the process captured Spanish forts at St. Marks and Pensacola. Seizure of the forts violated his orders, whether or not it could be justified by strict military necessity.

The departments immediately concerned were those of state and war. For six months Calhoun had been trying to enforce his authority over generals who were inclined to disregard orders. He naturally proposed making an example of Jackson for his insubordination, a course in which the President and all of the cabinet except Adams at first concurred. The Secretary of State, as in the Monroe Doctrine five years later, eloquently argued for a bolder solution: surrender the forts, but neither disavow their capture nor repudiate Jackson. At length he won the other cabinet members over to this compromise.[9]

Adams argued that Jackson's summary action could be satisfactorily justified on the grounds of self-defense, and that it was ideal for the purpose of convincing Spain that her delay in selling Florida to the United States might result in her losing it without compensation. The alienation of the General, he pointed out, would destroy the popularity of the administration with a public that loved Old Hickory more than the President. This undoubtedly was the convincing argument, but political repercussions were soon evident. Foreseeing Jackson as a dangerous presidential rival for the support of the West, Clay attacked the administration for its failure to censure him and warned the republic of the dangers of military tyranny.

Clay's resolution of censure was overwhelmingly defeated, but it led to numerous investigations of the war department and to the later reduction of the army. During the excitement Jackson made a triumphant trip to Washington. Though cordial to Calhoun, he regarded Adams as his special champion. Secretly the New Englander exulted, for he was planning to capitalize on the General's popularity by making him his running mate in 1824. Calhoun, realizing that congressional censure would reflect on him no less than on Jackson, aided in the defeat of the resolution and now admitted that the General had been honest and patriotic in his objectives. But the truth of the cabinet opposition to Jackson eventually leaked out through Crawford, and the Tennesseean revived the issue in 1830 as a dramatic pretext for breaking with Calhoun, who at that time had become obnoxious to him for other reasons.

*   *   *

The central event of these years was the depression, of which Calhoun was personally and politically aware, particularly after it ruined his ambitious program. "Calhoun is gloomy," wrote Adams in his diary after one of their numerous heart-to-heart talks. "He says there has been within these two years an immense revolution of fortunes in every part of the Union; enormous numbers of persons utterly ruined; multitudes in deep distress; and a general mass of disaffection to the Government, not concentrated in any particular direction, but ready to seize upon any event and looking out anywhere for a leader ... resulting in an impression that there was something radically wrong in the administration of the Government."[10]

Well might the Carolinian have been gloomy, for it boded ill for his political aspirations which depended for success upon a continuation of unity and nationalistic sentiment. Practical politicians were already endeavoring to capitalize upon this discontent. Clay attacked the administration even more vehemently; Crawford became a staunch advocate of economy and state rights. Local politicians who were soon to cluster under the Jackson banner were becoming convinced that the successful candidate in 1824 must be a man of the people free from the taint of responsibility for the current conduct of national policy.

The controversy over Missouri and the expansion of slavery, Calhoun told Adams, was like the debate on the tariff of 1820 a symptom of this undercurrent of discontent.[11] The compromise bill, proposed by Senator Jesse B. Thomas of Illinois, settled two basic questions. By the admission of slave Missouri and free Maine the South was guaranteed a parity in the Senate that she was to enjoy until 1850, thus insuring her of a means of vetoing legislation hostile to slavery originating in the House where her representatives were in a minority. The remaining territories to be formed out of the Louisiana Purchase were divided by the 36° 30′ parallel into slave and free areas.

Under pressure from his Virginia friends to grasp this opportunity to take an uncompromising state-rights stand, Monroe was so disturbed about the constitutionality of the measure that he submitted the question to his cabinet, requesting opinions in writing. He phrased his query in such a form as to inquire whether in the cabinet members' opinions the prohibition of slavery north of the line applied to that area only while it was territorial in status, or whether it would prohibit states later admitted from that area from adopting slavery. On the latter point the three southerners in the cabinet agreed that it did not, and only Adams believed in the constitutionality of such interference with the right of a state to decide for itself the status of slavery within its borders.

The question was crucial, for if the federal government were granted the power to restrict slavery in one state, the same power could be used by a congressional majority to abolish it in all. Calhoun proposed an adroit dodge. The President's question should be revised into the simple query as to whether the act was constitutional. All could say yes, and the southerners could later claim that they understood the prohibition to apply only to *territories* north of the dividing line, not to *states*. Such was the outcome, and Calhoun discussed the whole slavery problem in a surprisingly abstract fashion on a walk with Adams. Recognizing as "just and noble" the New Englander's assertion that slavery was contrary to the Declaration of Independence and an abuse of the rights of the governed, his southern friend tried to show Adams why Negro slavery was a social necessity to the South. "Domestic labor was confined to the blacks, and such was the prejudice, that if he, who was the most popular man in his district, were to have a white servant in his house, his character and reputation would be irretrievably ruined.... It did not apply to all kinds of labor — not for example to farming.... And it was the best guarantee of equality among the whites."

The answer to this reasoning which Adams confided to his diary was prophetic. By their arguments on Missouri the southerners "betrayed the secret of their souls. In the abstract they admit that slavery is an evil...but when probed to the quick upon it they show at the bottom of their souls pride and vain glory in their condition of masterdom." He and Calhoun speculated about the future. The southerner did not think the question would end the Union, but if it did the South would have to ally itself with England.

Adams asked if the North would not resist such a move by force, to which Calhoun replied that the South would then "find it necessary to make their communities all military."[12] Here they reached an impasse.

*   *   *

There is no doubt that Calhoun clearly foresaw that the formation of northern and southern parties would defeat the nationalistic program he regarded as essential and ruin his chances for the presidency. He immediately sought to calm the South and to check the growth of Crawford's sectional party. The senators from South Carolina, particularly his bitter foe William Smith, had sided with the Crawford forces in Congress against him from the beginning, but with the assistance of Lowndes he was able for a while to keep the younger political leaders in his state, like George McDuffie and Robert Hayne, true to the spirit and policy of nationalism. The attack on the admission of slave Missouri, he insisted somewhat with wishful thinking, was merely a bid for power by a small, selfish group of northern politicians. The people of the North generally were by no means hostile to southern prosperity. If southerners would keep their heads, the Missouri agitation would soon be forgotten as a temporary flare-up. But if they retaliated by attacking northern interests and forming a southern bloc, they would unite the entire North in hostile opposition and numerical superiority.

In Cassandra fashion he predicted the fatal consequences of the course into which he himself was later to lead the South. "We of the South ought not to assent easily to the belief," he wrote Senator Charles Tait of Georgia, one of Crawford's campaign managers, after a trip to New York and Boston in 1820,

> that there is a conspiracy either against our property or just weight in the Union. A belief of the former might, and probably would, lead to the most disastrous consequence. Nothing would lead more directly to disunion with all of its horrors. That of the latter would cooperate, as it appears to me, directly with the scheme of a few designing men to the north, who think they see their interest in exciting a struggle between the two portions of our country. If we, from such a belief, systematically oppose the North, they must from necessity resort to a similar opposition to us.

Our true system is to look to the country; and to support *such measures and such men*, without regard to sections, as are best calculated to advance the general interest.... Should emancipation be attempted it must, and will be resisted at all costs, but let us be certain first that it is the real object, not by a few, but by a large portion of the non slave holding states.

In another letter to Tait a year later he again decried the appeal of the "Radical" party to southern prejudice. "Distrust must engender distrust. We will not trust them, they will not trust us. Conflict must follow, thence violence and then disunion."[13]

Calhoun, it should be emphasized, did not recede from his nationalism during his cabinet years. Not only was he in complete agreement in 1824 with Clay and Adams as to the extreme powers of the federal government, but he even based his hope for the presidency upon the belief that he was generally regarded as more nationalistic than they. His major interest during these years was in internal improvements. He took care not to embarrass the President, who regarded construction of roads and canals by the federal government as unconstitutional. But no doubt existed in his own mind that the Constitution gave ample power to Congress for such a program, though he accepted the meaningless qualification that such power should not be exercised without the consent of the states concerned.[14]

In order to allay particularism in South Carolina which might cause him embarrassment, however, he attempted to use methods of indirection on the tariff similar to the artful dodge he had proposed in the cabinet on the Missouri Compromise. The facts that the South voted 40 to 3 against the Baldwin tariff of 1820 and that the bill was defeated by only one vote in the Senate made him fully aware of the dynamite latent in the question. In 1820 the citizens of Charleston had drafted a memorial to Congress, protesting in moderate language any increase in duties. Therefore, when Monroe's second inaugural message was being discussed in the cabinet in 1821, "there were expressions favorable to the manufacturing interests, to which Mr. Calhoun made some objections, and which were slightly modified."[15] His earliest biographer states that he also objected to Monroe's advocacy of an increase in protection in the annual messages of 1822 and 1823.[16] Another indication of his bid for southern support was his suggestion that the President confidentially inform Congress that influential Cubans had declared themselves ready to rebel from Spain and to request admission to the Union.

In these actions and in his letters of the period, particularly in one written in 1824 to Robert S. Garnet of Virginia, it is evident that he was beginning to hedge on the questions of the tariff and state rights. But John Taylor of Caroline, high priest of the Virginia state-sovereignty group which Calhoun visited in 1823, pointed out the Carolinian's inconsistency in a letter to Monroe. Calhoun was not preferable as a candidate to Adams, despite his being a southerner, argued Taylor. Though the Secretary declared that the distribution of powers between the states and the federal authority constituted a distinguishing pre-eminence in our form of government, he immediately destroyed that pre-eminence by endowing the federal government with a supremacy over the state governments whenever they came in conflict.[17]

CHAPTER SIX

A Young Man in a Hurry Has to Wait

CALHOUN had no hobbies and only two interests, his political career and his family. "I find my children the great solace of life," he wrote to his brother-in-law John Ewing Calhoun,[1] and before the end of his cabinet days he had sired a total of seven, two of whom died in infancy. When he was elevated to the cabinet, Floride and the family joined him in Washington. In 1817 they lived with the Lowndes, but the next year they rented a house of their own in town. Later they moved out to the heights of Georgetown to a residence (Dumbarton Oaks) which Floride's mother had purchased. In 1824 they returned to the Carolina piedmont because of the persistent illness of their children.

The War Secretary's expenses at this time were tremendous, for his position forced him to entertain frequently and his later campaign for the presidency undoubtedly cost him heavily. His salary was insufficient and he constantly requested funds from his brothers-in-law who were handling his cotton and his Carolina properties, including those of his wife which he fully controlled. Apparently Floride enjoyed her new social position. Her mother lived with them and may have embarrassed the young couple by her religious · zeal in seeking converts among their friends for the Presbyterian Church during a revival in 1822 at the height of a cholera epidemic. Floride attended the fashionable Episcopal Church, but her husband

75

assisted in founding the first Unitarian congregation in the capital.[2] It was perhaps a slap at her son-in-law's deism when Mrs. Calhoun stated that if "her candidate" Jackson were elected in 1824, she would spend the next winter in Washington just to see a President who went to church.

As a young man rapidly rising in affairs of state, Calhoun naturally attracted the professed admiration and friendship of many, yet only with Lowndes, and with John Quincy Adams for a short period, was he really intimate. He could not unbend, and conversation with him was generally a monologue on his part. "I never heard him utter a jest," wrote one friend of the family. "There was unvarying dignity and gravity in his manner; and yet the playful child regarded him fearlessly and lovingly."[3] He did not repel people with whom he came into social contact; they were aware of his intent to be friendly, but he did not bind them to him by any warmth of personality or mutual interest in life. He never read for pleasure or played cards. Work was both vocation and avocation, and during his early years in the cabinet he often spent fourteen to fifteen hours a day at his desk.

*   *   *

During the sixteen years after he took the lead in the nationalistic legislation of the postwar Congress, Calhoun's ambition and his primary objective was his own elevation to the presidency. Under the congressional caucus, still customary in 1816, the cabinet was a road to the presidency. Probably this was his chief reason for accepting the secretaryship of war under Monroe. In his ambition and his objective the Carolinian was by no means alone. William Crawford of Georgia and John Quincy Adams, his colleagues in Monroe's cabinet, and Henry Clay who chose a different road to the common goal by remaining in the legislative department as Speaker of the House, all had identical aspirations.

Like Adams and Clay, Calhoun hoped to ride into the coveted White House on the wave of the new nationalism with which he had so unreservedly identified himself. Unfortunately for his plans there were others, besides Adams and Clay, prominently associated in the public mind with the new spirit of unity: Andrew Jackson of Tennessee, hero of the battle of New Orleans who shortly chastised those other enemies of the republic, the Seminoles and the Spaniards; De Witt Clinton of New York, who was building the Erie Canal; and William Lowndes of South Carolina, whose popularity in the House was equal to Clay's and even greater in his native state than that of Calhoun.

Nevertheless, in December, 1821, against the advice of many of his friends, he formally announced his candidacy. Adams, Clay, and Crawford had already accepted nominations from their respective states. Had the various sections of the country been guided by reason alone, as Calhoun believed at the time, none of his rivals could have exceeded him in national appeal. Both in war and in peace he had taken definite stands on current issues favorable to special interests of each and all sections. As a southerner, he had no doubt that he could defeat Crawford in the South. By his vigorous advocacy of internal improvements, a tariff, and a strong military policy; he hoped at worst to divide equally the Middle States and the West with Clay. In time he convinced himself that he could hold his own in New England against Adams, who was none too popular with its influential minority of Federalists or, for that matter, with anyone. Calhoun's defense of the merchants against the restrictive system during the war had impressed the shipping interests, as well as his more recent efforts for sound money by the rechartering of the bank; and the rising industrialists of that section could not be unaware of his support of the 1816 tariff bill.

When Calhoun announced his candidacy for the presidency in the last days of 1821, despite his recent assurance to Adams through an intermediary that he had no intention of so doing, the New Englander regarded the move as deliberate treachery. During the bitter months of the presidential contest which followed, he secretly poured out his venom on the unsuspecting War Secretary in his diary. In its pages every action of the Carolinian was recorded as that of a self-seeking, hypocritical, and scheming politician. This diary was published in the 1870's and used by Hermann Von Holst as the basis for his hostile biography of the famous southerner. Thus in the Reconstruction Era, Calhoun seen through Adams' biased eyes became the personification of the unprincipled and wicked South plotting rebellion years before she tried it.

Most of Calhoun's later biographers have portrayed him as the symbol of the purity of southern motives.* In their eyes both Cal-

*Margaret Coit, *John C. Calhoun: American Portrait* (New York, 1950) is the only biography that places its major emphasis upon the man's personality. Her interpretation is psychographic and highly sympathetic.

houn and the South are above reproach, never motivated but by the loftiest incentives. Calhoun the man has remained in the clouds, symbolic of the Lost Cause. As a natural consequence the fiction persists that his great contemporaries, Jackson, Clay, and Webster, were ambitious men who used every means within their power to attain the presidency. But the Carolinian, willing in his high patriotism to accept high office because he so conspicuously had the interests of the whole nation and not himself at heart, never stooped to low personal ambition nor to any of the sordid methods of his rivals.

The letters and papers of Calhoun lend a superficial support to this thesis, but there is a much stronger case for a contrary interpretation. Calvinistic in mental habit and temperament, as was Adams,* Calhoun could never admit personal ambition but had to rationalize his policies and his every political act exclusively in terms of national interest. His shift in the middle of his career from extreme nationalism to an extreme state-rights position made rationalization all the more essential, not merely for his own mental comfort but also to convince the nation of his intellectual integrity. Webster made an identical shift in the opposite direction about the same time, yet he was not subject, in any such degree, to an urge for self-justification. Jackson and Clay, since their appeal was more to men's hearts, never bothered themselves about the matter of consistency. While much of this rationalizing on Calhoun's part was unconscious, it satisfied his peculiar complex and it has been accepted by his biographers for the most part at face value. But why should he not be exposed to the same critical philosophy of human behavior with which biographers have approached his contemporaries? To explain his career in terms of enlightened self-interest can be regarded as condemnation only by those who persist in identifying the fleshless symbol with the man.

Clay, it is generally admitted, wanted all his life to become President and took practical measures to achieve that objective. When in sectional crises he threw the whole weight of his influence and energy into successful efforts at compromise to save the Union, his patriotic course enhanced as much as it hindered his chances for the highest office. Calhoun, it might similarly be argued,

---

*Henry S. Foote, senator from Mississippi, pointed out this similarity between Adams and Calhoun in his *War of the Rebellion* (New York, 1866), 91-92.

equally wanted the presidency all his life and within the limits of his own inhibitions took what he regarded as practical steps towards that end. That he frequently differed with Clay by no means proved that he was any less patriotic or less desirous of preserving the Union — in fact he argued that acceptance of his proposals was the only sure method of such preservation.* At no stage in his career can it be clearly proved that he consciously placed his own fortunes above those of the nation. Yet he was always able to convince himself that the course most convenient to his own aspirations was also best suited for the general welfare of all the American people. As his personal traits differed from those of Clay, so did his methods. Lacking the Kentuckian's ability to charm his fellows by warmth of personality, he was naïve by contrast in his analysis of human conduct. Confident that all men were rational, he assumed that he would be able to win them by the persuasion of logic alone.

*   *   *

Calhoun's entrance into the contest in 1821 and his definite hope for the Democratic nomination as late as 1847 leave no doubt of the depth and persistence of his presidential ambitions. In regard to what might be called his methods of indirection, certain facts must be faced. The highly eulogistic campaign biography published by Harper and Brothers in 1843 was generally assumed to have been written by R. M. T. Hunter, a Virginia congressman. In 1854, however, Robert B. Rhett wrote that Calhoun himself had written all of it but a page or two and had in vain urged him to accept the nominal authorship.† The similarity of this work to an earlier biography published in New York prior to the election of 1824, entitled *Measures, Not Men*, supposedly the work of General Joseph G. Swift, suggests the possibility that Calhoun might have composed the earlier book also.

Certainly in 1828, at a time when the knowledge would have injured his standing in the Democratic Republican party, he kept

---

*George W. Julian, a contemporary and an opponent of Calhoun, wrote that "politically, he has been singularly misunderstood. He was not, as has been generally thought, a dis-unionist. He was the champion of State Sovereignty, but he believed that this was the sure basis and bond of the Union." — George W. Julian, *Political Recollections* (Chicago, 1884), 87.
  †See Appendix.

secret his authorship of the "South Carolina Exposition." He did not claim it as his own until several years later, when it had become a political necessity that he do so. As a member of the cabinet he used his influence to reward his friends with office. Contrary to Monroe's neutral policy he sought to bring administration pressure to bear on congressmen to prevent the re-election as Speaker in 1821 of the New Yorker J. W. Taylor, who had joined Clay and Crawford in defeating his military program.[4] Angered by the personal attacks upon him by the Crawford forces, he may have inspired his friend Ninian Edwards, as Thomas H. Benton infers,[5] to write the "A. B." letter charging the Georgian with misconduct in the treasury. At any rate he exulted in the congressional investigation of his enemy which followed, and he sought vainly to defend Edwards when he was attacked in the cabinet.

These actions certainly indicate that Calhoun did not hesitate to use methods identical in spirit with those for which other public men of the day have been criticized. On this point the impressions of his contemporaries in the early 1820's, while he was still a nationalist and enjoyed a popularity outside the South that he lost after 1832, must be considered somewhat in detail. Granting that they must be discounted because they were colored by the passions of a heated political campaign in which he was a principal, they cannot be dismissed outright as purely partisan expressions.

"As a politician," commented Senator Elijah H. Mills of Massachusetts, "he is too theorizing, speculative, and metaphysical — magnificent in his views of the powers and capacities of the government, and of the virtue, intelligence, and wisdom of the *people....* From his rapidity of thought he is often wrong in his conclusions, and his theories are sometimes wild, extravagant, and impractical... and his schemes are sometimes denounced by his party as ultra-fanatical." In another comment Mills referred to the same trait: "He wants, I think, consistency and perseverance of mind, and seems incapable of long-continued and patient investigation. What he does not see at the first examination, he seldom takes pains to search for; but still the lightning glance of his mind, and the rapidity with which he analyzes, never fail to furnish him with all that may be necessary for his immediate purposes.... In his legislative career... his love of novelty, and his apparent solicitude to astonish were so great, that he has occasionally been known to go beyond even the dreams of political visionaries, and to propose schemes...

which he seemed to offer merely for the purpose of displaying the affluence of his mind."[6]

His friend and colleague in the cabinet, Attorney General William Wirt, recorded that he was advised by Calhoun "to study less and trust more to genius; and I believe the advice is sound. He has certainly practiced on his own precepts." Henry A. Wise of Virginia called him "a giant of intellect, who was a child in party tactics." Thomas Cooper, college president and staunch Carolina state-righter who early fought Calhoun in his native state, wrote to Van Buren that the New Yorker could easily displace the Vice-President as Jackson's successor: "Calhoun is too pretending, too fond of the brilliant, the magnificent, too calculating, how all his sayings and doings will work with respect to his own honor and glory."[7]

But there was general agreement that he possessed ability and even genius. In the presidential contest Joseph Story of Massachusetts, Supreme Court justice, regarded him as perhaps too young but "superior to most, if not to all of the candidates." Webster supported him while he was still in the race and, unwilling to concede Adams any credit, thought Calhoun the only candidate who had a chance of defeating Crawford. Probably with an ulterior motive, Van Buren stated that the Carolinian was Monroe's preference. On the other hand Albert Gallatin, Crawford's running mate, called Calhoun "a smart fellow, one of the first among second-rate men, but of lax political principles and a disordinate ambition not over-delicate in the means of satisfying itself."[8]

*   *   *

It is difficult to avoid the conclusion that Calhoun's decision to enter the presidential race in December, 1821, when he was still under forty, was based upon poor political judgment and over-estimation of his popularity. Adams was in the field from New England, Clay and possibly Jackson from the West, though at the time the General insisted that he had no intentions of running. Crawford had the support of most of the South and of Van Buren in New York, and South Carolina had just unanimously nominated Lowndes in opposition to the Georgian. In all sections, including the South and his own state, he was no more than second choice at best. Undoubtedly he was counting upon the certain support of Pennsylvania as his trump card.

John C. Calhoun

When he decided, after trips to New England, New York, and Pennsylvania during 1820 and 1821, that he was more popular in those sections than Adams and Crawford, he was simply believing what he wanted to believe. He characteristically chose to ignore the warnings of friends, such as his Washington neighbor William W. Seaton of the *Intelligencer*, that his candidacy was premature and unwise. Such overconfidence was natural in a young man who in a decade had risen so rapidly and brilliantly. The recent setback to his defense program in Congress he regarded as pure political obstruction from Crawford and Clay that would be repudiated by the public, whose confidence in himself he fondly believed was supreme. In contrast to his later years, there was as yet no caution in his mind nor iron in his soul.

During Monroe's first term Calhoun's cabinet colleagues Adams and Crawford had been jockeying for position. Narrowly defeated by Monroe in the caucus of 1816 by a vote of 65 to 54, William Crawford had stood aside for the last of the revolutionary generation in line for high office. Regarding Calhoun at first as a potential rival and later as committed to Adams, he was well aware that his economy drive would check the Carolinian's influence. But his attack on the defense program had a more positive purpose: namely, to capitalize upon the dissatisfaction with the administration that had resulted from the depression. Originally a nationalist who had fought for the recharter of the bank in 1811 and who had championed the implied powers of the federal government, Crawford now veered strongly back to the state sovereignty of the Virginia school. Such a move was designed directly to obtain the support of his own state, and of North Carolina, Virginia, and New York as well, in his bid for the presidency. What he offered to a South still shocked by the Tallmadge amendment of 1819 (which passed in the House) to restrict slavery in the West was a southern party bolstered by Jefferson's old New York alliance. His long association with the Republican party, his experience in the government, the patronage of his department, and his not un-related influence in Congress gave him the inside track over Clay and Adams. At the beginning of 1822 he was definitely the man against the field.

Adams, too, had worried about Calhoun as a rival and had subtly offered him the ambassadorship to France. But the attack of Clay and Crawford on the defense program had thrown the Carolinian into his arms. He thought he had assurance that Calhoun, having decided to wait, was amenable to his still nebulous ticket of Jackson for Vice-President and Calhoun for Secretary of State. Ninian Edwards of Illinois, who sounded out the Secretary of War on Adams' behalf, reported his disposition as "excellent" and that he "had no views for himself for the next Presidency." The Secretary of State was counting on the fact that he was the only northern candidate as well as the only contestant from New England. He relied upon the nationalism of his foreign policy, both in regard to Florida and as later expressed in the Monroe Doctrine of 1823, to win sufficient votes from Crawford in the South and West. With quiet confidence he assiduously wooed his war colleague during 1821. "I spoke to Mr. Calhoun...yesterday," he recorded in his diary, "and told him that on this or any other...subject of general consulation by the whole Administration, if he had any preference of views with regard to measures, I should always take pleasure in concurring with them and supporting them." All Calhoun asked was the French mission for Lowndes if Gallatin still wished to retire. Was he giving Lowndes the same treatment that Adams had sought to apply to him?[9]

At any rate Lowndes, who had best expressed the attitude of the early nineteenth century in regard to the proper conduct of presidential aspirants when he stated "the Presidency is not an office to be either solicited or declined," was soon to figure prominently in the contest. On December 18, 1821, a caucus of the South Carolina legislature voted by the close margin of 58 to 54 that it was expedient for the state to nominate a presidential candidate. Since most of those who dissented were Calhoun supporters, they obviously knew, as he therefore must have, that there was no chance of his being nominated by the state. Then the dissenters joined with the majority in a unanimous nomination of Lowndes to defeat what they regarded as the unwise sectional party of Crawford.[10*]

Meanwhile the unsuspecting Lowndes was on his way to the capital to take his seat in Congress. Upon his arrival Calhoun informed him that, in order to stop rumors that he would run as the second candidate on the Adams ticket, he had decided to announce his own candidacy for the presidency. Lowndes replied that he would "greatly prefer his election to that of any of his

---

*South Carolina's preference for Lowndes over Calhoun is obvious in a letter of Jan. 21, 1822, from Hayne to Lowndes, quoted in Jervey, *Hayne*.

competitors." On the evening of December 28 Calhoun gave his consent to a group of congressmen, largely from Pennsylvania and New York, who asked him to accept their public support for the high office. A day or so later Lowndes received word in a letter from James Hamilton, Jr., that he had been nominated by South Carolina. Immediately he had a friendly conference with Calhoun, and they both decided to remain in the race. "The friends whom he had consulted," wrote Lowndes to Hamilton, "think it impossible that he should now retract what he has done.... I am not surprised at the conduct of Mr. Calhoun's friends. I know him and estimate him too well to be mortified by any preference which they may express for him."[11]

The coincidence of these events suggests the definite possibility that their relation was not entirely accidental. Calhoun's bitter enemy Senator William Smith charged that his "nomination" by a group of congressmen was a trumped-up affair. Several months before, Calhoun had gone to western Pennsylvania where he may have seen Dallas, Samuel D. Ingham, and the group who thought it controlled the vote of that state and who strongly favored the candidacy of the Secretary of War because of his definite stand for the tariff and internal improvements. It is not beyond reason that they assured him he could expect a "nomination" from congressmen at the proper time should it develop that such a move would not be made by South Carolina. Judging by the action of his friends in the legislature, Calhoun surely knew in December that if his state decided to nominate he would not be its choice. It is even possible that he received word of Lowndes' nomination before the latter did himself. In that case it was imperative that he be already in the field before news of the Lowndes nomination was received in Washington. Otherwise, by accepting some later "nomination," he would appear disloyal to his closest friend and in opposition to the expressed preference of his own state. His South Carolina supporters rationalized the outcome by arguing that two candidates in the field from that state would improve the chances of defeating Crawford. No so Calhoun, who pronounced the nomination of Lowndes "rash and foolish."[12]

He was able to persuade Lowndes that his own entrance into the contest was ethical, but not Adams, who had been relying heavily on his colleague's influence to carry the Middle States for him. When the rumor of Calhoun's candidacy got around, Adams sent his friend William Plumer to interview the Secretary of War. In a long conversation Calhoun told Plumer that he was running because such a step had become necessary to ensure Crawford's defeat. He stated that he and his southern friends had for four years been in favor of Adams, but that they had recently come to realize that the New Englander was unpopular in his own section and that he would apparently lose New York and Pennsylvania to the Georgian. It became essential, therefore, that some more popular man than Adams enter the race to save the South and the Middle States from Crawford.[13] Adams rejected this lame explanation entirely. Though he outwardly maintained friendly relations with his former friend, who suspected no change in attitude, more and more he confided to his diary his bitter suspicions.

If Calhoun honestly wanted to block Crawford rather than win the office for himself, and if his doubts about Adams' prospects at the time were sincere (it must be remembered that Adams eventually received most of New York's electoral votes), then the more logical course would have been to back the popular Lowndes rather than to split further the opposition to Crawford by becoming a candidate himself. An impartial weighing of all the evidence leads to the simple conclusion that Calhoun wanted the presidency badly, that he convinced himself during 1821 that his own prospects were good, but that he had to resort to circuitous methods in order to get himself properly "nominated." If he was sincere in the defense of his conduct he gave Adams, then he was unbelievably naïve. It is more plausible that some event of the fall of 1821, possibly the defeat of Crawford's candidate for the governorship in Georgia, resulted in his decision to enter the race. By so doing he placed himself in a position of appearing to have misrepresented his intentions to Adams, and he contrived the best explanation possible under the circumstances for an about-face which simply could not be explained to Adams' satisfaction.

*   *   *

Having acted upon his decision, Calhoun became an active and energetic candidate from December, 1821, until he was defeated in Pennsylvania by Jackson in February, 1824. During the intervening period two events occurred which vastly improved his prospects. In May of 1822 Lowndes died at sea on his way to Europe to recover

85

his failing health, and a year later Crawford suffered a serious paralysis from which he did not recover before the election, resulting in the widely held belief that he was permanently incapacitated. Eventually the South Carolina legislature nominated Calhoun almost unanimously, and Crawford's illness served to increase the Carolinian's strength in the Southeast.

For many months the central struggle of the heated campaign was the fight between the Calhoun and Crawford forces, both in Congress and in the newspapers. The immediate consequence of Calhoun's entrance was the reduction of defense appropriations and of the army, the defeat of his Indian policy, and incessant inquiries into the conduct of his department. These developments had the effect of severely decreasing the considerable patronage previously at his disposal, and he was definitely vulnerable in regard to the Mix contract* connected with the fortification projects. His association with the bank was used against him in the West, where the continuing depression was popularly blamed entirely on the "Monster." His defense of the Indians hurt him in Georgia, as did his nationalism in Virginia and his sympathy for protection in the South at large.

Nevertheless, he soon launched a strong counterattack. In the summer of 1822 the Washington *Republican and Congressional Examiner*, under the editorship of his former assistant Thomas L. McKenney, appeared as his official organ. The *Franklin Gazette* of Philadelphia ran installments on his life, probably written by his Pennsylvania lieutenant, George M. Dallas; and the *Virginia Times* of Richmond, the New York *Patriot*, and the *New England Galaxy* of Boston all espoused his cause. The *Republican* kept up a steady barrage on Crawford, and in the short session of Congress in 1822-23 the "A.B" charges† put the Georgian on the defensive for a change.

*In 1818 the war department had awarded a contract to Elijah Mix to supply stone for two fortification projects. Though neither Calhoun nor Christopher Van Deventer influenced the award, the latter was Mix's brother-in-law and bought a half-interest in the contract, without Calhoun's knowledge and contrary to his specific advice. Eventually Van Deventer sold his interest, but when his chief later discovered what he had done, he informed him that if any question should arise in the future in regard to the matter he would have to resign. The sequel to this incident is discussed in Chapter 8.

†On January 20, 1822, an anonymous letter charging Crawford with mismanagement of treasury funds was printed in Calhoun's *Republican*. A long congressional investigation ensued, but Crawford was exonerated. Calhoun's friend and supporter, Ninian Edwards of Illinois, was later revealed as the author of the "A. B." letters.

George McDuffie's efforts for Calhoun in Georgia involved him in two duels, but the appointment of the War Secretary's supporters, John McLean of Ohio as Postmaster General and Samuel L. Southard of New Jersey as Secretary of the Navy, increased his prestige.

His analysis of the determining factor in the campaign proved correct, but not his optimism. "It is certain that the election is with Pennsylvania and New York," he predicted to his Maryland lieutenant Virgil Maxcy in March, 1823. "If they unite they choose their man; if they divide their respective candidates must become the rival candidates. This simple view combined with my known strength in Pennsylvania places me on high ground. . . . I may be mistaken, but it appears to me my prospect was never better. I stand on the great republican cause free alike from the charge of federalism or radicalism."[14]

His strategy was clear. He maintained cordial relations with Jackson and thought he was doing so with Adams. "Keep separate, but attack none, save only the Radicals [Crawford's party]," was his advice to his followers. This meant that, after taking the South from Crawford, he was counting on falling heir to the Jackson, Clinton, or Adams strength in other sections should any of them withdraw. As a matter of fact an understanding existed between the Jackson and Calhoun managers that in the event of either one's withdrawal, the other should receive his support in the South and West. In the course of the campaign various proposals of coalition were apparently made. Crawford supposedly offered the vice-presidency to Adams and then to Clay. Colonel Richard M. Johnson of Kentucky approached Adams with an offer, alleged as coming from Calhoun, of a joint ticket of Adams, Jackson for Vice-President, Clay for Secretary of State, and Calhoun for the treasury.[15] All such rumors Calhoun denounced as tricks of the enemy. "It is a report wholly destitute of fact to support it," he informed his brother-in-law as to a report that he had withdrawn. "I stand wholly on my own basis, and shall continue so to stand. The prospect is good. The election will be left as it ought to be to the people."[16]

But his Pennsylvania lieutenants dared not risk an attempt to force his endorsement upon the legislature of that state, and suddenly towards the end of 1823 Adams' *National Journal* began an attack on the Carolinian. His election was unthinkable, explained Adams privately to Ingham of Pennsylvania, because none of the men older than he could serve under him as President, and if he was honest in what he stated to be his main objective, he would have supported Adams from the beginning. John McLean and other close friends of Calhoun had urged him all along to be content with the vice-presidency.[17] Jackson, carefully handled by the "Nashville Junto," at last consented to be drafted. The boom of his popularity among the masses, who now with the increasing adoption of manhood suffrage actually held the balance of power, had quickly enticed local politicians all over the country to his bandwagon. Calhoun, it so happened, was the first casualty of this significant development which he and the other "professional" candidates long underestimated.* About the time of Adams' attack, the Carolinian's staunch backer Duff Green was writing Ninian Edwards of his intention to support Jackson should his chief be out of the running.[18]

The end came quickly. The opposition to Crawford, failing in their attempt to prevent a congressional caucus, stayed away from the meeting and a rump of sixty-six members in February, 1824, gave all but four votes to the Georgian. This proved a pyrrhic victory for Calhoun, who was largely responsible for the small participation, since it forced his own lieutenant Dallas immediately to propose as a countermove a union of the anti-Crawford forces in Pennsylvania under the Jackson banner. When the Harrisburg convention met soon afterwards, the General received 124 out of the 125 votes for the presidency to Calhoun's 87 for Vice-President.

*   *   *

For the moment the loser could not bring himself to admit that this was the fatal blow. "Our friends have come to the conclusion," he advised Maxcy, "that we ought to hold our position and wait events.... Had Penna decided favorably the prospect would have been most fair. Taking the U.S. together I never had a fairer prospect than on the day we lost the state." But soon Floride's friend, the capital gossip Mrs. Margaret Smith, was remarking that

---

*Calhoun wrote his brother-in-law in the spring of 1822 that "my friends think my political prospect good, in fact better than any other who is spoken of. There is no doubt of Pennsylvania, which must go far to decide the contest.... My own opinion is that the contest will be between Adams, Crawford, and myself."

"he does not look well, and feels very deeply the disappointment of his ambition."[19]

During the remaining few months of the campaign he sought to add Adams' support to that of Jackson for his vice-presidential candidacy, but he constantly refused in return to come out for the New Englander against the General. Adams finally gave in on the point and Calhoun remained officially neutral until after the election. By no means a mere face-saving gesture, this strategy placed him in a strong position. The General, if elected, might die in office or, since he had committed himself to one term, might easily be induced to favor the Carolinian as his successor in 1828. Should Adams win, Calhoun could join forces with him and thus become his heir apparent. So young a man could well afford to wait. Some evidence suggests that he secretly preferred Adams, but the strategy of neutrality was essential to his future. Since the outcome was so unpredictable, he would have been foolish to offend the next President of the United States by coming out at the last moment for his rival, particularly when such an action was unnecessary to his own election. Upon the counting of the ballots it was found that in the electoral college Calhoun had received 182 votes to 30 for his nearest rival, but no presidential candidate had a majority. Jackson received 99 votes, Adams 84, Crawford 41, and Clay 37.

Adams carried all of New England and New York. Jackson divided the Middle States with him, the West with Clay, and the South with Crawford; clearly he was the victor in the nation as a whole since he won eleven states to Adams' seven. But the House, voting by states, had to select the President from one of the first three. Unfortunately for the General, his enemy Clay enjoyed a position of great influence in the House, which voted after weeks of dickerings and wild rumors. The congressmen of six additional states, some of whose legislatures had directed by resolution that their vote be cast for Jackson, went over to Adams, allegedly at Clay's urging. The New Englander received the thirteen states necessary to election on the first ballot. When the new President shortly appointed Clay as Secretary of State, the enraged Jackson forces raised the cry of "bargain and corruption" which embarrassed the incoming administration, ousted it four years later, and probably ruined forever the presidential hopes of Henry Clay.

No conclusive evidence of an actual bargain between the principals has been found, but it may be presumed that they arrived at an understanding of mutual objectives. Evidently Clay decided that his chances for the succession were better with the support of a northern and western coalition, which his union with Adams seemed to assure him, then with the backing that would have resulted from Jackson's good will. It was not the state department but the presidency of which he was thinking. Calhoun at once realized the significance of these events, and he had no choice but to ally himself hastily and unreservedly with the opposition. In order to block Clay he must become Jackson's recognized heir apparent, even if it did mean an eight-year wait unless the General should die before 1832. Quickly the Vice-President took his new tack, "I see in the fact that Clay has made the Pres't against the voice of his constituents," he wrote to his friend General Swift, "and that he has been elevated by him by the first office in his gift, the most dangerous stab, which the liberty of this country has ever received. I will not be on that side. I am with the people, and shall remain so."[20]

Martin Van Buren of New York, Crawford's campaign manager, saw the same light, and he too moved over to the side of the people and Andrew Jackson. Aware of the New Yorker's ambition, Calhoun nevertheless for some time remained optimistic because his strategy appeared highly successful. "I was a candidate for reelection on a ticket with General Jackson himself," he later wrote in regard to the outlook in 1828, "with a certain prospect of the triumphant success of the ticket, and a fair prospect of the highest office to which an American citizen can aspire."[21]

CHAPTER SEVEN

Nationalism and Sectionalism: Background of Nullification

AT first glance the personalities of the public men of the Jackson Era appear to be the determining factors in its changing political fortunes. Actually in any given instance the course of individual careers can be traced to the impact of certain broad economic and social changes which were unfolding in a young but rapidly growing nation. The multiplicity of candidates in 1824, the disappearance of the Federalists and the breakup of the victorious Republicans into the National Republican and Democratic Republican parties, the Jacksonian Revolution, and the miscarriage of Calhoun's careful plan to succeed the General in the White House — all were political consequences of the underlying forces which leaders might successfully follow, but which none of them could control.

There were really five more or less distinct sections in the nation, not three: New England, the Middle States, the Southeast (Old South), the Northwest, and the Southwest. The entire West was growing rapidly, but since the war with England both the Southeast and New England were relatively losing population. The Middle States were increasing at the average rate of the nation as a whole. Since representation in the House was based on population, the political power necessary to the enactment or rejection of legislation was vastly affected by this westward movement.

John C. Calhoun

U. S. POPULATION GROWTH BY SECTIONS, 1820-30

SECTION	POPULATION IN 1830	PER CENT OF TOTAL	PER CENT OF GROWTH, 1820-30
United States	12,866,000	100	33
New England	1,955,000	15	18
Middle Atlantic	3,588,000	28	33
Southeast	3,646,000	28	19
East South Central	1,816,000	15	53
East North Central	1,470,000	11	85
West South Central	246,000	2	47
West North Central	140,000	1	111

Source: U. S. Census Bureau Reports for 1820 and 1830

The eleven states admitted to the Union between 1789 and 1821 had twenty-two senators; the original thirteen had twenty-six. Virginia and Massachusetts may have been the poles of the old Federalist and Republican parties, but on certain basic issues a new political alignment arose in Congress during the Era of Good Feeling: the Middle States and the West against New England and the Southeast. This alignment was clearly evident in the vote on the tariff and internal improvements, both of which the last two sections opposed as detrimental to their current economic interests and their future political power.

Clay's American System was a clever appeal to the self-interest of the growing sections, the West and the Middle States — an appeal which could well be justified on the high grounds of national self-sufficiency. The tariff would protect young manufactures from ruinous competition and give employment to eastern farmers who could not compete with the rich lands of the West. The revenue thereby obtained would be used to construct roads and canals binding the east coast to the interior, thus giving the western farmer a home market. Decreased costs of transportation would enable him to buy his manufactured necessities more cheaply and at the same time to make a greater profit on his crops. The eastern merchant and manufacturer, by selling a greater volume of goods to the West, would also make more profit.

But New England and the Southeast — the first thinking of her shipping which still represented a larger investment than manufacturing, and the second of her cotton and rice — both wanted an increased rather than a decreased trade with England. To both a tariff meant an increased cost of production; they regarded it as a tax which would fall heavily on them for the disproportionate benefit of the other sections. By the encouragement of internal improvements to the already alarming westward migration, land values in these older sections would be further depressed and their political power in the House further reduced by loss of population. It was already becoming apparent that New York, Baltimore, Philadelphia, and New Orleans, and not the proud old colonial ports of Boston and Charleston, would largely monopolize western trade.

This particular sectional alignment did not solidify into political parties because there were other economic issues on which the sectional division formed a different pattern, as well as other motives which determind men's political affiliations. On the bank question all the propertied interests of the seaboard, including those of the Middle States, united against what they regarded as the ruinous inflationary consequences of the state banks of the West. After the depression in 1819 the entire West, even its financially conservative residents like Jackson, regarded the Bank of the United States as a monstrous device to deny them necessary credit and to make them pay excessive interest rates. As for the proposal of a cheap price for the millions of acres of western land in the possession of the federal government, again the business interests of the Middle States joined New England and the Southeast in opposition because they were aware that the resulting increase in migration from the seaboard would compel them to pay higher wages and would decrease land values. On the question of the expansion of slavery, which was only one of the several sectional issues that arose in this period, the division was one of South against North. On this issue the Southwest, which differed with the Southeast on western land and internal improvements, supported the stand of the older section.

Since none of these five sections was static, but in transition, even the near future was unpredictable. South Carolina voted for the tariff of 1816, and Calhoun in 1820 did not regard the effort to restrict slavery to the Old South as a danger. Moreover, by the end of Monroe's second term two new elements had been added to the mechanics of obtaining a congressional majority for legislation: the voting power of the class-conscious common man who, with the general adoption of white manhood suffrage, for the first time began to exercise the franchise; and the growing political strength of a consciously powerful West.

In the two emerging national parties, Whigs and Democrats, all sections were well represented; so far as there was a tendency towards a geographical division the Democrats were stronger in the West and the Whigs in the East. Individual congressmen supported their party on certain issues, but on others voted with their section regardless of party. In the two decades after 1815 the various sections were no means unanimous or even consistent in their stand on all the economic legislation introduced in Congress. For example, New England representatives voted 17 to 10 in favor of the tariff of 1816 but 23 to 16 against the bill of 1828. Southern votes against the measure increased from 35 in 1816 to 47 in 1828, while the Middle States supported both, 42 to 5 and 56 to 6.

ANALYSIS BY SECTIONS OF THE HOUSE VOTE ON BASIC ISSUES

ISSUE		YEAR	NEW ENGLAND	MIDDLE STATES	SOUTH-EAST	SOUTH-WEST	NORTH-WEST	TOTAL
Tariff		1816	17-10	42-5	16-35	3-3	10-1	88-54
		1820	18-17	55-1	5-49	0-7	12-3	90-77
		1824	15-23	57-9	4-56	2-14	29-0	107-102
		1828	16-23	56-6	4-47	0-16	29-1	105-93
		1832	17-17	44-17	31-25	22-6	18-0	132-65
	(low)	1833	10-28	15-46	57-2	27-1	10-8	119-85
	(low)	1846	9-19	17-44	34-9	24-13	30-10	114-95
Internal Improvements		1824	12-26	37-26	23-34	43-0		115-86
Missouri Compromise		1820	7-33	8-46	58-0	17-0	0-8	90-87

Source: H. J. Carman & H. C. Syrett, *A History of the American People.*

On the Survey Bill of 1824 (internal improvements), New England voted in opposition, 26 to 12, as did the South, 34 to 23. The Middle States favored it by a vote of 37 to 26; but 24 of the negative votes came from New York, which already at its own expense had constructed the Erie Canal and therefore objected to taxation by the federal government for a program of roads that would benefit its rival Pennsylvania. On the same bill the entire West voted unanimously in the affirmative, 43 to 0. On the Missouri Compromise the Southwest joined the Southeast in casting a unanimous affirmative vote of 75 to 0.

Thus from an analysis of the votes in the House during this period, a general sectional pattern on the major issues becomes apparent. The Middle States and the Northwest gave the tariff an almost unanimous support, but a majority from New England, the Southeast, and the Southwest were in opposition. Internal improvements were unanimously approved by the Southwest and the Northwest and by a majority from the Middle States, but a majority from New England and the Southeast opposed them. Congressional prohibition upon the westward expansion of slavery was unanimously opposed by the Southeast and the Southwest, but favored by all except a small minority in the three northern sections.

*   *   *

It is obvious, therefore, that no section acting alone in Congress possessed sufficient strength during this period to enact or block specific measures. To accomplish its purpose it was necessary for a section to form temporary alliances, now with one section, now with another, to pass or defeat a particular bill. There was some tendency for these alliances to become permanent; each section, in order to attain success on those measures it regarded as most vital to its interest, would yield on less vital measures to insure the necessary support. It was all a matter of effecting and preserving a congressional majority for or against particular legislation on which there was acute disagreement throughout the nation.

Precedent and the Constitution were much involved, but not morality. Under such circumstances the inevitable question arose long before South Carolina nullified the tariff in 1832. What recourse existed for a section which found itself hopelessly and apparently permanently outvoted on legislation that it considered ruinous to its prosperity? It was this question, as old as the Constitution itself, which eventually led to an overt attempt to dissolve the Union. Towards its solution Calhoun directed most of his energy and attention during the latter half of his long political career.

The delegates at the Philadelphia convention in 1787 had given major consideration to this very problem. Probably the primary purpose of the system of checks and balances which they had interwoven in the frame of the new government, as Madison clearly pointed out in his contributions to the *Federalist Papers,* had been the protection of a minority economic interest from the potential onslaughts of a political majority. For this protection three checks were included within the federal government itself.

Since two senators were chosen by each state regardless of population, the senate was a minority's first line of defense. The upper

95

house could reject a measure passed by the lower house, in which representation was based directly on population. Thus the Baldwin Tariff of 1820, after passing the House, was defeated by one vote in the Senate; the Tallmadge Amendment of 1820 restricting slavery in Missouri, successful in the House, was also rejected by the Senate. A second check was the President who might veto a bill, as Madison, Monroe, and Jackson did those on internal improvements, with the result that a two-thirds majority of each house would be required to override the veto. But by the 1820's the effectiveness of this check was severely limited due to the failure of the original plan for the election of the executive to work as it was intended in 1787. The same political majority which controlled the House could elect the President, and unpopular vetoes might defeat him and his party in the next election.

Potentially far more powerful as a check on the majority was the Supreme Court, free from any necessity of re-election and changeable only by impeachment, death or retirement, or congressional increase of its membership. Acting on its power as the final judge of the constitutionality of federal acts (formally pronounced in the Marbury vs. Madison decision of 1803), the Supreme Court could simply declare that the power upon which a particular bill in question rested had not been delegated to the federal government by the Constitution. Under the broad construction of John Marshall's numerous decisions, however, in case after case the court had increased the power of the federal government and limited the powers of the states, notably in the McCulloch vs. Maryland decision of 1819. By increasing the powers delegated to the federal government in every instance prior to the Jackson Era, the court actually insured the supremacy of the political majority in Congress over the minority.

It was natural, therefore, that in the early years of the new nation minorities should attack both the assumption of power by the Supreme Court as the ultimate judge of constitutionality, as well as the validity of specific decisions handed down by the court sanctioning the right of Congress to legislate on such matters as the bank. Two Virginians in particular, John Taylor and John Randolph, conducted for decades a running fight on Marshall's broad construction and on what they regarded as the unwarranted assumption of power by the federal government. From 1800 to 1815 they received much assistance from a New England which found itself in a minority, notably from Daniel Webster. Despite all that was said and written about the rights of states, however, with the exception of the action of the New England states during the critical war years, minorities had gained relief from obnoxious measures only by inducing a majority in Congress to favor repeal.

The first formal instance of state action came when the legislatures of Kentucky and Virginia declared the Sedition Act of 1798 (passed for partisan political purposes by the Federalists at the height of a war scare with France) null and void because it violated the first amendment of the Constitution. The famous Resolutions written by Jefferson and Madison argued that the Constitution was a compact among the states, each of whom retained "an equal right to judge for itself, as well of infractions as of the mode and measure of redress." No other state supported these two, however, and no act of state interposition was attempted. The Resolutions may have been designed by their authors primarily as a political maneuver. The Sedition Act was in force for only two years; when the Republicans defeated the Federalists in 1800 they simply let the measure expire. It was not state action but rather the Republicans' acquisition of control of the federal government which brought relief.

In order to prevent war with England, Jefferson pushed through the Republican Congress at the end of 1807 an Embargo Act which immediately ruined most of New England's shipping profits and shortly involved the entire nation in a serious depression. Almost in identical words the Massachusetts legislature revived the argument of the Virginia and Kentucky Resolutions, but again it was not state action but federal power which brought relief. So acute was the depression that New York bolted the Republican party, and representatives from that state joined the Federalists in voting to repeal the measure fifteen months after its passage.

When the Young Republicans succeeded in winning a small majority for a declaration of war against England in 1812, New England states resorted to more than protest. Governors refused to subject their militia to the orders of the war department, citizens refused to buy bonds offered by the national government, and merchants openly sold supplies to the enemy forces. In the darkest days of the war the New England states met in a convention at Hartford to organize for joint action, both against the federal government which was threatening to draft their citizens and against the British enemy which at last was invading them. Taking advantage of the crisis in which the nation found itself and using secession as a tacit threat, delegates from the convention were instructed to proceed to Washington and demand certain amendments to the Constitution which would check the power of the Republican majority. Negro slaves would no longer count as a basis for representation, thus considerably reducing southern influence in the House of Representatives. A two-thirds vote of both houses would be required for the admission of new states, a declaration of war, or the prohibition of foreign commerce. Presidential tenure would be limited to one term, and successive Presidents could not be from the same state. The news of the Peace of Ghent prevented the submission of this ultimatum, though it removed the immediate cause of New England's discontent.

Prior to 1832, therefore, minorities accomplished some success without any basic changes in the Constitution and with a minimum of state action. In each instance time worked to their advantage. The party in power might eventually be defeated or at least split on crucial measures; by combining threats with bargains, a determined minority might gain its point or a tolerable compromise. In essence and in outcome the nullification crisis of the early thirties was not without precedent. A southern minority objected strenuously to the high tariffs of 1828 and 1832, which their legislatures formally declared violations of the Constitution. When South Carolina, acting alone under Calhoun's leadership, took drastic action which confronted the nation with the threat of civil war, a frightened majority yielded on the issue and hurriedly approved a satisfactory reduction of rates. Again an aroused minority, by a threat forcibly to defy a federal act and possibly to secede from the Union, induced a congressional majority to accede to its demands.

But in her major objective of obtaining recognition of the right of nullification, which would have afforded the minority a more extensive check upon federal legislation than the Hartford proposals, South Carolina did not receive the support of a single state. Had her contentions been accepted as a valid interpretation of the Constitution, a minority of just over one fourth of the states (and possibly an even smaller numerical minority of the total population) could have set aside a disputed federal act by the simple device of rejecting an amendment delegating to the federal government the power to legislate on the matter in question. Both New England and South Carolina met total defeat in their efforts to establish a formal procedure for the greater protection of the minority. The Senate, the President, and the Supreme Court remained the only accepted checks upon the action of the absolute numerical majority in the House.

*   *   *

It was the tariff which led to the first formal attempt of a state at nullification, a procedure suggested by Jefferson and Madison which Calhoun borrowed and developed. The various tariff bills of this era were far more the work of politicians than of manufacturers; the facile conclusion of the 1850's that the early tariffs were a tribute forced on the agrarian South by an industrial New England was an anachronism. The young nationalists in the postwar Congress, Calhoun no less than Clay, had staunchly favored the tariff in order to protect the nation's infant industries as well as to provide revenue for the payment of the war debt and for the construction of essential internal improvements. The divergent economic development of his own section forced Calhoun later to hedge on this program. Henry Clay, on the contrary, continued enthusiastically to advocate the "American System" and expected to ride on its popularity into the White House.

From 1816 to 1832 tariff bills were passed every four years by Congress, with the single exception of the year 1820 when the measure was defeated by a one-vote margin in the Senate. The average rate of protection was raised in 1824 to 37 per cent, almost twice that of the original bill of 1816. As each successive tariff bill in the twenties won majorities in the House, it seemed impossible to defeat any general tariff measure (a bill to extend special protection to a specific item, the Woolens Bill of 1827, failed in the Senate when Vice-President Calhoun cast his vote with the opposition to break the tie which existed). It had become so obvious that an increasing majority of Americans were strongly in favor of the tariff that no prospective candidate for the presidency — not even Jackson himself — dared be suspected in protariff areas of opposition to the general principle of protection.

The strongest sentiment for the tariff came from the Northwest and the Middle States, Pennsylvania in particular; the fact that the rate of population increase in these states was the greatest in the nation made the prospects of defeating it slim. Not until 1828 did Webster, having decided that the wind had definitely shifted in New England, become a convert to the protectionist faith. Tariff adherents consisted mainly of two groups: those who for any purpose wanted a subsidy from the federal government (such as the western states for roads and canals) and those who produced either raw material or finished goods which met competition in the home market from foreign imports.

Thus Missouri favored the tariff because it protected lead, Louisiana because of sugar, and Kentucky because of hemp. The whole business became a matter of simple but effective log-rolling. Practically every local interest in the nation, except planters and shipowners, were convinced that they profited from the tariff. As a matter of fact the cotton-goods manufacturers were probably the only group who derived any definite financial benefit, but both politicians and the people in general were won over to the idea. Whatever profit woolen-goods manufacturers derived from the increased price of their finished product was offset by a proportionate increase in the cost of raw domestic wool, which resulted from the same tariff bills. In the writing of no bill was there any objective attempt to determine the ultimate effect of the numerous schedules upon the whole economy of any section, state, or major economic interest.

Senator Benton of Missouri, who in 1828 persuaded his colleagues to add an additional 100 per cent duty on lead, unintentionally but clearly revealed the secret of tariff success: "My personal position was that of a great many others in the three protective sections — opposed to the policy, but going with it, on account of the interest of the State in the protection of some of its production." The 100 per cent additional duty on lead "might be thought high; but he could say that it was not too high for the benefit of Missouri and Illinois; and if rejected, there would be nothing in the bill to induce him to vote for it."[1]

Shipowners and planters regarded the tariff as injurious because the reduction of the market for European goods in this country automatically reduced their own large foreign markets, particularly in England. To this cause southerners traced the severe drop in cotton prices in the middle twenties. At the same time the tariff increased their cost of production by raising the price of rope and sail used by the shipbuilder and of clothes and numerous other articles bought by planters from the North. Southerners also believed that it made them bear a disproportionate share of national taxation.

New England shipowners howled, but in time they were outnumbered by manufacturers in their own region; the wiser among them began gradually to transfer their capital into industry. Cotton planters throughout the South howled louder, since they could not shift their capital, but only those in South Carolina adopted a formal program of resistance. The complicated factors in this development were both economic and political in nature.

Largely as a result of the competition of cheap but fabulously rich land in the western South, a depression more severe than that of 1819 hit the Southeast in the middle twenties. Tremendous overproduction of cotton caused a drop in price from an average of 25 cents a pound in 1825 to an average of 12 cents in 1826 and 9 cents in 1827. As migration from the section increased, land values continued to decline. Population in the Southeast ceased to increase, though it was rapidly doubling in a large part of the nation. As a natural consequence of the abolition of primogeniture in South Carolina forty years before, the estate of the average well-to-do resident was much smaller than in the golden past. Imports into Charleston declined 50 per cent during the six years from 1823 through 1828, while exports from the state dropped from eleven to eight millions in value between 1825 and 1827. At the very time the state was thus forced to raise its cotton on the narrowest of margins, even the slightest increase in the cost of necessities purchased from other parts of the Union became glaringly noticeable.[2] The populace seethed and the politicians raved. The simple cause of all these ills, thundered the latter, was the tariff — a diabolical plot on the part of the North to cheat proud and superior Carolinians of their well-deserved prosperity.

Certain of the South Carolina leaders, however, saw in the tariff the prelude to an attack upon slavery, the central institution of their society no less than of their economy. The Tallmadge amendment of 1820 had convinced them of a deep-seated design in the North eventually to abolish slavery throughout the entire Union. The not unsuccessful opposition in the state to Calhoun and his nationalism, led by Senator William Smith and by Thomas Cooper, was motivated largely by this fear. A slave-insurrection plot was discovered in Charleston in 1822. During this decade the American

Colonization Society was growing rapidly and becoming bolder in its program. Resolutions were introduced in the legislatures of nine northern states and in Congress proposing compensated emancipation, with the proceeds from the sale of western lands as a source of the necessary revenue.

The Smith group violently opposed internal improvements and the tariff — particularly the principle of "consolidation" upon which both measures rested constitutionally. A tariff which was protective in intent and in effect could not be challenged in the courts as long as it produced revenue. The approaching extinction of the national debt, by reducing the need for revenue, might result in a lower rate of taxation. But in no way would a lower tariff remove the ultimate menace to slavery. A congressional majority was taxing the people of South Carolina to build western roads and to increase the profits on Kentucky hemp and Connecticut woolens. A subsequent congressional majority, unchecked by the Supreme Court, could cite such legislation as a constitutional precedent for taxes to compensate slaveowners for the freeing of their bondsmen.

To these disturbed Carolinians the tariff was a popular issue upon which to arouse the public in their own state and in the whole South to the larger danger which lurked in "consolidation." Thus was a small snake to be scotched before it attained sufficient poison to do irreparable damage.

*　　　*　　　*

During the turbulent years of the later twenties Calhoun was in the vice-presidency, where one could usually be safely noncommittal but where he might also be easily forgotten. This period proved in retrospect to be the crisis of both his political and intellectual life. As a presidential aspirant during the John Quincy Adams administration he had three objectives: first, to aid in the defeat of the Adams-Clay party in 1828 and the election of Jackson; second, to endear himself to the General and to make certain that Jackson and his party, then in the process of expansion, would honor his claim to the succession in 1832; and third, to establish himself firmly as the candidate of South Carolina and the whole South, without losing his popularity in Pennsylvania and the northern states. Ultimately these objectives conflicted with one another; the Vice-President found himself in the impossible position of attempting to ride two horses which were heading in opposite directions.

His efforts to accomplish his first two objectives will be discussed below. His steps towards the attainment of the third, the preservation of his own popularity in both North and South, can be understood only against the background of his simultaneous exertions towards the realization of the other two. The nomination of Jackson in 1826 by a caucus of the South Carolina legislature as their candidate in the next election³ ended Calhoun's chances for a campaign in his own interest before 1832 at the earliest. This delay was inevitable, but fatal to his hopes. Actually there were dual contests in 1828: the primary one between Jackson and Adams, a grudge-fight sequel to the bitter race of 1824; and a secondary struggle behind the scenes between Clay, Van Buren, and Calhoun as successor to the victor. It was clear to Calhoun that despite an immediate defeat of Adams and the National Republicans, the popular Kentuckian might bounce back four years later; but he certainly underestimated the competition of Van Buren to himself as heir apparent among the Democratic Republicans.

Because of his unquestioned dominance in South Carolina during the years after 1833, it has been falsely assumed that Calhoun's leadership in his native state prior to that date was equally great. The facts prove the contrary. Lowndes, not he, was its choice for the presidency in 1822; his leading opponent, Senator Smith, though defeated by Hayne in the same year, returned to the Senate three years later. Just prior to his re-election at the end of 1825, Smith induced the Carolina legislature to pass a set of resolutions, rejected by that body in previous years, condemning both internal improvements and the tariff as unconstitutional.⁴ An unmistakable repudiation of the policies which Calhoun had conspicuously championed for a decade, this amounted almost to a personal repudiation by his own state. It was a significant victory for Smith's group, known as the Radicals, which was simply the particularist southern party against the formation of which Calhoun had manfully struggled at the height of the Missouri controversy.

As a matter of fact, for years before and after this defeat he was under constant attack in South Carolina. Cooper in 1824 had anonymously published a pamphlet, "Consolidation," which was largely a bitter diatribe on Calhoun. "Mr. Adams, Mr. Calhoun, and Gen. Jackson," charged the author, "supported to the utmost of their power a principle and a measure which from the very moment of party differences has decidedly characterized the Federal Party — consolidation is the motto of their flag."[5] As late as the summer of 1827 the local state-rights group regarded him as an opponent. "Who toast him?" asked one of them. "Who claim him? Why, the old Federalists, whose doctrines he illustrates." But he was equally unpopular with the "Unionists." In July, 1828, the Unionist *City Gazette* of Charleston stated that he was the author of all the ills which had fallen upon the South, that he veered about like a weathercock, and that as a dangerous intriguer and politician he should be retired to private life.[6]

At first Calhoun had won the younger Carolina politicos — Robert Hayne, George McDuffie, and James Hamilton, Jr. — to his broad nationalism, but early in the twenties they began to follow public opinion in their state and deserted to the southern rights party. In the Senate, along with Webster, Hayne made one of the leading speeches against the tariff of 1824 which he declared to be unconstitutional. Hamilton and McDuffie became even more vociferous state-righters than they had formerly been arch-nationalists, but they had neither a long congressional record to embarrass them nor presidential ambitions to be guarded. It was they, rather than their former mentor, who were fast becoming the spokesmen for South Carolina. Not only were they slipping from under his influence, but they were even attacking his program and surpassing him in local popularity.

*   *   *

Retreat was never easy for Calhoun, and the year 1825 found him still defending the broad national program in which he had conspicuously participated in Congress and in the cabinet. In speeches at Augusta, Georgia, and his home town of Abbeville, he reviewed with pride his record. "No one would reprobate more pointedly than myself," he stated at Augusta, "any concerted action between States, for interested or sectional objects. I would consider all such concert, as against the spirit of our constitution."[7] But the passage of the hostile resolutions by the legislature and Smith's election shocked him into an acceptance of reality. About this time he must have realized the two fundamentals of his situation. His weight with Jackson and the party depended basically upon his ability to hold South Carolina and the South in line; and if he wished to retain any following in his state and the South he must either come out strongly against the tariff, or by some stratagem get the tariff lowered in such fashion that he, not his younger rivals, would receive the credit. Yet how to do this without alienating his tariff friends in Pennsylvania and the West?

An opportunity in this direction presented itself early in 1827 as a result of a deliberate trick on the part of Van Buren, who clearly recognized the Carolinian's vulnerability. Van Buren arranged it so that a bill to increase protection of woolens, having passed the House, received a tie vote in the Senate. The motion, introduced by Hayne, was to table the bill, which of course meant its defeat. Calhoun as Vice-President could either withdraw, and thus be non-committal, or vote to table it and thus risk displeasure in Pennsylvania. Quickly he chose the latter course, in order to give evidence to South Carolina that he was belatedly sound on the issue of the moment. Apparently he lost no immediate popularity in Pennsylvania, for the woolens industry was concentrated in New England. By no means could he fairly be regarded on the basis of this vote alone as having recanted his earlier favorable sentiments for protection.

Shortly a more serious crisis arose. In the summer of 1827 a monster protectionist convention of one hundred delegates from thirteen states was held at Harrisburg, Pennsylvania, to agitate for an even higher tariff than that of 1824. Early the following winter the Adams forces introduced in Congress a bill incorporating the proposed increases. Since the new Jackson party was a North-South coalition like that of the original Republicans forty years before, this was a clever move to split the General's followers. The latter, being in the majority on the House Committee on Manufacturers, revised the bill by increasing the duties on certain raw materials with the design of forcing New England manufacturers to oppose it. This ruse was probably the work of both Van Buren and Calhoun; its purpose was to permit the General to dodge the trap and remain all things to all his men. Congressmen from the western and middle states could support the bill, as they would be compelled to do if they wished to remain in office. Those from the South could vote against it for similar reasons, and the measure would be defeated by New England votes, with the result that discredit would boomerang on the administration. As McDuffie stated, "This is what is sometimes called 'fighting the devil with fire,' a policy which, though I did not altogether approve, I adopted in deference to the opinions of those with whom I acted."[8]*

McDuffie's doubts proved correct. The Jackson forces had agreed to oppose all amendments, which the administration would naturally introduce to restore the bill to its original character.[9]† When the Senate voted, however, enough of the various amendments were supported by Jackson's followers (Benton, Van Buren, and Eaton voting in the affirmative) so that the bill was accepted by the New Englanders as better than nothing, and it became law. Such was the origin of the "Tariff of Abominations."

All of these events had been closely followed by the nation. Various southern states had protested against the tariff and resolved that it was unconstitutional, but passions in South Carolina had reached the frenzy state. At an antitariff meeting in Columbia in response to the Harrisburg Convention, Cooper reached the pitch of his rash eloquence. "The avowed object now is, by means of a drilled and managed majority in Congress, permanently to force upon us a system whose effect will be to sacrifice the South to the North, by converting us into colonies and tributaries." Logically, therefore, the South would "ere long be compelled to calculate the value of our Union," in which "the South has always been the loser and the North always the gainer."[10]

But it was Robert J. Turnbull in his widely read pamphlet, *The Crisis*, who pointed to specific action. The state should exercise its prerogative of sovereignty and simply resist the unconstitutional federal action. Force should be met by force. "To talk of resistance to the tariff by all *constitutional* means, is to talk to no purpose.... Let us say distinctly to Congress 'Hands Off! — Mind your *own* business.' It is not a case for reasoning or negotiation. It must be a *word* and a blow."[11] Meanwhile Hamilton and McDuffie were similarly foaming at the mouth.

All of this inflammatory talk must have disturbed Calhoun far more than the current success of the protectionists. The last thing he wanted was precipitate, radical action by South Carolina alone; such an event might lead to a possible rupture of the Union, which he still valued highly and it definitely would kill his presidential

---

*This statement is strong evidence of Calhoun's responsibility for the strategy behind the Tariff of Abominations.

†In his speech of Feb. 23, 1837, Calhoun gives the full background of the Tariff of Abominations as he saw it.

chances. Rumors common at the time and still given uncritical credence held that it was he who inspired all the early moves of the "Nullifiers." Probably he was actually busy trying to retard and at the same time to catch up with them.

*   *   *

Since Calhoun naturally kept his moves at this time secret, it is impossible to determine his actions in day-by-day detail. But his private correspondence of this period exudes concern and a somewhat labored confidence in a peaceful outcome. In a long, confidential letter to his brother-in-law during the summer of 1827 he stated that the selfish efforts of the protectionists had created a crisis which tended "to make two out of one nation," but he hoped the South "would not be provoked to step beyond strict constitutional remedies." As significant evidence that he had for once been doing some serious thinking about the Constitution, the perfection of which he had theretofore conveniently taken for granted, he admitted the "great defect in our system" was the obvious fact that "the separate geographical interests are not sufficiently guarded." For the first time in his life John Calhoun was arriving at the point where James Madison had begun his thinking four decades before. As if frightened by this revelation to his close relative (and it would have proved embarrassing, if not seriously injurious, to the reputation of such a great patriot if the newspapers had published it) he characteristically added: "This for yourself."[12]

The following year he wrote again to his brother-in-law while the Senate debated the Tariff of Abominations which had already passed the House. After referring to the widespread excitement in the South over the tariff he admitted that he felt "confident that it is one of the great instruments of our impoverishment; and if persisted in must reduce us to poverty, or compel us to an entire change of industry."[13] In July, 1828, two months later, when he may already have commenced writing his famous "Exposition," he expressed himself in similar fashion but with less frankness to James Monroe who he knew was hostile to nullification.

The Tariff excites much feelings in this and the other Southern States.... It is not surprising, that under this impression, they should exhibit some excess of feelings, but I feel confident, that the attachment to the Union remains unshaken with the great body of our citizens. Yet, it cannot be disguised, that the system pushed to the present extreme acts most unequally in its pressure on the several parts.... I greatly fear, that the weak part of our system will be found to consist in the fact that in a country of such vast extent and diversity of interest, many of the laws will be found to act very unequally, and that some portions of the country may be enriched by legislation at the expense of others. It seems to me that we have no other check against abuses, but such as grow out of responsibility, or elections, and while this is an effectual check, where the law acts equally on all, it is none in the case of the unequal action to which I refer. One thing seems to me certain, that the system is getting wrong and if a speedy and effective remedy be not applied a shock at no long interval may be expected.[14]

Here he was withholding his true sentiments from Monroe, for a year before he had written his brother-in-law in plain language as to the crisis which was developing: "It must lead to defeat or oppression or resistance, or the correction of what perhaps is a great defect in our system."[15] And he was definitely not honest with Monroe when he told him that he saw no check for the abuses except the ballot box, for six days after his letter to the former President he wrote another to Bartlett Yancey of North Carolina specifying the correction which, as a last resort, must then have been uppermost in his mind. He hoped that Jackson, when elected, would remedy the situation, but if he failed to do so there must be an appeal to the states. "That they have adequate power, when all other fails to apply Constitutionally an efficient remedy I do not doubt. The Virginia Report and resolutions in '98 are conclusive on that point."[16]

This would seem to indicate that at this time he still expected a happy outcome not too far distant in the future. He hoped that the new President, with his assistance of course, would grant the South the relief it was demanding. Should this not occur, and he did not overlook the fact that the other wing of the Jackson party had voted for the amendments responsible for the passage of the latest tariff, his quick mind had envisaged a situation in which he would supply a brilliant correction for the great defect in our political system and lead the Children of Israel out of the wilderness.

Calhoun was absorbed in plans for his own political future and in the immediacy of the difficult problem which he feared might lead to a serious crisis in the life of the nation. It is foolish to regard him, despite the dispassionate language of his "Exposition," as a political scientist abstractly theorizing about the nature of the Union. With him political considerations were foremost, for his own fate and that of his America and his South were at stake. It was this very time that Calhoun, though he did not immediately admit it to himself, ceased to be a democrat. He had always argued that the admittedly great power which he advocated could safely be granted to the federal government because the wisdom and the virtue of the people would ensure its being used wisely and justly. The protectionists convinced him that the majority is neither wise nor just, but is motivated by pure self-interest which is usually not enlightened. From the politician's habit of long standing he still occasionally referred to his confidence in the virtue of the people, but in his mind he had already decided the contrary. He now found himself in the disturbing dilemma of having worked half his life to create what turned out to be a Frankenstein's monster.

As a matter of fact, as early as the summer of 1827 he had clearly and succinctly stated the nature of the problem (the danger of power) with which as a practical politician he was to wrestle for the rest of his life. "The wisest men of the country," he commented in the first letter to his brother-in-law referred to above,

> have divided in opinion, how far Congress has the power, and admitting they possess it, how far, on principle, encouragement may be given to domestic manufactures, as connected with the great consideration of the defense and independence of the country. But whatever may be the diversity of opinion among the wise and patriotic, as to the discreet exercise of this great power of changing the capital and industry of the country, there cannot among such, be any doubt, *that the power itself is highly dangerous* and may be perverted to purposes most unjust and oppressive. Through such an exercise of it, one section of the country may really be made tributary to another; and by this partial action, artful and corrupt politicians may use nearly half of the wealth of the country to buy up partisans, in order to acquire, or retain power.*

When the din of nullification ended in what Carolinians regarded as a victory, Calhoun soon realized that he had just begun to fight Goliath.

*Italics added.

CHAPTER EIGHT

The Little Magician Wins a Bout on Points

AN identical logic forced Calhoun to ally himself with Martin Van Buren, and Van Buren with Calhoun, in supporting Jackson against President John Quincy Adams and his administration. Both wished to remove Henry Clay as a presidential rival, yet they could strike at him only by striking at Adams. Necessarily they must cooperate in electing the General in 1828. Since Adams and Clay had gotten into power by a union of forces, it was natural that the several defeated factions and candidates should similarly unite in temporary opposition to "throw the rascals out." But bitterness between the Crawford-Calhoun, Crawford-Jackson, and Van Buren-Clinton groups persisted beneath the surface of the coalition.

Clay quickly sensed the situation. When Adams' ineffectual attempts to win over certain of the defeated factions had failed, the Secretary of State decided to counterattack before they could cement their union of necessity. As Calhoun was the more vulnerable and perhaps the more vital figure in the new coalition, he bore the brunt of the administration's counteroffensive. "We must be identified with the administration," wrote the Vice-President to his friend Swift, "and give an unqualified support or be denounced as in opposition. We must go farther, we must pledge a support to Mr. A's reelection.... If we do not oppose them, they must oppose us. Be it so." He would accept the challenge. "Occupying as we do, the great Democratic principles, on which our whole political institution rests, I do not fear, that our position can be forced or turned."[1]

Forthwith he made his overture to the General. In June, 1825, he gave John Henry Eaton a letter for Jackson, in which he pointed out that events of the next three years would settle the issue of whether presidential power and patronage or the expressed will of the people would govern the political system. It was his sincere wish that providence would preserve Jackson as the instrument "of confounding political machinations and . . . of perpetuating our freedom." He added that he was fully willing to accept any consequence of such a victory.

"I know that much of the Storm will fall on me," he concluded, "but so far from complaining I deem it my glory to be selected as the object of attack in such a cause. If I had no higher object than personal advancement, my course would be easy. I would have nothing to do, but to float with the current of events. I feel, however, that such a course would be unworthy of the confidence which the American people have reposed in me. . . ."[2] These high-sounding sentiments did not fool the recipient and his close advisers, for they knew that the Vice-President could not remain neutral and that he joined them in self-defense. On the other hand they were aware of their own need for him and his influence. As a new group in national politics they could well use his social and intellectual prestige, his established reputation, and the votes he controlled both in and out of Congress. "I trust that my name will always be found on the side of the people," answered Jackson, "and . . . that we shall march hand in hand in their cause."[3]

For the next four years, therefore, with the dual purpose of ousting the rival party and of improving his own position as a future presidential candidate, Calhoun became an ingenious and active participant in partisan attacks on the President. His comment on Adams' inaugural message, which would formerly have received from him an enthusiastic approval, indicated his new tack: "Those, who in the main, advocate a liberal system of measures, think that the message has recommended so many debatable subjects at once, as to endanger a reaction even to those measures heretofore adopted and apparently acquiesced in."[4] He immediately conspired with Van Buren to defeat the confirmation of delegates to the Panama Congress which the administration proposed as an

111

implementation of Adams' and Clay's previous efforts to establish the nation as the leader and protector of the American republics, and which would increase both men's prestige. Opposition to this measure was also conveniently in accord with his new policy of identifying himself with southern particularism, for the South feared the southern republics because of their current trend towards emancipation as well as their potential rivalry as producers of cotton.

*   *   *

It was to be expected that Calhoun would attempt to clothe the vice-presidency with a new dignity and importance. Fate aided him in this project, for the preceding Congress had transferred to the chair the appointment of all Senate committees (the former system was restored two years later). Under the guise of impartiality he at once gave control of eight of the fifteen important committees to the administration and of seven to its opponents. In interpreting the rules of debate he permitted senators the widest liberty, taking the position that the "right *to call to order,* on questions touching the *latitude* or *freedom* of debate, belongs exclusively to members of this body, and not to the Chair."[5] His power in this regard was, according to this interpretation, purely appellate. Consistent with this position he refused to check Randolph in his scurrilous attacks upon the President and the Secretary of State. Shortly the Virginian's dramatic reference to the bargain "of Blifil and Black George ... the puritan and the black-leg" led to his bloodless duel with Clay, for which many held Calhoun directly responsible.

His conduct of his office elicited a series of scathing attacks in the public prints from Adams himself, who chose the pseudonym of "Patrick Henry," to which Calhoun replied at length under the pen name of "Onslow." The reputation of both men undoubtedly suffered from such undignified carping on the part of the two highest officials of the Republic; the Alexandria *Gazette* observed that it was no longer an honor "to be in a Senate where a monster of depravity presides." Rumor even had it that Clay and Calhoun had fought a duel in which the latter was killed.[6]

In numerous other ways Calhoun struck telling blows upon the administration and furthered the Jackson cause with all the resources and energy at his command. He marshaled his southern friends in the House to defeat even minor administration measures, and was probably more responsible than can be proved for the complex stratagems of the opposition. Certainly he aided Van Buren in cementing a North-South alliance as the nucleus of the Jackson coalition. As we have seen, he helped plan the ruse of 1828 which enabled the General to avoid a possibly fatal commitment on the tariff. At some risk to himself he tried to prevent any embarassing action on the tariff in South Carolina prior to the election.

Yet he kept his eye on his main chance and worked for himself as well as for Jackson. His transparent efforts at flattery amused John Randolph, who wrote that after a certain debate "Mr. C. sent for me, and said, that the question had assumed a new and important aspect — required solemn consideration and decision — my views were strong and important, etc., etc. He then sent for Mr. B[enton] and told him much the same. He electioneers with great assiduity." The mad Virginian was alleged to have begun one of his speeches in the Senate: "Mr. Speaker. I mean Mr. President of the Senate and would-be President of the United States, which God in His infinite mercy avert...."[7] The very fact that Randolph and many others regarded most of Calhoun's actions as "electioneering" revealed the Vice-President's complete inability to give other people the impression of himself he wished them to have.

Granting the strategic necessity of his opposition to the administration and his union with the Jackson forces, it should not be overlooked that he suffered as much damage as he caused. The Clay-Randolph duel, the attacks of "Patrick Henry," and the petty partisanship in which he indulged were injurious to his stature. Nor were these the only incidents. The administration charge that he claimed undue credit for the earlier reforms in the war department led to a public squabble between the Vice-President and his former officers, to whom considerable credit was justly due. The accusation was formally made that he was guilty of complicity in the notorious Mix contract. Thereupon he temporarily "resigned" as chairman of the Senate and demanded an investigation by the administration-controlled House which, though it absolved him of any dishonesty, by no means satisfactorily cleared his record.

Thus in these years he was increasingly on the defensive, both in Washington and in South Carolina, because of a political record in regard to which he was unduly sensitive. These attacks upon his reputation, regardless of the nature of his defense, tended to lessen his influence with the Jackson party and with southerners, and to weaken his position should he decide upon an independent canvass for the presidency. Furthermore, his position in the new party was by no means secure. He could not have been unaware of the power and of the personal rivalry of Van Buren, however much he over-estimated his own strength. There were other Crawford men, absorbed in the new party, who had old grievances against the Carolinian. More serious still, the General's intimate advisers from Tennessee were jealous of Calhoun from the start. John Eaton and William Lewis resented the patronizing attitude of the Vice-President and his "eastern" associates who confidently took over the party which the Tennesseeans felt they had originated. They were closer to Jackson than his newer friends and far more cognizant of his peculiar psychology; time was soon to prove what dangerous enemies such relatively unknown men could be.

At making friends and influencing people, Calhoun was a babe in arms compared to Martin Van Buren. The New Yorker was under no allusions about his Carolina rival, whose value for the moment and whose weaknesses he fully appreciated. When his own state upon the construction of the Erie Canal changed its sentiment on internal improvements, he seriously considered the advisability of an attack both on Calhoun and the administration. "You must advise me," he wrote a friend in December, 1826, "whether I can safely make my constitutional speech and therein reprobate strongly but respectfully the heresies of Messrs. Calhoun and Clay on the subject of the powers of the Federal Government before my election."[8] Apparently he later decided that an open break with the Vice-President before the election of 1828 was premature; but he carefully distributed his ammunition where it would be most useful later. He may have been partly responsible, along with the administration, for some of the numerous attacks on Calhoun.

The Vice-President's opponents within the party tried to drop him from the ticket in 1828. Crawford made such a demand as the price of his support of Jackson, but evidently it was decided that such action was too risky. Van Buren attempted without success to set up Thomas Ritchie, Virginian and former Crawfordite, as editor of a second Jackson paper because Duff Green, editor of the potent party organ, the *United States Telegraph*, was pro-Calhoun. The theft in the winter of 1826-27 of a letter from Calhoun's files, written to him by Monroe on the subject of the Seminole campaign, revealed the existence of a plot to embroil him with the General. Correspondence between the three principals dragged for months. The matter was dropped not because of Jackson's satisfaction, but because of the fear of his advisers that the personal dispute might disrupt the coalition.[9]

Again Calhoun was on the defensive. "Honest and patriotic motives," he explained to Jackson, "are all, that can be required, and I never doubted but that they existed on both sides."[10] But he did not admit that it had always been his opinion that the General had disobeyed the letter of his orders and that in 1818, in the secrecy of the cabinet, he had recommended an inquiry into his conduct. Even before 1828, then, the stage was set, and when the Little Magician should decide the moment proper, out would go John C. Calhoun from the confidence of Andrew Jackson.

*　　*　　*

The unexpected passage of the Tariff of Abominations was a blow to Calhoun and to southern congressmen generally. The wave of protest in the South reached the proportions of consternation in South Carolina. Mass meetings throughout the state resolved to boycott both northern manufactures and western livestock; many were already dressing in homespun. In a gathering at Walterboro young Robert Barnwell Rhett harangued for immediate, forceful resistance to the law and the summoning of a special session of the legislature to formalize such action. While Calhoun secretly opposed revolutionary tactics, he joined in these protests upon his return to the state in the summer. At a dinner in his honor at Pendleton he gave a toast to "The Congress of '76 — they taught the world how oppression could be successfully resisted, may the lesson teach rulers that their only safety is in justice and moderation."[11]

Immediately upon the act's passage, South Carolina's representatives in Washington — except Senator Smith and Calhoun — met at Hayne's residence to decide upon a course of action.[12] Hotheaded Hamilton wanted to resign at once from Congress, but was dissuaded by his colleagues. At length they decided against any action prior to the presidential election in the fall, since they regarded the tariff issue as far more vital than the mere choice between Jackson and Adams and wished to exert pressure upon both candidates. Meanwhile they would return to their districts, keep in touch with one another by letter, and reassemble in the fall at Columbia when the legislature convened. But in their discussion long-range contingencies were considered and speculation arose about the ability of the state militia to repel a possible attempt by the federal government to coerce the state. This, of course, was contemplation of treason.

The exact details of Calhoun's conduct during the three critical years from 1828 to 1831 cannot be established. While he secretly wrote the "South Carolina Exposition" in the early fall of 1828, he never avowed his authorship nor officially committed himself to nullification until his public letter of July 26, 1831. As to his actions during the intervening period, neither his own later testimony nor that of his contemporaries is reliable, colored as both of them were by the relevant fact that he did become the leader of the nullification forces in 1832. What he can be proved to have done is far more significant than what he and others stated later that he did.

In his autobiography written in 1843 Calhoun said that he was consulted by many citizens at his home during the summer of 1828, "with all of whom he conversed freely, and expressed the same sentiments." These sentiments were the assertion that he could see but two possible remedies "within the limits of the Constitution; one, the election of General Jackson . . . and the other, State Interposition or Veto, the high remedy pointed out in the Virginia and Kentucky resolutions as the proper one, after all others had failed."[13] Though this statement can reasonably be discounted as ex post facto, it is supported in part by much stronger evidence. In the summer of 1830, a year before he was forced to show his hand, he wrote to his friend Maxcy that because of his official position in the federal government he had "not intermingled with the great contest between it and the State, except so far as might seem advisable to direct the eye of the state to the constitution, instead of looking beyond it, for the redress of its wrongs."[14] This, too, might be discounted on the grounds that Calhoun rarely showed his hand in his letters. Yet one of the toasts given at a Unionist meeting in Charleston on July 4, 1831, read: "The Vice-President of the United States: His political intimates have declared their sentiments on Nullification, — will he *shrink* from an *open* exposition of his own?"[15]

On the other hand, before Calhoun submitted his "Exposition" to the legislature, Hamilton proclaimed the full-fledged doctrine of nullification in October in a speech at Waterboro. Even prior to this speech the same doctrine was less ably set forth by an unknown "Sydney" in a series of letters to the Charleston *Mercury*.[16] It has frequently been alleged that Calhoun used Hamilton and "Sydney" as mere puppets and that he was the secret leader of the Radicals who all along directed their every action. Both extreme hypotheses, that Calhoun did little or that he did everything, can be refuted. The safest assumption is that he attempted to use Hamilton, Hayne, McDuffie, and the other Radicals for his own purposes, since they were essential to his political future and had it in their power to put him in an uncomfortable spot. The Unionists in the state were at first equally strong, and it required four years of agitation for the Nullifiers to gain the two-thirds control of the legislature necessary to call a convention. The vice-presidency gave Calhoun a certain immunity, but the Unionists and the Nullifiers were both busy trying to use him, and he them. Not until it was obvious that the Nullifiers would be victorious in the state did he join them openly, and then only because they forced his hand.

One of the citizens who visited him at Fort Hill in the summer of 1828 was William C. Preston, a member of the state legislature, who apparently asked him to write a report for the Committee on Federal Relations. The result was the "South Carolina Exposition" which the committee, with many omissions and minor changes, submitted to the legislature in December as its own, along with a protest to the United States Senate, also written by Calhoun. The protest was passed by both houses and actually presented in the Senate by his old enemy Senator Smith. But the state legislature, still sensible enough to realize the danger of any independent action (other than talk) by South Carolina alone, refused to approve the "Exposition." To save face the committee induced the lower house to order the printing of 5,000 copies of the document that it refused to ratify.[17]

*   *   *

The "Exposition" itself was generally misunderstood at the time and has frequently been since. Rather than being a conscious justification for secession, it was avowedly an attempt to preserve the Union; it advocated a supposedly constitutional method by which

South Carolina could disobey a tariff passed by Congress and still remain in the Union. When Calhoun wrote it in 1828, it was certainly his hope and probably his expectation that the application of the doctrine would never become necessary. For three years he never publicly admitted his authorship, and not until 1831 did he take any overt action towards inducing the state to attempt nullification. It can be proved that when he took his stand in the summer of 1831, he was forced by political necessity to lead the movement. Once he made his decision, however, he threw all his energy and his persuasive powers into the successful effort to have the tariffs of 1828 and 1832 nullified by South Carolina. Thereafter he published several lengthy elaborations of his original thesis.

The "Exposition" consisted of three major points. The first was a realistic survey of the economic effects of the tariff, stating the numerous reasons why it was unconstitutional. The second was a detailed description of the allegedly constitutional method by which South Carolina could reject the tariff, yet remain in the Union without fear of coercion from the federal government. But the third point, and for the moment the most significant, was the assertion that the state would delay nullification, though it was clearly her constitutional right, in the hope that the majority would come to its senses and grant her relief. The basis for this hope was the anticipated election of General Jackson, who would restore "the pure principles of our government." Should he prove unable to do so, however, South Carolina would proceed with "her sacred duty to interpose; — a duty to herself — to the Union — to the present, and to future generations, — and to the cause of liberty over the world."[18]

Calhoun's motives in writing the "Exposition" and in his subsequent conduct were by no means self-evident, and they are still a subject of much dispute. Probably the simplest explanation is that of the leading scholar on the question, Frederic Bancroft, who regards the whole business as merely another instance of Calhoun's jockeying for the presidency. The Vice-President "believed that he could slip on Jefferson's clothes of 1798 and, soon or late, walk into the White House."[19] But there is some evidence to support the contrary position that Calhoun was sincerely concerned for the welfare of the South and the preservation of the Union, and was willing to subordinate his personal ambitions. The tariff was a tremendous burden, if not ruinous, to the South; anticipating the frontal attack upon slavery soon to come, he was also attempting to establish nullification as a defense in advance of that attack. If the preservation of the Union was his major concern, he was indirectly striving to avoid a situation where a disaffected minority might in desperation take action which would lead to dissolution or to civil war. This he would do by simply giving the minority sufficient power to protect itself against the tyranny of the majority.

It is much more plausible, however, that to Calhoun's mind these three objectives — his political ambitions, the welfare of the South, and the preservation of the Union — were supplementary. Always striving for his own elevation to the presidency (at least unconsciously), he could easily have convinced himself that the best method of protecting the South and preventing disunion was the election of John C. Calhoun as chief executive. If this was vanity, it should be remembered that Thomas Jefferson adopted the identical method in 1798 to save the nation from Federalist despotism.

This conclusion is fully supported by the long letter to Maxcy, mentioned above. The fact that it was written in September, 1830, a year before Calhoun was compelled publicly to announce his support of nullification, lends it more significance than his later statements defending his actions. He begins by chiding his friends for regarding the matter purely from the viewpoint of his (Calhoun's) own political future: "In this, as well as in all the other trying situations, in which I have been placed, I must merge my interest, in the higher sense of duty; and to do that, which with the best lights I have, may seem right, regardless of consequences." He was not indifferent to his "future advancement . . . but, I trust, however strong may be my ambition, my sense of duty is still stronger." By his own admission, he had not subordinated his ambitions but had *merged* them.

Next he informed Maxcy that he had done nothing except direct the attention of the state to the Constitution for a method of redress. He realized that many of his northern friends expected him to check the nullification movement, but that was beyond his power. Only Jackson, in his opinion, could do so, by lowering the tariff and granting the Nullifiers what they were threatening to accomplish by independent state action. "If, I really believed, that civil discord, revolution, or disunion would follow from the measure contemplated, I would not hesitate, devoted to our system of government, as I am, to throw myself in the current with a view to arrest it at every hazard, but believing that the State, while she is struggling to preserve her reserved powers, is acting with devoted loyalty to the Union, no earthly consideration would induce me to do an act, or utter a sentiment, which would cast an imputation on her motives."

Finally he stated that the tariff was merely the occasion of the controversy, but that the "peculiar domestick institution of the Southern States" was the basic cause. Slavery as well as the soil and climate placed the South as a minority in a position vulnerable to the current legislative program of the congressional majority. In his opinion, "if there be no protective power in the reserved rights of the States, they [southerners] must in the end be forced to rebel, or submit to have their permanent interests sacrificed, their domestic institutions subverted by Colonization and other schemes, and themselves and children reduced to wretchedness."[20]

*   *   *

Whatever may have been Calhoun's conscious objectives in writing the "Exposition," there were three definite consequences relative to his own political future. Undoubtedly he had in mind Jefferson's tactics of 1798 when the Republican leader, as a Vice-President hostile to the current administration, secretly wrote the Kentucky Resolves and gained the presidency for himself two years later. Calhoun's immediate purpose was, in Bancroft's words, "to obtain secret and at least partial control of the radicals and to retain inconspicuous general leadership in South Carolina." The prominent Carolina Radicals believed that he had come over to their position and probably expected that at the proper time he would come out into the open.

At once this precluded the possibility that a hothead like Rhett or Hamilton might, before the election in November, create a situation that would compel Jackson to commit himself on the tariff and thus lose potentially crucial votes in the North or the South. At the same time the Vice-President temporarily won the confidence of the Radicals; should their cause eventually become popular he could always claim an early conversion. Yet, because his authorship was kept secret and was not generally known in South Carolina or outside for several years, he by no means lost the support of the Carolina Unionists or of his national following in the North and West. He had greatly strengthened his position without an official commitment of any kind.

An equally fundamental objective of the "Exposition" was to put pressure on Jackson, after his election, to reduce the tariff. Such reduction, Calhoun fully realized, was essential to southern support for his own candidacy in 1832; without such support even an endorsement by Jackson and the northern wing of the party might prove insufficient. The Vice-President had recognized the significance of the votes cast by Van Buren and Eaton for the amendments to the tariff of 1828. He correctly feared that the General might forget his desire for tariff reduction should it appear unpopular with the majority wing of his party or with the general public. Here he was building a backfire. He desired and encouraged the threat of independent action in South Carolina for tariff reduction with the expectation that Jackson's fear of alienating southern support — or possibly of civil war — would influence him to force a lower tariff through Congress regardless of northern opposition. And if Jackson lowered the tariff, Calhoun felt certain of his own election in 1832.

He probably expected his plan to work, but he may also have written the "Exposition" with full awareness of the potential value of nullification as a campaign platform in an uncertain future. Not that he actually anticipated the break with Jackson or the possibility of the General's deciding to run again in 1832, but he sensed the ominous nature of contemporary politics. Even the best of plans might miscarry, as his own had in 1823 and 1828, and there was some chance that he might lose out with the northern wing of his party. Certainly he felt that the coming struggle over slavery would contain more political dynamite than the current one over the tariff.

Consequently in the back of his mind he may have advanced nullification, secretly and without commitment at the moment, as a sort of trial balloon and at the same time an insurance against an unpredictable future. If it caught on in the South and the West — and the Webster-Hayne debate lends the weight of strong circumstantial evidence to this hypothesis — then he could come forth boldly as its champion and its originator. After all, he had ample time and sufficient leeway with which to act — in fact until 1832. Were nullification repudiated, even in South Carolina, he could still drop it and return to a moderate nationalism. Or he could take a middle ground, as he was actually planning when his hand was forced in the summer of 1831, and win support from all sides as the statesman who could arrange a compromise between seemingly irreconcilable interests.

*   *   *

Jackson easily defeated Adams in 1828, but open conflict soon broke out among the several factions of his party. The selection of the cabinet was bound to cause hard feelings. Calhoun, re-elected as vice-president, later stated that the President never consulted him in the matter, though Van Buren's lieutenant James A. Hamilton alleged that the Vice-President in a formal interview recommended Littleton W. Tazewell of Virginia for the state department.[21] Since Van Buren was as valuable to the party as Calhoun, Jackson logically appointed the New Yorker to that important post. It was natural also that the General should desire one of his older Tennessee friends in his official family, but Eaton was not selected for the portfolio of war until his fellow Tennessean Hugh Lawson White had refused it. Ingham and John McLean of Ohio were actually Calhoun's only friends in the cabinet. Ingham was given the treasury, though the Vice-President preferred that he be Postmaster-General; and McLean was soon appointed to the Supreme Court. The Carolinian's staunch supporter Duff Green, editor of the party newspaper, aided him greatly in the scramble for patronage. But Calhoun did not recommend John M. Berrien and John Branch; not until the Eaton affair did they become his intimates. His opposition and that of his friends to certain of Jackson's choices, notably to Van Buren and Eaton, aroused the General's suspicions.

When he assumed his duties as President in the spring of 1829, Jackson was a deeply embittered man. Among the many vilifications of the recent campaign was a repetition of the old attacks upon the character of his wife Rachel (they had married on the incorrect assumption that the state of Kentucky had granted her a divorce from her first husband). Mrs. Jackson died soon after the election, and the General was convinced that the recent slanders had hastened her death; in particular he held Clay personally responsible. "May Almighty God forgive her murderers," said the new Executive, "as I know she forgave them. I never can!"[22] At this point another woman appeared on the scene: Peggy O'Neill Timberlake Eaton. Daughter of a Washington tavern keeper, the voluptuous Peggy created the situation which Martin Van Buren used to oust Calhoun and ingratiate himself in the General's confidence.* With the best of intentions Jackson seems to have induced Eaton to regularize by marriage his association with the notorious widow. But the wives and daughters of other cabinet members, as well as Washington society in general (including Jackson's niece Emily Donelson who was serving as his hostess), refused to accept Mrs. Eaton socially. In the eyes of the widowed General this was persecution identical with the tribulations of his Rachel, who had given Peggy her love and blessing. He conducted his own investigation of the charges, presented the evidence to a cabinet meeting called for that purpose, and pontifically pronounced her as "chaste as a virgin." Peggy defeated all efforts to solve the embarrassing situation by transferring her husband to a less conspicuous job, as she was determined to enjoy sweet victory over her feminine enemies on the ground in Washington. "Her Ladyship," confided the Virginian David Campbell to his wife, "is *decidedly* the greatest fool I ever saw in a genteel situation."[23]

Loyal to the memory of his wife and to his friend Eaton, Jackson refused to budge in his defense of slandered virtue. It is but another instance of his stubborn determination that ultimately his cabinet was compelled to resign, Emily Donelson left the White House, and Calhoun was ousted from the succession. For two years, however, the Eaton "malaria" split the party and made the administration appear ridiculous. Indeed, it was Van Buren's masterpiece that he contrived to rid the President, not merely of Calhoun and his new cabinet friends, but of Peggy and her spouse as well. When most members of the cabinet failed to assert their domestic authority to compel the acceptance of Mrs. Eaton, Jackson ceased to consult them; instead he turned to unofficial advisers and most of all to Van Buren. Widowed and daughterless, the Secretary of State remained cordial to the Eatons. Thus he won the admiration of his chief and became his close confidant. On their morning horseback rides together the two men frequently discussed both official and unofficial matters.

In this manner the President, who at first blamed Clay for the conspiracy against Peggy, was subtly led to believe that Calhoun was the real instigator. Apparently Floride Calhoun led the purity

*According to Adams (*Memoirs*, VIII, 116), Calhoun and Van Buren clashed immediately.

123

campaign; if her husband at first preferred otherwise he was unable to control her actions. When his break with Jackson became public, the Vice-President did pronounce the successful ostracism of Mrs. Eaton a "great victory that has been achieved, in favor of the morals of the country, by the high-minded independence and virtue of the ladies of Washington." Thus he accepted full responsibility and may have been pressing the issue for some time. Enjoying the discomfort of all concerned, Adams commented that "Calhoun heads the moral party, Van Buren that of the frail sisterhood."[24]

*   *   *

Tension between the Calhoun and Van Buren factions increased from the moment the new administration began, but Maxcy wrote the Vice-President in the summer of 1830 that Jackson had satisfied him as to his honest intention to remain neutral in the contest between them. Already Major Lewis of Tennessee, who with Mrs. Eaton's influence had obtained the post of second auditor of the Treasury, was taking the proper steps to get the General "drafted" for a second term as a method of blocking Calhoun's ambitions. These efforts, in which Van Buren undoubtedly participated, culminated in the spring of 1830 in letters written by Lewis to members of the Pennsylvania legislature urging them to renominate Jackson immediately.

Such a move, he argued, was the

> most effectual if not the only means of defeating the machinations of Mr. Calhoun and his friends, who were resolved on forcing General Jackson from the presidential chair after one term. The peculiar position of the Vice-President, it was believed, made this necessary. He was then serving out his second term, and as none of his predecessors had ever served more than 8 years, his friends thought it might be objected to and perhaps would be injurious to him, to be presented to the nation for a third term. . . . It would not do for him to retire to the shades of private life for 4 long years. He could not run for a third term, and they dare not run him in opposition to General Jackson.[25]

This intrigue bore fruit. On one of their horseback rides in the fall of 1830, the President actually proposed to Van Buren that he become his running mate in 1832. Jackson would resign shortly after the election and thus elevate the New Yorker to the presidency. The Secretary objected so strongly that his chief dropped the plan for the moment, but the President continued throughout his first term to press this proposal. Certainly his desire to pass the office on to Van Buren was a major factor in his decision to stand for re-election, and was a main objective of his second term.

Long before this proposal, however, the conspirators had succeeded in alienating Jackson from Calhoun. In December, 1829, the President suffered an illness which his friends feared might result in a fatal attack of the dropsy. At Lewis' suggestion he wrote a "political" will in the form of a letter to his old Tennessee friend John Overton:

> Permit me to say here of Mr. Van Buren that I have found him everything that I could desire him to be, and believe him not only deserving of *my* confidence but the *confidence* of the *Nation*. Instead of his being selfish and intriguing, as has been represented by some of his opponents, I have found him frank, open, candid, and manly. As a Counsellor he is *able* and prudent ... and one of the most pleasant men to do business with I ever saw. He, my dear friend, is well qualified ... to fill the highest office in the gift of the people.... I wish I could say as much for Mr. Calhoun. You know the confidence I once had in that gentleman. However of him I desire not now to speak.[26]

Eaton, Lewis, and Van Buren had done their work well. By harping upon Calhoun's opposition to Jackson's cabinet appointees and his attempts to monopolize the newly vacated offices for his friends, they gradually convinced the General that the Vice-President was using the Eaton affair to discredit him personally and exerting himself to prevent Jackson's possible candidacy for re-election. Conveniently at this point came reports from Pennsylvania that Ingham was furthering Calhoun's cause at Jackson's expense.

But the most important link in the chain of circumstantial evidence convicting the Carolinian was a letter from John Forsyth of Georgia, dated February 8, 1828, which had been deliberately solicited by Van Buren's friend James A. Hamilton. According to Crawford, the letter stated, it was not he but Calhoun who sought to persuade the cabinet back in 1818 to punish Jackson for disobedience of orders. Surely Van Buren, as one of Crawford's lieutenants in 1824, knew the sentiments of his former chief, and though he protested his innocence until his death, it is probable that he was behind Hamilton's action. In the winter of 1828 Hamilton had seen Forsyth and shortly thereafter received from him the letter in question. On the same trip he saw Calhoun in Washington and naïvely asked if anything had been said in the cabinet sessions about arresting the General for his conduct of the Seminole War.

"Never," replied Calhoun. "Such a measure was not thought of, much less discussed." But when Hamilton later asked him for a written confirmation of this statement, he began to smell a rat and refused, for he suddenly recalled the letter which had been stolen from his files.[27]

Forsyth's letter was held in reserve from February, 1828, until November, 1829, a month before Jackson sent his will to John Overton. It so happened that Eaton and Lewis attended a dinner given by the President in honor of Monroe, at which Marshal Tench Ringgold told the two that Monroe had been the General's only friend in the discussion of the Seminole crisis. They feigned surprise and stated that they had always understood that Calhoun had been Jackson's staunch defender. Later in the evening, when the two were left alone with the President, he asked them what they had been talking about with Ringgold. Thereupon Lewis told him about the Forsyth letter. He insisted upon seeing it at once, but Hamilton would not surrender it without Forsyth's consent. Five months later, on May 12, Jackson was given a letter from Crawford, dated April 30, 1830, in which the Georgian confirmed his earlier statement to Forsyth. It was this letter that Jackson used for his formal break with Calhoun.[28]

Since the President had decided as early as December, 1829, to drop Calhoun in favor of Van Buren, his subsequent actions in 1830 must be considered against this background. Thus the Maysville veto in May of that year, inspired by Van Buren and in accordance with his earlier plan to attack internal improvements, was probably aimed more at Calhoun than at Clay, though both had always advocated federal subsidy of roads and canals. Prior to the veto had occurred the Webster-Hayne debate, which Jackson correctly regarded as an effort by the Vice-President to win the West over to nullification. Without doubt the President's famous toast at the Jefferson Birthday Dinner, "Our Federal Union: it must be preserved," was directed at the Carolinian. Jackson, the strict constructionist who had supported Georgia in her open nullification of John Marshall's decisions protecting the Indians, was in this later instance consciously taking a stand against Calhoun.

The Vice-President's reply was an anticlimax: "The Union, — next to our Liberty most dear. May we all remember that it can be preserved only by respecting the rights of States and distributing equally the benefit and the burthern of the Union."[29]

*　　　*　　　*

One month after this banquet Jackson received the Crawford letter, which he immediately forwarded to Calhoun with a request for an explanation. The Vice-President answered briefly the same day, and two weeks later he attempted to refute the charges in a 52-page epistle. What he could not explain was the fact that he had let the General believe throughout the years that he had been his defender from the first. Shortly after the cabinet crisis in 1818 Jackson had offered his famous toast, "John C. Calhoun, — an honest man, 'the noblest work of God,' " and had written in 1825 that "Calhoun was the only friend I had in the cabinet."[30] The fact that Calhoun had not been completely candid about his actions in 1818 placed him in a vulnerable position.

On the other hand Jackson had no legitimate grounds of complaint. Calhoun logically argued that cabinet discussions were state secrets and that he had, in the end, concurred with the majority in the decision not to press charges against him. The letter, as he pointed out, was an act of vengeance on Crawford's part, and certainly his own devotion to the General's cause in the years since 1824 was sufficient proof of loyalty for any reasonable man. The conclusion is inescapable that Jackson, having already decided to break with his lieutenant, merely used, and may possibly have deliberately obtained, the Crawford letter as an excuse for reading the Vice-President out of the party and the succession. Much of his indignation was probably feigned for this specific purpose.

For six months the break was not publicly known. Yet in the fall of 1830 he referred to Calhoun in a letter as "an ambitious demagogue [who] would sacrifice friends and country, and move heaven and earth to gratify his unholy ambition." And to his old friend Overton, from whom there was no reason to hide his true feelings, he voiced the same sentiment: "You know the confidence I once had in that gentleman.... I have a right to believe that most of the troubles, vexations and difficulties I have had to encounter,

127

since my arrival in the city, have been caused by his friends. But for the present let this suffice. I find that Mr. Calhoun objects to the apportionment of the surplus revenues among the several states, after the public debt is paid. He is, also, silent on the bank question, and is believed to have encouraged the introduction and adoption of the resolutions in the South Carolina Legislature relative to the tariff."[31]

At this point occurred one of the strangest episodes of Jackson's life. He had fired Duff Green for his pro-Calhoun efforts and, upon the advice of the Kitchen Cabinet, had selected Francis P. Blair of Kentucky as editor of the new party organ, the Washington *Globe*. But it was noticeable that the *Globe* took care not to offend the Calhoun faction, and suddenly in January, 1831, it was announced to Van Buren that the President had agreed to a reconciliation. The unfriendly correspondence between the principals was to be destroyed, and Calhoun would appear at a White House dinner.[32]

Had Jackson discovered suddenly that Lewis and others had engaged in an intrigue against Calhoun? Or did the growing danger of nullification in South Carolina, or possible plans for a war on the bank, along with the realization of the damage done by the Eaton malaria to his prestige and party, convince him that the support of Calhoun and his followers was essential to his future political success? Or was it simply that since Calhoun was preparing a pamphlet on the whole matter for public release, he feared that the exposure of his unreasonable treatment of the Vice-President might place him in a bad light before the nation? His close friend Judge Overton was at the moment urging a policy of reconciliation upon the President, pointing out that Jackson, not Calhoun, would be hurt were the correspondence published. Overton even went so far as to defend the Vice-President's actions and motives.

Here Calhoun made a fatal move. Since he obviously had Van Buren on the run, he planned to finish his rival off quickly by publishing his pamphlet exposing the machinations of the Secretary of State. To make sure of Jackson's approval, Felix Grundy, acting for Calhoun, went over the manuscript with Eaton as the President's representative, so that the General would understand it was not directed at him. Just then Adams recorded that "there has been a very prevalent rumor that a challenge passed" between Calhoun and Van Buren. Eaton gave Grundy to understand that he had received the President's consent, and the pamphlet was published.

The Little Magician Wins a Bout

"They have cut their own throats," exploded Jackson. Eaton had effectively revenged himself upon Calhoun by never mentioning the prospective pamphlet to the President![33]

With Calhoun and Duff Green thus fortuitously eliminated from a position of influence with the President, the only remaining encumbrances upon the party were the Eatons and the members of the cabinet who had been driven into the Calhoun camp. When on one of their frequent rides the late unpleasantness was again discussed, Van Buren adroitly proposed to his chief that to relieve the latter of embarrassment he would tender his resignation as Secretary of State. This was touchy business, but the Little Magician was at last able to convince the President that his proposal was made in all sincerity, with the disinterested purpose of rescuing the administration from a dangerous situation. Reluctantly, after consulting Postmaster-General Barry, Jackson agreed.

The following evening, as Barry, Lewis, Eaton, and Van Buren left the White House, Eaton stopped suddenly and exclaimed, "Gentlemen, this is all wrong. I am the one who ought to resign." His companions said nothing, but later at dinner he repeated his proposal. When Van Buren asked what would be Mrs. Eaton's attitude, the Secretary of War replied that she would agree. But the New Yorker insisted that he must be sure, and the next evening Eaton informed him that his wife "highly approved" of the move. Soon Ingham, Berrien, and Branch, apparently under pressure, also submitted their resignations, all of which the President accepted. Later Van Buren was appointed minister to England and departed for the Court of St. James.[34]

The climax to the drama came when the Senate, which had not been in session when the appointment of Van Buren as minister was made, went into executive session to consider the nomination. A tie was contrived to give the Vice-President the sweet revenge of casting his vote in the negative. Benton heard Calhoun tell one of his friends, "It will kill him, sir, kill him dead. He will never kick, sir, never kick."[35]

But the Missourian's contrary prediction to Senator Gabriel Moore of Alabama, upon the announcement of the outcome of the balloting, proved instead to be correct: "You have broken a minister and elected a Vice-President." For the reaction of "King Andrew I" had been vehement. "By the Eternal!" he had exclaimed upon receipt of the news. "I'll smash them!"[36]

CHAPTER NINE

Calhoun Crosses the Rubicon

ACCORDING to the "Exposition" and its several elaborations composed by Calhoun during 1831 and 1832, each individual state was completely sovereign and the "General Government" merely an agent. This agent, created by a compact among these sovereigns for their mutual convenience, had been delegated certain powers. Each state, therefore, retained its reserved right to decide when the agent exceeded the specific powers granted to it by the compact (the Constitution). This right was in no way invalidated by the fact that the power of determining the constitutionality of laws had been usurped by the Supreme Court.*

The process by which a state could exercise this reserved right was simple. Its legislature would call for an election of delegates to a convention for considering the constitutionality of the federal act in question. If a majority of this convention voted that the act violated the original compact, the act became null and void

*Calhoun expressed his views on this point succinctly in a letter to Virgil Maxcy on Sept. 1, 1831. "The question is in truth between the people and the Supreme Court. We contend, that the great constructive principle of our system is in the people of the states, and our opponents that it is in the Supreme Court. This is the sum total of the whole difference; and I hold him a shallow statesman who, after proper examination does not see, which is most in conformity to the genius of our system and the most effective and safe in its operation."

in that state. Such a declaration was binding on both the federal government and the citizens of the state, as it placed "the violated rights of the State under the shield of the Constitution." At one point Calhoun implies that such action by one state would make the act null and void throughout the entire Union.[1]

If a congressional majority insisted upon the constitutionality of the nullified act, it must then initiate an amendment to the Constitution specifically granting the disputed power to the federal government. Such an amendment, of course, would require the affirmative vote of two thirds of the members of both houses of Congress and ratification by three fourths of the states. Were the amendment successful, the nullifying state must yield to the expressed will of her sister states or choose the logical alternative of secession.

Much of this argument of Calhoun was pure dialectic. The major premise upon which it was based was not the Constitution but rather the highly debatable doctrine of state sovereignty, which is even more difficult to read into the letter of the Constitution than the equally disputed doctrine of judicial review. This very question of the powers delegated to the federal government and those reserved by the states transcended the Constitution and was, therefore, constantly debated by the nation from 1792 to 1865. In the end the decision was rendered not by the Supreme Court, nor Congress, nor the President, nor even the states themselves. It was rather the consensus of opinion of the people of the United States which decided the issue.

Adroitly but distinctly buried in his major premise was Calhoun's conclusion. His only literal borrowing from the Constitution was the amending process by which a majority could attain constitutional sanction for the exercise of a disputed power — a sanction which could still be defied by the persistent state willing to risk the hazards of secession. Despite his close reasoning, he was here once again the pragmatist using the language of political philosophy. Assuming that his objective was the preservation of the Union, and that he regarded as essential to that objective the relief of the South from the economic ills attributed to the high tariff, Calhoun cleverly selected an innocuous premise which he could logically develop to the desired conclusion. Perhaps deliberately, he confused two fundamentally different questions: one, was nullification, as he maintained, a proper interpretation of the Constitution and in accordance with the intentions of its framers as well as with the circumstances of its adoption? and two, purely aside from its constitutionality, would it in practice prove desirable and useful as the basis of our federal system of government?

His mental process and his reasoning in this instance were similar to those by which, a decade before, he had justified high nationalism. In lawyer fashion he exaggerated the arguments which supported his conclusion, and ignored or glossed over those which refuted it. Just as he had previously contended that the wisdom and virtue of the people of the nation would prevent the abuse of the power he would grant the federal government, he now argued that the wisdom and the virtue of the people of any given state would prevent the abuse of the equally excessive power which nullification would confer upon the states. In this instance, as always, he experienced no difficulty in convincing himself of what he wanted to believe, and the unguarded soul who accepted his premise found himself caught in a locked vise of logic.*

*   *   *

This theory of nullification, advanced by Calhoun as the proper interpretation of the fundamental law of the land, was rejected in the early 1830's not merely by the North but also by all southern states except South Carolina. The Virginia and Kentucky Resolutions of 1798, a less positive expression of the state sovereignty theory, had been similarly rejected by a majority of the states. The outcome in the later instance resulted primarily from the fact that, despite Calhoun's sophistry, they understood his basic point and applied to it a *reductio ad absurdum*.

Of the twenty-four states in the Union in 1830, Delaware the smallest, with one half of one per cent of the total population, could arrest the operation of any law or treaty passed by Congress and even set aside a decision of the Supreme Court. Should the

---

*In a series of lectures on ante-bellum southerners delivered at the University of Wisconsin in the 1890's, William P. Trent denied that Calhoun "was a born leader of men, and therefore a born politician. Calhoun led thought rather than men, and lacking imagination, he led thought badly. [He] unconsciously started with the conclusion he wanted and reasoned back to the premises.... [Thus] he leads you willy-nilly to his conclusions." If one reads his treatises on government without first rejecting the assumptions of indivisible sovereignty and the compact theory, "the sure grip of Calhoun's logic will end by making one a nullifier or a lunatic, it matters little which." — William P. Trent, *Southern Statesmen of the Old Regime* (New York, 1897), 158, 169-71.

majority attempt to pass an amendment that would give constitutional sanction to a law previously nullified, the seven smaller states, containing eight per cent of the total population,* could defeat the amendment. Even the southern states refused to confer such tremendous power upon so small a minority. Many of them had benefited from legislation enacted by slight majorities or had in mind future measures vital to their interests. Apparently they saw in nullification a two-edged sword which could injure the wielders no less than their opponents.

Most of the southerners who regarded secession as a right of a state did not agree with the novel doctrine that a state could disobey a congressional act and still remain in the Union. To the great majority of citizens nullification appeared clearly to destroy the Constitution and all that had been accomplished under it since 1798. It meant to them a return to the days of the Confederation when little Rhode Island alone had blocked the amendment granting the central government the badly needed power to levy a small duty on imports. Like the Dutchman, Calhoun had simply proposed to rid the barn of rats by the effective device of burning the barn itself.

The jurist Edward Livingston, the venerable James Madison (author of the Virginia Resolutions of 1798), and numerous distinguished South Carolinians joined in a vigorous attack on nullification as a constitutional heresy.[2] To their contentions Calhoun replied at length, once he had finally committed himself in 1831 to an open support of his theory. The gist of his rebuttal, selecting only his arguments in support of the general as opposed to the constitutional validity of his doctrine, was somewhat as follows:

First, he reiterated his axiom of 1814: loyalty to a government depends upon the security of the governed. Increasingly aware of its insecurity, the South was definitely on its way to becoming a conscious and disaffected minority. The tariff was its current concern, but the basic issue was slavery. Southern states either could not or would not convert their economy to manufacturing; and even if they did so the social institution of slavery, vital to their internal harmony, would make them vulnerable to an unsympa-

---

*The seven least populous states in 1830 were Delaware, 76,748; Rhode Island, 97,199; Mississippi, 136,621; Missouri, 140,455; Illinois, 157,445; Louisiana, 215,739; New Hampshire, 269,328. Their combined population was 1,093,535 out of a total of 12,866,000.

thetic or hostile majority in Congress. The very preservation of the Union hung upon an adequate solution to this problem of security for the minority.

The excessive power then being exercised by the federal government (to which he more than most statesmen had contributed) could lead only to secession and possibly to civil war. This power must therefore be effectively curbed, and the value of the Union was so inestimable that no price, other than the loss of liberty, was too great to insure its continuance. But checks and balances within the federal government offered at best uncertain and insufficient protection. How could a minority that could not block ruinous legislation in the Senate obtain sufficient votes in Congress for an amendment specifically denying the disputed power to the central government? The only recourse was the exercise by the states of their reserved right of nullifying acts which exceeded the power delegated to the federal government, a right which Calhoun, citing Jefferson as his authority,* found clearly inherent in the circumstances under which the Union was established and the Constitution adopted. This right he admitted rested upon inference from the Constitution, but an inference so clear "that no express provision could render it more certain. . . . Like all other reserved rights [of the states] it is to be inferred from the simple fact that it is not delegated."[3]

While he refused to admit the slightest doubt as to the consti-

---

*Though Madison vehemently denied in 1832 that Calhoun's theory could be deduced from the Virginia and Kentucky Resolutions of 1798 drawn up by Jefferson and himself, the contract theory and state sovereignty concepts which they advanced were the premises with which Calhoun began. Madison argued that the resolutions were only appeals to public opinion—successful appeals since the American public voted the Republican party into power in the subsequent presidential election. He pronounced nullification by the state an "absurdity . . . in its naked and suicidal form." Like Jefferson Davis later, Madison believed that a state could secede, but that it could not constitutionally nullify a federal law and remain in the Union. See Mitchell Franklin, "The Unconstitutionality of Interposition," *Lawyers Guild Review*, XVI (Summer, 1956), 45-60.

Evidence discovered by Miss Adrienne Koch in 1947 reveals that Jefferson at one point was clearly planning strong action similar to that considered by South Carolina in 1832. "Determined," he wrote Madison on August 23, 1799, "were we to be disappointed in the repeal of the unconstitutional act by Congress to sever ourselves from the union we so much value, rather than give up the rights of self government which we have reserved, & in which alone we see liberty, safety & happiness."

tutionality of this procedure, Calhoun somewhat shifted his ground by arguing on the basis of consequences. Granting that in one case out of a hundred the dire predictions of the critics of his doctrine might come about, in the other ninety-nine cases, he argued, it would prove highly efficacious. Recognition of the sovereign right of the individual state to exercise its suspensive veto would in most cases deter the congressional majority from thrusting upon a helpless minority a bill certain to be nullified. On the other hand, a state for various reasons would hesitate to apply its veto, and the operation of certain automatic factors would prevent its abuse.

Calhoun enumerated these factors in detail, and though the nation remained unconvinced, subsequent events in South Carolina bore him out. Despite universal condemnation of the tariff in 1828, only after four years of strenuous campaigning did the Nullifiers succeed in electing a legislature pledged to calling a nullifying convention. When this convention met, the delegates provided for a considerable delay before nullification would become effective, partly to give Congress a chance to yield and partly because they feared a clash with federal authority. The effective date was later postponed an additional month, during which the tariff was reduced and the nullification ordinance was withdrawn.

The very factors which would check a liberal use of the nullifying power by the states — the economic disadvantages of separation from the Union, the danger of coercion, and the conflict in the loyalties of citizens of the state — would operate even more strongly against a resort to secession were nullification answered by a successful amendment to the Constitution. But since the power to nullify was derived from state sovereignty and the compact theory of the Constitution, Calhoun defended the equally logical power of a state to secede.

*   *   *

During the years of its historical development, the nullification movement was inextricably interwoven into the complex issue of the tariff and the complicated designs of Calhoun to attain the presidency in 1832. The prospect for tariff reduction during Jackson's first term depended, on the one hand, upon the positive influence which Calhoun (as heir apparent) and his southern bloc, with the aid of western allies, could exert upon the President and the party; and, on the other, upon the threat of independent state action should reduction not be attained during the next four years. Obviously, the first contingency faded with the open break between Calhoun and Jackson in 1831.

Though the course of the movement in South Carolina reflected a growing emotional intensity on the part of its citizens, neither they nor their leaders ignored considerations of expediency. Much depended upon the current interpretations of the President's actions as indicative of his ultimate position on the tariff, and as much upon his attitude towards nullification should it finally be attempted by the state. In turn, both Jackson's action and that of Carolina were influenced by the response of her sister states, not merely to the theory of nullification, but to nullification as a *fait accompli*. The majority in South Carolina did not vote to nullify until they were convinced that such a method was not merely constitutional but also reasonably safe.

Never at any time during his first four years in office, in fact not until he actually signed the tariff bill which passed Congress in the summer of 1832, was it certain that Jackson would not force a drastic tariff reduction. He was generally regarded in the West and South as an advocate of state rights. By his veto of the internal improvement bill in 1830 and the bank bill of 1832 he positively committed himself to strict construction. In his various messages, however, he was vague on the tariff, perhaps deliberately. In his message of December, 1830, he pronounced it constitutional but admitted that he favored changes in the current schedules. In his letter of June 14, 1831, to South Carolina, designed to strengthen the cause of the Unionists who were strenuously resisting the Nullifiers in that state, he called attention "to the fast approaching extinction of the public debt, as an event which must necessarily produce modifications in the revenue system."[4]

At first some, but eventually many, South Carolinians dismissed Jackson's various statements because of the President's more positive recommendation of the distribution among the states of the surplus which would shortly materialize in the treasury upon the final payment of the national debt. They realized that distribution would make tariff reduction even more difficult to attain because the tariff would then receive additional votes from states, previously unconcerned about the issue, who would be receiving valuable revenue from that source. Calhoun made a telling argument when he predicted that it would inaugurate a "system of plunder [which] was the most despicable of all possible forms of government." In such a traffic of interest the North would always beat the South. "We being the payer and they the receiver, they could outbid us with the West and always would do it."[5]

Consequently he advocated a continuation of protest, but a postponement of overt action against the tariff until the public debt had been discharged. As long as the income from custom duties was applied to payment of the debt, the tariff remained technically a revenue measure difficult to challenge on constitutional grounds. But even on this point Jackson was not uncompromising. In his message of December, 1831, he omitted for the first time any reference to distribution; in it he specifically recommended a reduction of the tariff to a revenue basis and an adjustment of duties "with a view to equal justice in relation to all our national interests."[6]

The President made no public pronouncement on nullification until his famous toast to the Union at the Jefferson Day banquet in April, 1830. This banquet, a sequel to the Webster-Hayne debate, was intended as a climax of the Nullifiers' campaign to win the support of the West and of other southern states to their cause. His vehement toast disappointed and surprised many of them, for in view of his reputation in the South as a believer in state rights they had taken for granted his sympathy, or at least his neutrality. A year later, in his surprisingly subdued letter of June 14 to the South Carolina Unionists in which he promised tariff reduction, he also promised, should it become necessary, to uphold the Union "at all hazards." Finally, in answer to South Carolina's ordinance of nullification, his proclamation of December, 1832, made clear his intention to compel obedience to federal laws.

Despite his strong and positive language, there was still a remote possibility that Jackson was merely raising what he regarded as Carolina's bluff, that he was answering threat with threat. Certainly he had permitted Georgia to nullify completely Marshall's decision protecting the Cherokees. Carried away by wishful thinking, some Carolinians convinced themselves that no matter what he said, when the matter changed from the stage of words to the stage of action the President would not dare coerce a state. But the majority of their leaders seemed to have acted upon the more realistic premise that it was not a matter of what Jackson would do, but of what he could do. Would her sister states, even though they rejected the theory of nullification, actually permit the President to coerce South Carolina? Were they willing to risk a civil war? Would Jackson carry out his drastic proposal of coercion if the cooperation of a majority of states, or even of the southern states, was doubtful?

*   *   *

When the General's first year in office ended without any indication that he would initiate legislation to lower the tariff, and when McDuffie's bill for reduction was tabled without discussion in February, 1830,[7] certain South Carolina leaders decided that it was time to increase the pressure on the administration by a more drastic type of action. The antitariff movement of the past several year, both in the state and in the rest of the South, had been intense but amorphous, despite wild talk about independent state action even before the appearance of the "Exposition." During the lull which followed Jackson's election, the remedy proposed by the "Exposition" had been heatedly discussed in South Carolina, but the refusal of the legislature to adopt it in 1828 had revealed that such a course was considered entirely too drastic. Positive action had consisted of protests from the legislature, appeals to other states, and the threat of unified southern action if relief were not forthcoming.

During 1830, however, the radical party, including among its leaders Hamilton, McDuffie, and Hammond, began an active campaign to win the West, the South, and the state of South Carolina to the support of nullification, or at least to a program of concerted action rather than verbal protest. Apparently their original objective was a convention of states to consider the questions of the tariff and the Constitution. On all three fronts their offensive ended in failure.

Pronouncing nullification "peaceful, safe, and efficacious," but keeping it in the background, they called themselves in South Carolina the "State-Rights and Free-Trade" party and clamored merely for the calling of a state convention "where the people in their sovereign capacity should decide what ought to be done." This ruse did not deceive the Unionists, who resisted so bitterly that the state seemed on the verge of an internal civil war. The intense feeling which resulted broke personal friendships of long standing and destroyed previous political associations. When the votes for legislators were counted in the autumn of 1830, the Nullifiers were found to control a majority, but not the two thirds necessary for calling a convention.[8]

The opening gun in their battle to convert the West was the Webster-Hayne debate in the spring of 1830. Senator Foote of Connecticut had previously introduced a resolution to limit the sale of lands to those already on the market. Benton of Missouri attacked the resolution as another instance of eastern hostility to the West. Hayne, seeing an opportunity of a political alliance between the South and the West directed both against the tariff and against restriction on land sales, joined Benton with an attack on the resolution and on New England, emphasizing that section's disloyalty during the War of 1812. Aware of the danger of alienating the West, Webster arose to defend his section, but shrewdly singled out the southerner as his opponent. He pointed out that the Northeast had joined the West in voting for internal improvements, opposed by the South. Consolidation, which Hayne had attacked as an evil resulting from the policy of using the public lands as a source of revenue, he defended as the major objective of the Founding Fathers. The charge of New England disloyalty he cleverly dodged by expressing confidence that the Carolinian was not among those in his native state who were currently stating that it was time to calculate the value of the Union.

Hayne snapped up the bait. Echoing the reasoning of the "Exposition," he boldly defended the doctrine of nullification and asserted that it was in complete accord with the Constitution and the Republican doctrine of 1798 as expressed in the Virginia and Kentucky Resolutions. But Webster adroitly shifted the debate into an argument for nationalism against nullification, for Union against disunion, thereby turning the sympathy of a large majority of westerners, and even of southerners, against the radical leaders of South Carolina.

By their emphasis upon the Jeffersonian principles of 1798 as the authority for their views upon the nature of the federal government, the Nullifiers were seeking to capitalize upon the prestige of the dead Republican hero in the Old South and beyond the mountains. More specifically, they were making a strong bid for the support of Virginia. As a climax to what the twentieth century would call a propaganda campaign, they planned to use the dinner in celebration of Jefferson's birthday on April 13, 1830, as a grand finale. Here they hoped, by paeans to the revered Virginian and by praise of Georgia and Virginia for their defense of state rights against tyranny, to cinch their conquest of public opinion. But Jackson's unexpected toast, following closely upon Webster's glowing peroration to nationalism at the conclusion of his debate with Hayne, dealt their cause before the nation a fatal blow. And when James Madison, author of the Virginia Resolutions of 1798 and still very much alive, refuted their claim that his doctrine in any way supported nullification, their isolation was completed.

The South Carolina Radicals, therefore, ignoring the contentions of Madison, Webster, and Jackson, began at once to use milder language, at least outside their own state. Jackson's veto of the Maysville Bill in the month after the Jefferson banquet made their fears of consolidation seem exaggerated to many. Still insisting upon the constitutionality of their position, they stressed their devotion to the Union and the moderation of their proposal. In June McDuffie wrote, according to Thomas Ritchie of the Richmond *Enquirer,* that "the most the politicians of S. C. had thought of doing was to declare the Tariff null and void by a Convention, and then leaving it to her Juries to refuse giving Judgments on the Revenue Bonds. He seemed to think that even this course would now be abandoned ... his tone is much softened down."[9] Several months later Hayne informed Van Buren that the nullification plans were much exaggerated. Calhoun, though at this time he had not publicly associated himself with the movement, wrote in the same vein to Maxcy, in the letter of September, 1830, already quoted.

What had sobered them was the realization that not a single southern state would support them in their original program. It is evident from their later actions, however, that these assurances of peaceful intentions were designed as a ruse to quell the storm they had aroused and to lull the opposition into a sense of false security. Even the observant Ritchie was taken in. "I have almost lost all fear," he informed his brother, "of a *storm from the South.*"[10] In realistic fashion they abandoned hope for a unified southern movement while Jackson was in office. In his letter to Hammond in January, 1831, the still officially aloof Calhoun expressed a conclusion at which they had previously arrived: "We must next look to action of our own State, as she is the only one, that can possibly put herself on her sovereignty."[11]

They had simply decided, come weal or woe, that they would

drive their own state alone into nullification by electing to the next legislature in 1832 the necessary two thirds pledged to such action. Their successful agitation towards this end forced the unwilling Calhoun to join the movement in July, 1831; it compelled Jackson to drop distribution of surplus revenues and to recommend tariff reduction in his message of the following December. When a political dilemma caused the President to sign the lowered but still protective tariff bill of 1832, the Nullifiers gained control of the legislature. At once it called a convention that passed the nullification ordinance.

*   *   *

Assuming that Calhoun, with mixed motives, had written the "Exposition" in 1828 as a trial balloon, he now found himself in a most uncomfortable dilemma. The rejection of nullification by most of the nation early in 1830 made it apparent that if he openly espoused the doctrine he could not hope for nomination in 1832. But with his own state so bitterly divided on the question, he was in constant danger of being forced to take a public stand in South Carolina which would destroy him nationally. To increase the pressure on the administration and to maintain his influence in the state, he continued a private contact with the Radicals and even encouraged them in the early stages of their campaign.

Here he was attempting the impossible. He had helped build a backfire which he assumed he could control, without officially committing himself to the movement; ultimately the backfire became a raging conflagration which swept him before it. When he balked at the Radicals' drastic strategy in the summer of 1831, they simply went ahead without him and thereby forced his hand.

Despite the contemporary suspicion of certain individuals and many ex post facto statements of others that he led the Nullifiers from the beginning, there is evidence to the contrary. Adams expressed surprise in August, 1830, when Joel Poinsett, staunch Carolina Unionist, told him that Calhoun was at the bottom of the whole business. Judge John P. Richardson, another Unionist, wrote at the same time in his public address against nullification, "whatever obscure rumor there may be on the subject, we cannot trace the principle up to any direct sanction of our esteemed Vice-President." Certainly the Unionist toast directed at him on July 4, 1831, expressed doubt as to his position. When he did commit himself later in the month, editor Duff Green wrote that "his friends had been taught to believe that he was not a nullifier." Commenting on this commitment and Calhoun's earlier authorship of the "Exposition," an anonymous "Civis" in the Charleston *Courier* was more specific: "It is believed that Mr. Calhoun was anxious he should be concealed. It has been frequently denied that he was the author, and both he and his friends indulged a hope that it could not be fastened upon him."[12]

During this period Calhoun had much more on his mind than these developments in South Carolina. Naturally he was disturbed by the possibility that Jackson might run again in 1832. On this point he wrote, shortly after the President's toast at the Jefferson banquet, that it was "perfectly uncertain, whether General Jackson will offer again or not. Some who regard their own interest more than his just fame are urging him to offer." The rivalry of Van Buren he completely and fatally underestimated: "His strength, which was never great, has been steadily declining all session, and he may be now pronounced feeble. I see no cause to fear him."[13]

Hayne's attack on New England and Calhoun's later decisive vote against Van Buren's confirmation as minister to England proved to be major blunders. Many public men in Washington regarded Hayne as spokesman for the Vice-President. One southerner told Adams that he had warned the Carolinian of the "injudiciousness of the violent attacks of his partisans against New England; and that Van Buren was taking advantage of it, and might have the whole Eastern influence thrown into his scale by it, which otherwise Calhoun might expect for himself. He said Calhoun seemed to be exceedingly at a loss what to do; said that he had been obliged by his position to take the lead in the opposition to Mrs. Eaton; that he did not know what things were coming to."[14] It is highly significant that Calhoun did not take his stand for nullification in Souh Carolina until his break with Jackson was irreparable and until it was fairly certain that the President had selected Van Buren for his running mate in the next election.

Confronted with these unpleasant facts, Calhoun repeated his error of 1822 by refusing to face them and by convincing himself that his popularity with the nation would overcome all odds. On one occasion he told a northern journalist, M. L. Davis, that he was the strong man of the South and would win the votes of all southern states except Georgia. Davis received the impression that he intended to enter the field against Jackson, and Calhoun later wrote in regard to the President that he "had it in his power to annihilate him — but would act on the defensive." To his old friend Van Deventer of the war department days he expressed himself more freely: "I will in the coming contest act second to no one. I feel that it would degrade me. I will stand on my own ground, which I know to be strong in principle and the public support. I do not fear to carry the whole South with me, acting as it becomes my duty, which I will take care to do. I never stood stronger. I have the strongest assurance of a decided and successful support in Virginia which in the present state of things is all important."[15]

This was written at the end of May, 1831, and inspired by the attention the Vice-President had received on his way home from the capital. This confidence is all the more amazing in view of the fact that he had been told by Hammond two months before that his candidacy would not be supported by the Carolina Radicals. According to Hammond's careful account of this conversation, which took place in March, Calhoun had decided to abandon nullification and to propose instead a compromise on the issues in conflict between the various sections. This sudden decision was the consequence of his final break with Jackson the month before, and there can be no doubt that he hoped by his compromise to win the presidency.

Calhoun naïvely told Hammond that an amazing revolution of party lines was about to take place. He stated that even Tennessee had unanimously supported him in his recent fight with the President, who was everywhere losing the confidence of the party. With him against Jackson, he claimed, were three fourths of Congress and the states of Kentucky, Pennsylvania, and Virginia with minor exceptions. Clay, on the other hand, was about to lose the support of the tariff men, who feared that he would go too far with protection. "The members from Kentucky had gone home resolved to push the election against Clay, though not in favor of Jackson. Should they succeed Mr. Clay was gone, and his partisans hating General Jackson and Mr. Van Buren as they did, would unite upon any man to put him out. They would even take him (Mr. C.) with nullification upon his head."[16]

For the time being, therefore, it was his opinion that the South should not commit itself to a candidate. But because of the danger to the Union, he thought the time had come to reconcile "the three great interests of the Nation, the North, the South, and the West." This he believed could be done, and the plan he proposed was almost identical with the one currently advanced by Clay. For the West he would amend the Constitution to authorize internal improvements, using for this purpose the income from the sale of public lands. These internal improvements would make Charleston the great city of the South, and the proposal would satisfy the East by protecting it from the danger of free western land.

Ultimately he was in favor of direct taxation, but for the present he would reduce the tariff merely to a revenue basis. "He said he was no radical in this and thought the government should be liberal in its constitutional expenditures. The Tariff at this point might be so adjusted as to suit the Northern people better than it did now.... He would propose to single out some of the most important articles and giving them a liberal protection, enhance their profits still further by lowering the duties upon all [or] nearly all the other articles of necessary consumption." By this appeal to self-interest, he "thought the Northern people might easily be induced to lower the Tariff to the revenue point and thus reconcile the interests of North and South.... He thought it practicable — at all events worth trying. If it failed or matters continued going forward as they now did he looked upon disunion as inevitable."

After proposing this complete abandonment of nullification to his surprised lieutenant, he revealed his true intention. "Mr. Calhoun took his hat and we walked together for some distance. He then hinted pretty strongly that if things went right, he might be placed in nomination for the Presidency next fall." But Hammond refused to fall into the trap.

> I told him candidly that such a step would be imprudent at this moment both at home and abroad, and should not be thought of at this time. At this rebuff the Vice-President hastily retreated.
> He agreed with me. He said his object was to throw himself entirely upon the South if possible to be more Southern.... To many of his projects I could not yield my assent, and his fine theory — if sound and republican — I fear will be found inpracticable.... He is much less disposed to harangue than usual. There is a listlessness about him which shows that his mind is deeply engaged and no doubt that it is on the subject of the Presidency. He is unquestionably quite feverish under the present excitement, and his hopes.

When Hammond reported this conversation to Hamilton and the other Radicals, they quickly decided that the time had come to smoke Calhoun out. They would support neither him nor his compromise, and he must either join them publicly in support of the cause, regardless of his own ambitions, or take the consequences. Several months later Hamilton wrote Hammond that Duff Green had approached him about the compromise,

holding out the most alluring probabilities of Mr. Calhoun's success and of the willingness of the Manufacturers to compromise with us on the principle of his speech of 1816. I have replied very explicitly to him that in no shape lot or scot would we be included in the arrangement, that we would take no part in the presidential election and that I was quite sure that Mr. C's prospects were as hopeless as his ruin would be certain if he was brought to give his countenance to such a compact.... We [would] go on and abate not one jot of our zeal in support of our principles, which we would sacrifice to the elevation of no Man on earth. That as for surrendering Nullification, which he kindly recommended, that this was ... impossible. ... I have no doubt he moves in this matter with Calhoun's sanction.[17]

*   *   *

In keeping with these sentiments, the Radicals planned an incident which served their dual purpose of dramatically opening the campaign for nullification by the independent action of South Carolina alone and of forcing Calhoun to join them publicly. A visit of McDuffie, their most fiery orator, was used as the occasion for a dinner in his honor at Charleston, on May 16. The electric effect of his violent speech at this banquet whipped the community into a frenzy for nullification as the sacred revolutionary right of an oppressed people, and at once evoked a rousing denunciation from the press throughout the nation.*

This development caused Calhoun no little embarrassment outside the South and, in fact, ended any chance of his entering the presidential race as a proponent of sectional compromise. To his friends Green and Ingham, who at once voiced their protests by letter, he replied truthfully that "the occurrence in Charleston to

---

*Hamilton told Hammond that Green wrote him asking "if we were all crazy at McDuffie's dinner, if we intended to start into open rebellion and insure the empire of the whore of Washington (Mrs. E I suppose)."

me was wholly unexpected.... I think it every way imprudent, and have so written to Hamilton. I see clearly it brings matters to a crisis; and that I must meet it promptly and manfully. I intended to wait for Mr. Crawford's movement on me, so as to have the great advantage of acting on the defensive." He went on to outline a tentative plan of a letter to some local newspaper, and he informed Ingham that if he came out he would avow his "opinions freely, but modestly, as by those of the Virginia Report, Kentucky Resolutions and your supreme court in the case of Cobbett in '98; and will also state my opinions on all the connected points, particularly that of our adjustment of the conflict."[18]

Assuming that the adjustment he had in mind was the one recently outlined to Hammond, this statement to Ingham could only mean that Calhoun had convinced himself for the moment that he could support both nullification and compromise, despite unmistakable assertions to the contrary from Hamilton and Hammond. He somehow believed, as Bancroft well puts it, that he "could run with the hare of nullification and yet hold with the hound of protection." Since the votes of Pennsylvania, Virginia, and South Carolina were essential to the success of his contemplated presidential candidacy, he at first refused to admit that he would lose them by such inconsistency.

Torn between his efforts at self-delusion and his subconscious recognition of his dilemma, Calhoun apparently postponed as long as he could the evil day of decision. In face of the obvious fact that his hesitation was alienating the Carolina Radicals and that a crisis was at hand as early as May, he dangerously delayed his public commitment to nullification until the end of July. This delay may have been due in part to uncertainty as to whether the Unionists or the Nullifiers would prevail in the state, or to apprehension of the effect of such a stand upon his possible nomination by a new third party, the Anti-Masons.* Yet he may have continued to hold

*The Anti-Masons, a local New York party in origin, began as a result of the abduction and murder of one William Morgan in 1826, allegedly because he exposed the secrets of the Masonic Order. Seized upon by politicians, notably William Seward and Thurlow Weed, it became a third party in the national election of 1832. Opposed as it was to both National Republicans and Democrats, to Jackson and to Clay (both of whom were Masons), it might have proved the ideal vehicle for Calhoun to use to obtain the presidency — by throwing the election into the House if no candidate received a majority — and to advocate the compromise platform he had just outlined to Hammond. Despite his protests to the contrary, either Calhoun made himself available

high hopes for the nomination until the actual meeting of the party convention in September. Soon after the publication of the July letter, Green optimistically wrote that "the Anti-Masonic nomination is all that is wanting to put Clay out of the field and to elect Calhoun," and later added (after the convention had chosen William Wirt) "but for the cry of Nullification Mr. Calhoun would have been nominated by the Anti-Masons."[19]*

On July 4 of this fateful summer both Carolina parties staged mass meetings in Charleston. Repeating the fiery sentiments of McDuffie's recent speech, Senator Hayne called upon all patriots to support the sacred cause of the Nullifiers. Their Unionist opponents dramatically countered with William Drayton's spirited refutation of the "Exposition," with young William Gilmore Simms' "National Ode," and with Jackson's recent letter quoting Washington's "Farewell Address" and promising tariff reduction. But the most significant event of the occasion was their demand, diplomatically presented in the form of a toast, that Calhoun publicly announce his position. Caught thus between the cross fire of rival parties in his own state, the Vice-President could no longer avoid an open declaration.

Three weeks later the Pendleton *Messenger* stated that he would shortly express his sentiments without reserve, and on August 3 published in his public letter, dated July 26 at Fort Hill.† In it he committed himself fully to nullification, simply rewording the arguments of his earlier "Exposition." "This right of interposition," he concluded, "... I conceive to be the fundamental principle of our

---

to the Anti-Masons or Duff Green did it for him. Though he stated in a letter of May 25, 1831, that he had had no correspondence with them, he continued in this fashion: "I am not a mason, and go farther. I am so far anti Mason, that I believe the institution not only useless, in the present state of the world, but also pernicious, and have always thought so; though at the same time, I cannot doubt, but that there are, and have always been, many honest and virtuous members belonging to the society."

*Adams mentioned several times in his diary Calhoun's aspirations for the Anti-Masonic nomination — which Adams hoped to receive himself.

†Not to be confused with the more famous "Fort Hill letter" of August 28, 1832. Calhoun in this period developed his doctrine in four essays. The first was his "Exposition" of 1828, to which his name was not formally attached and which was not adopted by the South Carolina legislature when a special committee reported it. The second was this letter of July 26, 1831, on the "Relations of the States and the Federal Government," in which for the first time he formally and publicly avowed his support of the nullification thesis. In November, 1831 (the following fall), he prepared a "Report on

system, resting on facts historically as certain as our revolution itself, and deductions as simple and demonstrative as that of any political or moral truth whatever; and I firmly believe that on its recognition depend the stability and safety of our political institution.... I yield to none, I trust, in a deep and sincere attachment to our political institutions and the union of these States. I never breathed an opposite sentiment."[20]

This belated confession of faith by no means restored him at once to the confidence of the Nullifiers. Two subsequent documents, a report and an address written by him for the legislature which met in the fall, were rejected by that body "greatly to his mortification."[21] During most of the following year Calhoun may actually have been struggling to regain his leadership in the state, the only remaining avenue for a political future open to him. Not until his election as senator and his resignation of the vice-presidency in the crisis of December, 1832, was it evident that he had succeeded in regaining a position of dominance in South Carolina.

Politically, Calhoun had crossed the Rubicon. Though he seemed never able to admit it to himself, his zealous leadership of the nullification movement permanently doomed any chances he may have had of attaining the presidency in the future. In fact, this consequence of his fatal decision was immediately predicted by his close admirer, Judge John McLean, who wrote prophetically in September, 1831: "Our friend Calhoun is gone, I fear, forever. Four years past he has been infatuated with his southern doctrines. In him they originated.... I have no doubt, he believed, that he could consolidate the South, carry Pennsylvania, and bring over the West. He will not sustain himself anywhere, not even in his own state."[22]

This last prophecy proved incorrect. Calhoun did sustain himself in South Carolina, but only because of the aid he received from his old enemy Henry Clay.

Federal Relations" for the legislature, but it was rejected. Finally, in August, 1832, at the request of Governor Hamilton he wrote his final letter on the subject, usually referred to as the "Fort Hill letter." Naturally, in his later speeches in the Senate and in the two works on government he was writing at the time of his death, he restated his original thesis and added to it.

CHAPTER TEN

Crisis and Retreat

HAD Jackson been able to carry out the degree of tariff reduction promised to the Carolina Unionists in his message of December, 1831, the nullification movement in that state would have died a natural death. The prospects of such an outcome increased when the President towards the end of his first term appeared to favor the policy, advocated for some time by a West-South alliance under Benton and Hayne, of combining cheap land with tariff reduction as an effective means of preventing a surplus in the treasury. In the summer of 1832 this plan was defeated in Congress by Clay and his followers, who presented Jackson instead with a tariff, still protective in principle, which he dared not veto with the presidential election upon him. For his American System, stated the Kentuckian, he "would defy the South, the President and the devil."[1]

Naturally Clay had observed with glee the Eaton malaria, the Jackson-Calhoun split, and the other troubles of the party in power. Even before his nomination by the National Republicans at the end of 1831 he had planned his strategy and had begun his second campaign for the presidency. His original program of tariff and internal improvements had been designed to win the support of both the West and Northeast, but gradually the Kentuckian trimmed his American System to appeal more strongly to the special interests of men of property on the Atlantic seaboard north of the

John C. Calhoun

Potomac. His platform in 1832, therefore, consisted of three measures which he had recently sponsored: the retention of the protective tariff, the rechartering of the United States Bank, and the distribution of the proceeds from the sale of public lands among the states on the basis of population. These same measures were to remain the major objectives of the Whig party for the next two decades.

The approaching extinction of the national debt had strengthened both the demand of the newer western states for reduction in land prices and the demand of the South for lower duties, since the federal government would no longer need the sizable revenue currently produced from those sources. But cheap land would result in higher wages in the East and a decline in land values in older western states like Ohio and Kentucky, no less than in Pennsylvania and Massachusetts. By his distribution bill of 1832 Clay thought he had found a solution to this dilemma. The price of public land would not be reduced, but the proceeds therefrom would be divided among the states. Ten per cent of the revenue would be given to the western states in which the land lay; the rest would be divided among all the states according to the ratio of their congressional representation, to be used for internal improvements, education, and similar projects.

This distribution bill, approved by the Senate in 1832 and pocket vetoed by Jackson when it passed both houses the following year, was meant to insure the success of the whole Clay program in several ways. Sufficient funds would be provided for internal improvements. By substituting the states for the federal government as agents of construction, the old problem of constitutionality was avoided. By removing public lands as a source of federal revenue, a permanent and sufficiently high tariff would become indispensable as the major source of governmental income. The property interests of the seaboard and the old West, who could not fail to appreciate the numerous advantages they would derive from such a measure, would be bound more closely to the Clay banner. To prevent the alienation of the new West, internal improvements and the 10 per cent bonus from land revenue were offered as a substitute for cheaper land.

Jackson was personally opposed, in varying degrees, to all the items of the Kentuckian's program, but the fact that a large minority of his own party favored each of them placed him somewhat on the defensive. Eager to take full advantage of this situation, Clay carried the fight to the President on the eve of the election by pushing through Congress the tariff and bank bills. Jackson vetoed the bank bill, which he regarded as the greater evil, but he dared not press his followers beyond their endurance by rejecting also a tariff which provided for considerable reduction in duties. Clay's strategy boomeranged and the President, largely as a result of the popularity of his bank veto with the democratic masses, routed his rival in the election.

This tariff of 1832 was not the measure which Clay originally introduced in the Senate, but a milder bill sponsored by Adams and his House Committee on Manufactures, specifically designed as a compromise offer to the South. It reduced duties on the average to the level of 1824 and deleted most of the "abominations" of 1828, but since reductions were almost exclusively on noncompetitive items it was in essence more purely protective than any previous measure. It received, nevertheless, a majority of the southern votes, including those of three South Carolina congressmen.

The other eight members of the South Carolina delegation, however, joined in an ominous statement to their constituents on the day before Jackson signed the measure: Convinced "that all hope of relief from Congress is irrevocably gone, they leave it with you, the sovereign power of the State, to determine whether the rights and liberties which you received as a precious inheritance from an illustrious ancestry, shall be tamely surrendered without a struggle, or transmitted undiminished to your posterity."[2]

*   *   *

In the state election of 1832, the climax to a long and bitter internal struggle, the Carolina Nullifiers won sufficient districts to control the necessary two thirds of the legislature, though their popular vote was only 23,000 to the Unionists' 17,000. Summoned at once into special session by Governor Hamilton, the new legislature called for an election of delegates to a convention. Acting rapidly in accordance with prearranged plans, this convention met in November and passed an ordinance declaring the tariff acts of 1828 and 1832 null and void in the state, effective February 1, 1833.

Numerous auxiliary acts were passed by the convention, and later by the legislature at the convention's direction, to make nullification effective. All state officers, except members of the legislature, were required to take a "test oath" to obey the ordinance and related laws. Appeal to the Supreme Court in cases involving the ordinance and federal tariff laws was forbidden. The governor was authorized to call out the militia if coercion was attempted, and funds were appropriated for the purchase of arms and munitions.

In justification of these actions, two addresses were promulgated, one to the people of South Carolina and the other to citizens of the "Co-States," affirming the constitutionality of nullification and denying any intent or desire for disunion. As a concession the state was willing to accept a tariff which placed the same rate of duties on all imports, provided no more revenue was raised than the amount necessary for constitutional expenditures. Should the federal government violate the Constitution by a resort to force, South Carolina would consider the Union thereby dissolved. Were she thus "driven out of the Union, all other planting States, and some of the Western States would follow."[3] A resolution was forwarded to the other states and to Congress proposing the early calling of a convention of all states to consider the questions in dispute.

In such manner were steps taken to transfer nullification into the realm of fact. The parallel between this action of South Carolina and the secession of the lower South three decades later is striking, and in neither instance is a simple explanation possible. The tariff of 1832, like the later election of Lincoln, was obviously a critical incident in a complex chain of causation, but neither to most contemporaries nor to posterity did it logically justify the drastic and dangerous resort to nullification. The majority of Carolinians, however, aroused to frenzy by what Hamilton called "five years of the most intense agitation and concussion of public mind,"[4] saw their situation in an entirely different light.

They had come to regard their state as a nation, to whom they gave their whole loyalty and allegiance. The young Union was to them a convenient league into which South Carolina had entered by a solemn compact with other sovereign states. The general government thus established, a mere creature of the states and as such devoid of sovereignty, had for years violated the terms of the contract by protective tariffs which subsidized lowly manufacturers and shifted the cost in the form of excessive taxation upon noble cotton planters. This to their minds was the cause of their state's alarming decline in prosperity in recent years.

In vain had they pled for justice and too long had they waited for a redress of grievances. The time had now arrived to assert their constitutional right of nullification, a peaceful legal procedure in which the certain support of their sister states would insure easy victory. The federal government would either not dare coercion, or would suffer inevitable defeat if it resorted to so foolhardy a move. If a struggle ensued, declared Governor Hayne,* South Carolina would be fighting not for selfish ends, but for the sacred cause of "the liberties of the Union and the Rights of Man."[5]

*   *   *

By the fall of 1832 these sentiments had become dominant in the state, though a large minority remained to the last immune to the mass hysteria and warned their brethren of the dangers to which their wishful thinking would lead. Carolina particularism had been in the process of development for years, the product of a combination of factors peculiar at the time to that state alone. Probably beginning as a movement having a broad popular base rather than as one superimposed upon the citizenry from above, it gradually made converts in the 1820's of most of the political leaders of the state, and none who opposed it to the end remained prominent in public life after the crisis. Almost the last to make public espousal of the faith,† Calhoun was later forgiven his tardiness when he became its courageous champion against Jackson in the hour of peril. Despite his hesitation to support independent state action until all other alternatives had proved unavailing, his conversion was by no means sudden and his ultimate acceptance of the creed was wholehearted and without reservation.

Most Unionists fully agreed with Nullifiers that the protective tariff was unconstitutional and unjust;‡ the issue over which they

*Senator Hayne was elected governor as successor to Hamilton in December, 1832.

†It is noteworthy that Benjamin F. Perry, a discerning contemporary, gave Hamilton the major credit for the movement. Hamilton, wrote Perry, "was the gallant leader of the nullification party in South Carolina. He originated the nullification clubs, which were established in every district of the state, and which carried the election that fall [1831], in two thirds of the election districts. Mr. Calhoun was the author of nullification in South Carolina, but Governor Hamilton made it a success throughout the State. But for him, it would have fallen still-born, or been crushed in its swaddling clothes."—Benjamin F. Perry, *Reminiscences*, 143.

‡A few regarded it as unjust only and not unconstitutional. "That [the protective tariff] is contrary to the spirit of amity and concession in which

divided was the proper method of combating it. Both within the state and later within the nation the controversy involved the recognition of the right of South Carolina to nullify any federal legislation which a state convention pronounced a violation of the Constitution. The tariff, wrote Calhoun in one of his later reports, was "of vastly inferior importance to the great question to which it has given rise, and which is now at issue in the controversy: the right of a state to interpose, in the last resort, in order to arrest an unconstitutional act of the General Government within its limits. This they conceive to be by far the most important question which can be presented under our system."[6] Already he was thinking of interposition as a defense against potential antislavery legislation, not just the tariff; for he warned in another address that the illegal use of the taxing power could be applied to "any purpose that the majority may think to be for the general welfare; — to the Colonization Society, as well as to cotton and woolen manufactures."[7]

His personal letters of 1832 make it clear that he had lost faith in his original belief that the mere threat of interposition would induce Congress to approve a reduction of rates. "It is now too late for that remedy," he wrote in May to the future editor of his works, Richard Crallé, "or any other, except the reserved rights of the States.... I no longer consider the question one of free trade, but of consolidation. If, after ten years of remonstrance and denunciation of the system, as unconstitutional, the Southern States should now yield their ground, where can a stand be hereafter made? When will such another opportunity, as that of the discharge of the publick debt, be ever again presented? Let the occasion pass, and it is easy to see, what must follow — corruption, oppression and monarchy."[8]

Long before the victory of the Nullifiers in the state election, Calhoun had outlined in detail their strategy and the reasons for their confidence in its success regardless of strong opposition. Once South Carolina had nullified the tariff laws by formal action, the only recourse of the protectionists would be to call a convention of the states to pass upon an amendment granting the power in

---

the Constitution was conceived," said James L. Petigru, a prominent Unionist leader, "and in which the government ought to be exercised, I freely admit; that it is injurious to the South I firmly believe, but that it is unconstitutional I wholly deny; and that it is ruinous in its operations, is no more than a rhetorical flourish." — Quoted in Henry D. Capers, *Memminger*, 61.

question to the federal government. The Unionists had proposed that the state delay action until such a convention had been called. On the contrary, argued Calhoun, South Carolina must interpose first, "as it is only by such action that a necessity of acting on the subject could be imposed on the other States, and without such necessity, nothing would be done."[9]

By thus forcing the protectionists to introduce an amendment, the antitariff group would need the vote of only one more than one fourth of the states to defeat it. Since all southern states except Kentucky and Louisiana had expressed their overwhelming opposition to the tariff, their negative votes in the convention would be more than sufficient to defeat the amendment. Regardless of any unwillingness on their part to accept the extreme Carolina doctrine, their action would constitute a de facto recognition of the right of nullification. It is no exaggeration to describe this plan of the Nullifiers as a trap, baited with the tariff, into which they confidently expected their sister states of the South to walk blindly.

In this confidence they were mistaken. An equal delusion was their expectation that the contest would be peaceful or that, at worst, an attempt at coercion would fail. Had this not become the confirmed conviction of a majority of South Carolinians, it is highly doubtful that they would have voted in the fall of 1832 to invoke what they regarded as their constitutional right of interposition. More than a year earlier, McDuffie had scoffed at the ridiculous "idea of bloodshed and civil war, in a contest of this kind."[10] Shortly before the crucial election Calhoun was called upon by Governor Hamilton for a final summary of the Nullifiers' case, and he replied with his "Fort Hill Letter" of August 28, 1832. Restating all his previous arguments as to the constitutionality of interposition, he insisted at length that force could not be used against the state because its action would be perfectly legal and would in no way dissolve the ties which bound South Carolina to the Union. Nullification, he reiterated, was "in its nature, peaceable, consistent with the federal relations of the State, and perfectly efficient, whether contested before the courts, or attempted to be resisted by force."[11]

*   *   *

The involved events of the crisis during the several months following the passage of the ordinance can be simplified by citing certain facts of basic significance. South Carolina never actually interfered with the collection of the obnoxious custom duties. The original effective date of February 1, 1833, was suspended on January 21 by an informal public meeting in Charleston, and on March 14 the reassembled convention repealed the ordinance by a vote of 155 to 4. Thus nullification was only threatened and was not put into actual execution at any time. The state yielded, said the Nullifiers, because she had accomplished her objective when Congress passed Clay's bill for a gradual reduction of the tariff.

On the contrary, in view of their earlier repeated assertions that recognition of their right of nullification was their major purpose, and of their later threats to secede if the Force Bill should pass, the outcome was a definite defeat for Calhoun and his colleagues. They used the compromise tariff as a face-saving excuse for the surrender of their original objectives, since all their expectations proved erroneous. Every southern state, even Virginia, rejected nullification as contrary to the Constitution, and no convention was ever called. By unmistakable words and acts Jackson prepared to use force against the state the moment overt interference with the collection of duties was attempted. His request for specific congressional authorization of coercion was almost unanimously approved in the Senate by a vote of 32 to 1.

Faced with the certainty of armed resistance from the large minority of Unionists at home and of invasion by a large force of militia from without, and doubtful of military aid from other southern states, South Carolina hastily chose the only avenue of escape by accepting a partial concession on the tariff. Through a desperate alliance which Calhoun arranged with Clay, she was spared the bitter indignity of yielding to Andrew Jackson — at the price of waiting ten years for a reduction in the tariff equal to that which the Verplanck Bill at the outset had offered in two.

The first retreat of the Nullifiers on January 21 was in part due to the unfavorable response of all the southern states. Mississippi, North Carolina, and Alabama rejected nullification flatly as "a heresy fatal to the existence of the Union," "subversive of the Constitution," and "leading in its consequences to anarchy and civil discord." Kentucky refuted it by copious quotations from the Constitution itself; Georgia abhorred it "as neither a peaceful or constitutional remedy." But the reply of Virginia completed the isolation of the Nullifiers and compelled them to backtrack. Virginia denied that her resolutions of 1798, which she still regarded as the true interpretation of the nature of the Union, in any way sanctioned South Carolina's recent action. Urging that state to withdraw her ordinance and Congress to reduce the tariff, she sent a commissioner to South Carolina to hasten a peaceful settlement. Ostensibly it was in response to this Virginia proposal of compromise that the Charleston meeting postponed the effective date of nullification to allow Congress time for final action on the Verplanck Bill.[12]

But this decision to retreat was at least equally influenced by the tremendous pressure on the Nullifiers resulting from the positive steps taken by the President in the interim to meet their challenge, which he regarded both as a personal attack directed against him by Calhoun and as a danger to the Union. Never an enthusiast for protection, in recent messages he had advocated a reduction of the tariff to a revenue basis. In his message of December 4, 1832, he again made such a recommendation, indicating his dissatisfaction with the bill of the previous summer which he had signed. Later in the month, probably upon Van Buren's advice, he consented to the introduction of a measure by Congressman Gulian C. Verplanck of New York for a series of reductions until rates reached an average of between 15 and 20 per cent by 1834. Thus he effectively reversed the Carolina strategy of translating antitariff into pronullification sentiment; by eliminating protection as an issue he reduced the controversy to the essential question of the right of the state to annul an act of Congress.

Already in his proclamation of December 10 he had thundered defiance to the heresy of his native state in clear and forceful words: "I consider, then, the power to annul a law of the United States, assumed by one state, incompatible with the existence of the Union, contradicted expressly by the letter of the Constitution, unauthorized by its spirit.... The Constitution ... forms a *government* not a league.... Those who told you that you might peaceably prevent [the execution of the laws] deceived you — they could not have been deceived themselves.... Their object is disunion; but be not deceived by names; disunion by armed force is treason."[13]

Jackson was not one to rely upon words alone. Surely the warrior who had executed Ambrister and Arbuthnot would, had the necessity arisen, have led in person a force to put down resistance to federal laws in South Carolina. Since early autumn he had maintained close contact by letter with Joel Poinsett, leader of the

Unionists in the state, and had taken numerous steps to strengthen federal forces around Charleston. It was his original plan, as soon as he received official proof that the legislature had passed military measures, to call upon the governors of certain states for sufficient militia to enforce the tariff laws.

Martin Van Buren, desirous of avoiding civil conflict and well aware that the President's proposed action would alienate from the party many southerners already disturbed by the excessive nationalism of his proclamation, argued with his chief for a more cautious policy. The mere raising of troops by a state was not actual treason, he contended, and the legal sanction for Jackson's plan was not sufficiently specific. It was wiser in his opinion first to isolate South Carolina, should coercion later become unavoidable, by appeasing state-righters elsewhere with a request for specific authority from Congress and an offer of tariff reduction. Reluctantly the President followed this advice. Although he had still received no official confirmation of formal military action in South Carolina, on January 16 he asked Congress for authority to use force in collecting the duties. But if it should fail to act in the two weeks that remained before the deadline, his intention was to proceed on his own initiative.[14]

A week later he wrote Poinsett that he would "in ten or fifteen days at farthest have in Charleston ten to fifteen thousand well organized troops well equipped for the field, and twenty thousand, or thirty, more in their interior." Volunteers from every state, he added, had offered their services and within forty days he could march two hundred thousand men to put down insurrection. Should Virginia attempt to prevent the movement he would arrest her governor at the head of his troops. "I repeat to the Union men, fear not, *the union will* be preserved."[15]

This determination of Jackson to suppress overt nullification by force frightened his friends no less than his opponents, and all neutral parties as well. It produced a dual effect of winning votes from protectionists as the only means of avoiding civil war and of placing the Nullifiers under a pressure they could no longer bear. All of these parallel developments — the prospect of invasion, the adverse response of southern states, the compromise efforts of Virginia, and congressional consideration of the Verplanck Bill — sobered them into their strategic retreat.

*　　　*　　　*

Early in the crisis the scene in Washington focused upon the personal battle between the President and Calhoun for the support of the Senate. In December the Nullifiers had recalled Hayne from the Senate and elected him to the governorship, and the legislature had promptly chosen the abler Calhoun to fill the vacancy thereby created. Having resigned the vice-presidency, the new senator began his journey north under great emotional tension, for among the various threats currently attributed to Jackson was a statement that "if one more step was taken he would try Calhoun for treason and, if convicted, hang him as high as Haman." Dismissing as legend the numerous contemporary stories of Calhoun's abject fright, there remains reliable evidence that he was highly excited. Certainly his journey to the capital required courage; the autobiography states that wherever he stopped on the way crowds gathered to see the man whom they expected to be arrested for treason. When he took his seat in the Senate on January 4, the gallery was packed with spectators.[16]

Despite his positive convictions and his powers of logic, the Senator faced almost insurmountable obstacles which, for all his self-delusion, he could not have ignored. It was already apparent that recent events had given the lie to all his earlier predictions; they made it clear that South Carolina was isolated and that the President was not bluffing. For fifteen years Calhoun had not indulged in public speaking, yet his chief antagonist in the Senate debate by which the outcome of the contest might well be determined was certain to be Webster, ablest orator of the day and ardent supporter of Jackson's bold stand for federal supremacy. Regarded by many of his fellow citizens as a traitor and by most of them as chiefly responsible for the ugly crisis at hand, Calhoun was facing political ruin. Upon his actions depended, in no small degree, the fate of his native state and his nation.

Surely he was consulted in advance in regard to the suspension of the nullification date by the Charleston meeting on January 21; it is not improbable that he suggested the move himself. Assuming that the Verplanck Bill then before Congress would pass, the Nullifiers could claim victory by asserting that their action alone had at last brought about reduction and that they had voluntarily called off their plan to nullify. At the same time the indefinite suspension of the date made federal use of force unnecessary, and would encourage the rejection by Congress of the President's request.

But Jackson would not permit Calhoun and his colleagues to retreat with such impunity. South Carolina had raised the issue by formal action; he demanded an equally formal repudiation of the right of a state to annul a federal law. He insisted upon his Force Bill to make it clear that federal authority was supreme and that the government had not been intimidated in the slightest. Upon this bill the Nullifiers at once concentrated their attacks. In their Charleston meeting they threatened secession if Congress should pass the President's "bill of blood." Were it approved, Calhoun told the Senate, "and an attempt be made to enforce it, it will be resisted, at every hazard — even that of death itself. Death is not the greatest calamity: there are others still more terrible to the free and brave, and among them may be placed the loss of liberty and honor."[17]

The Judiciary Committee of the Senate, to whom the President's request had been referred, reported the Force Bill on January 21. The following day Calhoun replied with three resolutions which summarized his contentions as to the nature of American government. Briefly, these asserted that the people of the United States had never formed and did not compose a nation; that the states alone were sovereign; and that they retained the sole allegiance of their citizens as well as the right to decide the powers which they had reserved to themselves and those which they had delegated by the compact of the Constitution. "He had drawn them with great care," he informed his audience, "with a scrupulous regard for the truth of every assertion they contained.... No impartial jury in Christendom could, on an issue, refuse to render a verdict in their favor."[18] Had the Senate acted favorably on these resolutions, the Force Bill would have been defeated in advance, but various contrary resolutions were at once introduced. Shortly a majority voted for the priority of the bill itself.

After much jockeying for position between the principals, in the middle of February began the great debate between Webster and Calhoun, less dramatic but far more incisive than the New Englander's earlier debate with Hayne. Each contestant resorted to the closest legal and historical reasoning, each refuted the other on many constitutional points, but they ended as they began with irreconcilable premises. In a tone of injured dignity and sincere conviction Calhoun defended in detail both his own actions and those of his state; she had not acted rashly, but her sister states tardily.

Senators listened respectfully but remained obviously unconvinced. When the final vote on the measure was taken on February 20, the Carolinian and other state-righters dramatically withdrew, leaving John Tyler of Virginia to cast the single negative.[19]

*   *   *

Early in the month Calhoun had foreseen the failure of his effort to defeat the Force Bill. In desperation he had sought out Clay to form with him an alliance against their mutual enemy Jackson, the purpose of which was to prevent the ultimate passage of the President's measure from appearing to the nation as a personal victory.[20] As a substitute for the Verplanck Bill, Clay would introduce a new tariff proposal which by their combined influence they would induce Congress to pass, thus producing the impression that reduction was accomplished against the wishes of the administration and in the face of its active opposition. South Carolina could then say that she had won a pronounced victory over Jackson on the fundamental issue of the controversy, and could scorn the Force Bill as an empty gesture on his part to disguise defeat.

This plan was speedily translated into action. On February 12 Clay introduced his bill and Calhoun took the floor to announce his full support. At the beginning of March both the Compromise Tariff and the Force Bill were finally approved by both houses of Congress and Jackson signed the measures. Several years later, when the Carolinian broke his alliance with the Kentuckian, each claimed he had forced the other to accept his terms in the earlier crisis. It is evident from the facts, however, that Clay's aid saved Calhoun from utter defeat and that Clay successfully demanded a high price for his assistance. Instead of swift reduction to a revenue basis in two years, as provided by the Verplanck Bill, reduction was to proceed slowly for eight years, according to the compromise measure, and then rapidly during the next two, until rates reached an average of 20 per cent in 1842. Calhoun abandoned his attempt on the floor of the Senate to remove some of the objectionable provisions of the bill when Clay threatened to let him "fight it out with the General Government."[21]

Actually Calhoun had no alternative to the subtle strategy which he followed. Otherwise both he and South Carolina would have suffered the bitter humiliation of abject surrender to Jackson or almost certain defeat in a military conflict. As it turned out, the state proudly claimed a significant victory, while Calhoun received its adoration as the hero who had worked the magic. Moreover, as an immediate consequence in the practical politics of the moment he had robbed Jackson and Van Buren, already designated for the succession in 1836, of credit for tariff reduction which would have strengthened their following in other southern states.

Like his fellow statesmen, Clay was anxious to avoid armed conflict that might disrupt the Union. Yet for him also the alliance proved advantageous, since the wide margin of his recent defeat by Jackson had given his pride and his prestige a severe blow. Though from the first he had denied the contentions of the Nullifiers and refused to oppose the Force Bill, his nationalistic thunder was being stolen both by the President and by Webster, his rival for the leadership of the National Republicans. His new stand against Jackson in defense of state rights won for him and his program the moderate support of many southerners, unwilling to espouse nullification but recently alienated by the President's ultra-nationalism, and prevented a restoration of their earlier alliance with the newer West.

As a matter of fact, this was Clay's initial step in the formation of an anti-Jackson coalition shortly to be organized formally as the Whig party. As anxious as Calhoun to rebuff Jackson and to embarrass Van Buren, Clay paid nothing for Calhoun's support. The mild compromise bill saved protection from the rapid reduction of the Verplanck measure; it allowed ample time, as he pointed out to his protectionist friends, for a subsequent Congress to restore rates before serious damage was done. The father of the American System now had to his credit a second great compromise,* a fact of no little influence among men of good will.

After Calhoun, with Clay's assistance, had obtained congressional adoption of his plan, there remained the serious question of whether South Carolina hotheads would accept its terms. So great was his anxiety on this score that Calhoun risked irreparable damage to his ailing health, by traveling night and day over icy roads, to defend in person his handiwork at the state convention already reassembled in Columbia. Fortunately for him, the committee on

---

*Clay was already popularly given credit for the Missouri Compromise, although it was not the act of 1820 but the second minor compromise of 1821 which he arranged.

resolutions recommended acceptance of a proposal from Virginia that the nullifying ordinance be repealed on the grounds that the new tariff fulfilled the original Carolina demands. "The effect of interposition," reported the committee, "if it has not equalled our wishes, has been beyond what existing circumstances would have authorized us to expect." Obviously the majority recognized the rashness of opposing the settlement, and even the fiery Hamilton, the president of the convention — who in January had advocated secession if the Force Bill were enacted — now voted in favor of acceptance.[22]

But a minority, critical of Calhoun's course and suspecting that secret commitments had been made to Clay, failed by only three votes in an attempt to interrogate their senator and congressmen on the full details of the compromise. Robert B. Rhett objected strenuously to a statement in the resolutions affirming devotion to the Union. For home consumption at least, therefore, specific reassertions of state sovereignty were formally pronounced. The convention passed a new ordinance nullifying the Force Bill and resolved pointedly that "the allegiance of the citizens of this State, while they continue such, is due to said State; and that obedience only, and not allegiance, is due by them to any other power or authority...."[23] In this spirit a new test oath was passed which continued to receive bitter opposition from Unionists until the state court of appeals annulled it a year later.

In their relief from the disaster which had been so imminent, Calhoun and the majority hailed the outcome as a triumph. The same Turnbull who had been the first to advocate forcible resistance now exulted, "with our one-gun battery of Nullification, we have driven the enemy from his moorings." Calhoun was less exuberant in his language. "I have no doubt," he wrote to an intimate northern friend in regard to the tariff, "the system has got its death wound. Nullification has dealt the fatal blow. We have applied the same remedy to the bloody act."[24] But when time brought a return of clearer vision, he reverted to the contrary sentiment which Rhett had expressed to the March convention.

"Let gentlemen not be deceived," said Rhett upon that occasion when the majority had defeated his attacks upon the compromise. "It is not the Tariff — not Internal Improvements — nor yet the Force Bill, which constitutes the great evil against which we are contending. These are but symptoms of the disease...but it is the despotism which constitutes the evil; and until this Government is made a limited Government, and is confined to those interests which are common to the whole Confederacy, there is no liberty — no security for the South."[25]

*   *   *

Viewing the results of the controversy from a longer perspective, regardless of what they said or believed at the time about the outcome, Calhoun and his colleagues were completely defeated in their attempt permanently to limit the power of the federal government by obtaining recognition of nullification as a constitutional procedure. It is an irrefutable fact that the doctrine was specifically rejected by the South* and that in passing the Force Bill Congress formally denied its validity. Never at any future date, even when more extreme views as to state sovereignty became general in the Cotton Kingdom, did a majority of southerners regard nullification as a reserved right of the states. As for the secondary issue of the tariff, the action of South Carolina was but the most important of several factors responsible for reduction. In view of the defeat of Clay and protectionist congressmen in the recent election, of Jackson's desire for reduction and his opposition to Clay's distribution plan, and most of all of the approaching surplus in the treasury, a considerable lowering of duties was imminent.

The controversy was the climax of Calhoun's career, and its various consequences fixed the pattern of his political future. For more than a decade it inclined him to caution in his tactics, lest he be caught out on the same limb again. Realizing that independent state action had proved impractical, he spent his remaining years in an effort to unite the whole South into a political bloc, trying at the same time other opportunistic stratagems by which he hoped to protect southern rights and thus preserve the Union. The virtue of nullification, to his mind, had been the fact that it would accomplish both these objectives. Not until 1850, the year of his death, when the South was fighting a losing battle against legislation fatal

---

*Hamilton, who had earlier threatened secession if the Force Bill passed, openly gave as his reason for voting for the repeal of the ordinance of nullification in the March convention the fact that "the whole force of the embodied public opinion of the South is against us." Beverly Tucker wrote in later years that after nullification Calhoun "fell back upon a cheating compromise which he knew was not to be observed in good faith, and then went home and pretended to regard the compromise as the triumph of nullification."

in his opinion to her security, did he reluctantly give serious consideration to secession.

By his defense of nullification Calhoun sacrificed the national political following which he had carefully cultivated during the past twenty years, but by the same action he achieved for the first time the absolute and undisputed leadership of his native state. In effect, South Carolina had proclaimed herself a sovereign nation and in the eyes of his fellow Carolinians he now became the incarnation of that sovereignty. His stature increased as the abolitionist attack upon slavery in the 1830's accentuated this sentiment of state-nationalism. With few exceptions the Unionist leaders who had opposed him in the crisis either migrated to other southern states, retired from politics, or became converts; his colleagues among the Nullifiers were soon dwarfed by his new prestige. South Carolina became in effect a pocket borough that followed almost without question where he led. Thus he easily defeated the effort of Senator William C. Preston to carry the state over to the Whigs contrary to his wishes, as well as the later movement for nullification or possibly secession, led by Governor Hammond and Rhett, in protest against the high tariff of 1842 and the Senate's rejection of the Texas annexation treaty two years later.

The possession of such tremendous power in the state aggravated a trait of personality that seriously hindered the realization of his political aspirations and objectives on the national stage. The adoration he received in South Carolina misled him into believing that expressions of admiration from his friends elsewhere in the South indicated a similar devotion on the part of all southerners. More and more he became accustomed in these later years to forming decisions with little regard for his local lieutenants, and to the usual acceptance of these decisions by his state without compromise or opposition. By his dictatorial manner he unintentionally alienated leaders of other southern states who were willing to cooperate but who refused to kowtow. Among the primary causes of his critical failure to win the full support of the key states of Virginia and Georgia, and of the Democratic party when he later returned to it, must be included a personality which grew more rigid and domineering with the passing of time.

John C. Calhoun

1. *Now when James, the son of James, had returned to his people, he gathered together the captains, and the wise men, and the rulers of hundreds, and the rulers of tens in all the land of Colleton, which is hard by Charleston.*

2. *And he cried aloud against John of Quincy, and against the statute, and against the tariff which he had ordained.*

3. *And he opened his mouth and said, "Ye men of Colleton! lo, the people of the East, who are called Yankees, have smote your land with a scourge; they have despoiled you of your substance and put chains upon your members; they have robbed your fields of their increase, and "the fox peeps forth from your ruined chateaus."*

4. *And the men of Colleton turned their eyes to the East and to the West, for they knew not the thing which is called a "chateau"; they felt their arms for chains, but they were free.*

5. *And they looked forth on the fields, but they were fresh with verdure, and the land was without scourge; and they marveled great at the words of James.*

6. *But James called aloud on the name of George the Prophet.*

7. *And George answered in a voice like the rushing of many waters and said unto the people, "Awake, stand up, O men of Colleton, who have drunk at the hands of the Yankees their cup of fury."*

8. *"Verily, I say unto you, that although your fields are green and your hands free, yet desolation and destruction and famine shall surely come upon you, for by the spirit of John, the Conjuror, I swear that great and inconceivable are the evils which the tariff of John of Quincy shall bring to pass.*

9. *"Wherefore, O men of Colleton, let not your hearts be faint, but hearken to the words of James and wax stronger in the faith — for lo! I will show unto you a hidden secret."*

10. *Then George waved his hand before the eyes of the men of Colleton, and they beheld in the air a host of Yankees bearing from the fields of the South "forty of every hundred parts" of the increase thereof.*

11. *And he gave them to drink of certain liquor, which James and his companions had procured from the kingdom beyond the great*

---

*A satire written by the South Carolina Unionist, Christopher G. Memminger, in 1830. (For the full work see Henry D. Capers, *Life and Times of C. G. Memminger* [Richmond, 1893].)

waters, even from the land of Champaigne, and they waxed warm, and they felt the chains and the shackles whereof James had spoken.

12. *And the men of Colleton were astonished at the power of George and of James, the son of James, and they bowed down to them and worshipped them.*

13. *So the words of James, which he had spoken, were made manifest to them, and they gnashed their teeth and shouted aloud.*

14. *On that same day James departed from among them and went down by the sea to the city called Charleston.*

15. *Now it came to pass that John of Quincy was gathered to his fathers and Andrew sat upon his throne.*

16. *And John the Conjuror, and Robert the Nullifier, and George the Prophet, and James, the son of James, feared in their hearts the power of Andrew, for he was a just man, and had the fear of the Lord before his eyes.*

17. *And they bowed before his throne, and spake in a loud voice to the people, saying: "We, even we, are the faithful servants of Andrew, and will do honor to his name."*

18. *But the heart of John the Conjuror was in secret turned against Andrew, and he was greatly wroth against him, and his countenance fell — for his soul coveted, strongly, the throne whereon Andrew sat.*

19. *Now when John the Conjuror had seen the power of George the Prophet, and of James, the son of James, made manifest upon the men of Colleton, he gathered unto him all the wise men, and the rulers, and the captains of his faction to take secret counsel together.*

20. *And George the Prophet was in the midst of them; and Robert and James, the son of James, were not afar off.*

21. *Then John opened his mouth and said: "Men and brethren, verily we have cried aloud against the Tariff ordained by John of Quincy, and my servants, George and James, have made ready the men of Colleton and of Edgefield, and we have sought to prepare all the provinces of the South.*

22. *"So that if it should come to pass that John of Quincy should continue to sit upon the throne we could rend from him the provinces of the South, and place a King to reign over them.*

23. *"Then should we all have honor, and power, and distinction, and glory; and my servants, George, and James, and Robert, would be set in high places.*

24. *"But now, men and brethren, behold, the people give more honor and love to Andrew than to me, and they bow down with*

veneration before him, and if we cry aloud against Andrew, as we did against John of Quincy, they will cast stones at us.

25. *"Wherefore let us go forth to all the provinces of the South, and let us confound the understanding of the people, and let us, with one accord, declare to them that the King's counsellors at the great city are seeking to despoil them.*

26. *"And we will arouse them to vengeance, and we will send forth George the Prophet, and Robert, and James, and there will be a mighty commotion.*

27. *"And we shall have meetings and feasts, and meat offerings, and drink offerings over all the land of the South; and when the hour shall come, then shall we cause the people to NULLIFY the statute which was ordained in the reign of John of Quincy.*

28. *"And peradventure Andrew the King will wax wroth thereat, and will send forth a power to enforce the statute and the ordinances of the realm; but we shall rejoice the more, for the South will become as a fiery furnace for Andrew, and people will be as tigers when their garments are stained with blood.*

29. *"Then shall we be able to send forth a multitude against Andrew the King, and we will do battle with him, and we will rend asunder his dominions, and we will take to ourselves the rich provinces of the South, and set over them another King and other Princes and Governors.*

30. *"And I, John, will cast for ye all a Graven Image, which shall be endued with great power to blind the eyes of the people, and to shut their ears, and ye shall set it up in a high place, and ye shall bow down before it and worship it.*

31. *"And the name of the Graven Image shall be called 'NULLI-FICATION,' which being interpreted is 'DISUNION,' and the place wherein ye shall set it up shall be called 'CONVENTION.'"*

32. *And the counsel of John the Conjuror seemed good to all the chief men, and the rulers, and the captains, who were gathered before him, and they departed straightway every man to do his allotted part.*

CHAPTER ELEVEN

The Whig Flirtation

THE transition of the National Republican and the Democratic Republican parties into the Whigs and the Democrats of the 1830's signified far more than a change in political nomenclature. The new names were, in fact, accepted slowly and reluctantly by a considerable minority. Yet early in Jackson's second administration, as a direct result of his actions in the bank and the nullification controversies, it was evident that a fundamental realignment was occurring in the political affiliation of leaders, of classes, and even of sections. By the end of this turbulent decade, when the Whigs ousted the Democrats from the presidency by a majority of 150,-000 in a popular vote of almost 2,500,000, the new alignments had solidified into fairly definite parties.

At the time of its origin in 1833 the amorphous "Whig" opposition consisted of National Republicans and a spontaneous coalition of individuals and groups alienated by Jackson, all clustered around the axis of the new Clay-Calhoun alliance. The regrouping of factions which continued in subsequent years was similar to that which had recently taken place when the General began his successful attack on the victorious Adams-Clay party in 1825. The new opposition was united only in its antipathy to the President and in the desire to drive him and his followers from office. Consisting of men alienated by one or more of his frequently inconsistent actions on the issues of the day, it included in its ranks groups holding diverse and even opposite views on specific matters of national policy: nullifiers, moderate state-righters, and nationals; national bank, state bank, and independent treasury advocates; opponents and supporters of the tariff, distribution, and cheap land.

Unable to agree on these basic items, the opposition found a popular least common denominator in attacking the tyranny of "King Andrew I," as the name "Whig" implies. Its major objectives in Jackson's second administration were the recharter of the bank and the defeat of Van Buren. The President's stands in these and in all other matters were attacked, not on their own merits, but on the grounds of the defense of liberty against the dangerous usurpation of power by the executive.

The original coalition consisted of four more or less distinct wings: former National Republicans led by Clay; the majority of northern Anti-Masons who united with Clay's group in 1834; Calhoun's group of extreme state-righters; and a moderate southern group, strong both in Virginia and Tennessee, who resented Jackson's preference for Van Buren over Senator Hugh L. White of Tennessee. Before 1840, however, two major shifts occurred among factions in the roughly equal national parties. Calhoun, who fully cooperated at first but never formally joined the Whigs, led his smaller southern group over to a similarly irregular position of cooperation with the Democrats shortly after Van Buren's election; and when Van Buren persisted in his advocacy of separating the government from connection with all banks, a wing of conservative Democrats led by Senators William C. Rives of Virginia and Nathaniel Tallmadge of New York went over to the Whigs.

When the General retired from the White House, it was becoming apparent to the discerning that a deeper distinction divided the parties than the mere opposition to his strong personality which had given the new alignment its original impetus. Like the Federalists who preceded and the Republicans who followed them, the Whigs were fundamentally men of property. A social as well as a political revolution was in progress; the rise of state labor parties and locofocoism* in the East indicated that the common man might

---

*"Locofocos" was the name given to the radical, workingman's wing of the Democratic party in the North, which developed during the fight over the bank in the 1830's. They favored hard money and the separation of the government from all banking connections.

use his recent acquisition of the ballot to effect a drastic redistribution of wealth. The ferment of the thirties, manifested in abolitionism, in the wild ideas of Fannie Wright and Robert Owen, and in numerous other equalitarian and humanitarian movements, threatened established social institutions no less than property.

Frightened by the noise of the lunatic fringe and the potential but as yet unrealized power of the masses under white manhood suffrage, conservatives flocked together in defense against the greater danger of radical democracy. Thus it was no accident, when Jackson and later Van Buren adopted the hard-money policy favored by the workingman and attacked Biddle's and all banks as a monopoly of the rich, that the money question became the central issue of the decade. With tacit understanding, a majority of planters, manufacturers, merchants, and bankers became Whigs, willing to compromise their former differences rather than risk a division of ranks. A majority of large slaveholders remained with the party long after the slavery controversy became paramount.

Since the Democrats were in power throughout the thirties, cleavages among the Whigs never rose to the surface, and even in the campaign of 1840 the party did not commit itself to a specific platform. It simply reiterated its condemnation of Jackson and Van Buren in the name of liberty, concealed its intentions on controversial matters of national policy, and finally turned the tactics of the Democrats against them by nominating a western military hero in the person of General William Henry Harrison. Clay's previous defeats prevented his selection, but he, and not Webster or Calhoun, won the confidence of the party and directed its strategy. Because the process of unity had not progressed sufficiently by 1836, three candidates for the presidency were put forward, White, Harrison, and Webster, in the hope that Van Buren would not attain a majority and that the House would determine the outcome. Four years later Harrison was chosen as the candidate with John Tyler of Virginia as his running mate. The appeal to the West and the South, coupled with general dissatisfaction arising from the depression that began in 1837, gave victory to the Whigs.

*　　　　*　　　　*

Though Calhoun took care to maintain a technical independence of the new party during Jackson's second term, he acted with its leaders in their incessant personal attacks upon the President and in their vigorous opposition to his executive actions and his legislative program. Not even Clay exceeded him in bitter denunciation of the tyranny and corruption of the administration, nor in energetic efforts to defeat its measures. For the time he seemed to regard executive rather than federal usurpation of power as the great danger to the republic. Such a course was tangent to his previous and his later position, but it was an entirely natural consequence of his recent quarrel with Jackson and Van Buren. Driven by disappointment and a desire for revenge, he was also committed to the opposition by his alliance with Clay, and he may have hoped ultimately to lead and to determine the policy of the new party. In any event, whatever the course he should later decide upon, his first step was to oust his enemies from power.

The central issues of the second Jackson term were the removal of deposits from the Second Bank of the United States and the inflationary spiral which it accelerated. Since the bank's charter did not expire for four years, in order to prevent Biddle from using his financial power to force a recharter upon Congress over his veto, Jackson decided in the summer of 1833 to transfer government funds to a number of state banks selected by himself (the House had recently passed a resolution declaring that the deposits were safe in the Bank of the United States). With this in view he had taken advantage of a vacancy in the cabinet to appoint William J. Duane Secretary of the Treasury; but when he formally ordered removal of the funds in September, Duane refused to comply. Thereupon the President dismissed his recent appointee and replaced him with Roger B. Taney, who carried out the order. The Senate passed resolutions censuring the President for both these actions, to which he replied with a vehement protest. Biddle retaliated with a stringent contraction of credit, and Congress was swamped with petitions to stop the war on the bank. But Jackson's party stood firm, and in the end Biddle was forced to retreat.

The depression which began as Jackson left the White House was the result of numerous conditions, but the President's action encouraged the inflation which preceded it. Within a few years the number of state banks doubled, and the deposit of the increasing government revenue in numerous "pet" banks permitted them to overexpand their note issues, much of which was loaned for the purchase of government land. This soon led to a vicious cycle, for the notes received in payment for land were deposited in pet banks and used as the basis for further expansion of credit. All prices soared except those on government land set by law; land sales jumped in two years from six to twenty million acres. With such increase of income the national debt was paid off early in 1835, and to check inflation the President soon issued his Specie Circular requiring gold or silver in payment for land.

On all these matters Calhoun spoke repeatedly and at length in the Senate. He bitterly attacked the President for the dismissal of Duane and the removal of deposits. He denied Jackson's right to protest the senatorial resolution of censure, which he himself had conspicuously supported. Defining the conflict as one between "a Bank of the United States incorporated by Congress, and that system of banks which has been created by the will of Executive," he joined Clay and Webster in an unsuccessful attempt at rechartering the former. He viewed the "question, in its true light, as a struggle on the part of the executive to seize on the power of congress, and to unite in the President the power of the sword and the purse."[1]

As chairman of the Committee on Executive Patronage he reported an extensive criticism of the spoils system and introduced several bills to correct its abuses. He was active in framing the bill for the distribution of the surplus, and later he sponsored a measure ceding public land to the states on the condition that they return to the government one third of the income derived from the sale. He equally denounced Jackson's diplomacy in the spoliations dispute with France, and with two minor exceptions he took vigorous issue with every action and proposal of the administration. The enmity between the two was personal as well as political; the General returned it with interest. In view of his almost paranoid treatment of the Carolinian, even a "cast-iron" man could hardly have been expected to react otherwise.

On most occasions Calhoun's language was as extreme as his logic. In his long connection with the government, he had never "conceived that such rottenness, such corruption, such abominable violations of trust could ever exist in any of its departments.... It exceeded anything in the history of the rottenest ages of the Roman Empire."[2] It is not surprising that his use of scathing invective involved him in two acrimonious controversies, one by letter with Jackson which he answered in the Senate, and one on the floor of that chamber with the President's champion, Thomas H. Benton.

Calhoun's new fear of the power of the executive soon became a phobia. He insisted upon viewing all these matters — the bank, appointments, surplus, and public lands — in their relation to what he charged was a deliberate conspiracy on the part of the President to keep his party in power by illegal means and to dictate the choice of his successor. In this belief he was by no means alone. From recent habit of mind he turned at once to the Constitution and by a process of close reasoning found proof that the President did not possess the power he had exercised. Congress alone of the federal departments had constructive or implied powers; the executive and his cabinet could do only what the Constitution or constitutional act of Congress expressly permitted them to do. The President, therefore, could not transfer the deposits or dismiss his own appointees from office without congressional approval,* since neither the Constitution nor Congress had specifically given him such power.[3]

The Carolinian was enthusiastic about his discovery. Its similarity to his previous distinction between the reserved powers of the states and the specific powers delegated to the federal government is obvious. But his new reasoning involved him in some inconsistency, as he had recently sought to limit the power of Congress. In his current enthusiasm he halfway argued that the bank was constitutional, for if Congress had the right to receive and pay out anything besides specie, it had the right to regulate the value thereof through the agency of a national bank.[4]

*   *   *

In view of the subsequent importance in national affairs of certain of these questions, Calhoun's attitude at the time must be considered in more detail. In his first speech on the bank in January, 1834, he argued that the alternative to the national bank was the complete divorce of the government from all banks, and he indicated his sympathy for an independent treasury system. Two months later, after conversation with the Whigs and friends of the bank, he reversed himself and supported recharter, for a period of twelve

---

*In his first speech on Jackson's removal of Duane, he pronounced the action an *abuse* but not a *usurpation* of power, as the President could dismiss his appointees. Upon further study, however, he came to the contrary conclusion.

years at least, rather than the six advocated by Webster.* A continuation of the bank was essential to restoration of "a safe and stable currency.... My impression is, that a new Bank of the United States, ingrafted upon the old, will be found ... to combine the greatest advantages, and to be liable to the fewest objections."[5]

The essence of the matter was not the bank but the currency, which he wished to place as soon as possible on a purely metallic basis. He proposed the twelve-year extension with this end in view, thus using the "bank to unbank the banks." There was a vast difference between doing and undoing an act, he told his state-rights friends, and even if the bank were unconstitutional, it was too dangerous to abolish it suddenly. By strict logic the purchase of Louisiana was unconstitutional, yet no one for that reason advocated the surrender of that territory; the compromise act of the last session was equally so because it temporarily recognized protection.[6]

One of the recommendations of Calhoun's Committee on Executive Patronage was the distribution to the states of any surplus in the treasury over five million dollars on January 1, 1837, and an amendment to the Constitution authorizing such distribution from that date until 1843,[7] when under the compromise act the tariff would finally be reduced to a purely revenue basis. A similar proposal had been made by Jackson in his first annual message in 1829, but he had soon abandoned the idea. Calhoun had then opposed it because the resulting deficit in the treasury would necessitate a high tariff. The surplus of the middle thirties was produced by income from the tariff, the rates of which he did not wish to change for fear of upsetting the terms of the compromise act, and by increased proceeds from land sales. He now adopted Jackson's original proposal primarily to eliminate the possibility of the federal government's spending the surplus and thus increasing its patronage and popularity. His former objection to distribution had been removed by the compromise, since presumably the tariff would remain at a revenue basis after 1842.

On several occasions after the President's veto in 1833 Clay rein-

---

*Professor Thomas Govan has suggested the possibility that it was at this time that Calhoun learned that there might be gold on his Georgia property, and that his decision to support the bank and the "specie amendment" which he introduced on the divorce bill of 1837 were aimed at increasing the price of that metal. The only evidence for this contention is circumstantial.

troduced his bill, which would have solved the problem by distributing the income from land sales among the states on the basis of population, but the certainty of executive disapproval prevented its repassage. The advent of a tremendous surplus after 1835, however, produced such a popular demand for some form of distribution that neither Jackson nor Calhoun was willing to incur disfavor by futile opposition. The attitude of both was determined by considerations of expediency. The President was probably afraid that uncompromising opposition to distribution on his part might prevent the nomination and election of Van Buren. Calhoun wished to provide funds for the ambitious railroad projects which South Carolina and Georgia were enthusiastically planning at the time, thus strengthening his local popularity. So eager was he for its passage that he dropped his proposal for a constitutional amendment; when Jackson refused to approve the distribution of funds as a gift to the states, Calhoun successfully proposed the substitution of the word "deposit" in the original bill.[8]

The final measure, after being kicked around by both administration and opposition forces, called for the transference as a loan to the states of an estimated surplus of $37,000,000 which would accrue during 1837, in return for certificates of indebtedness which they would transmit to the treasury. Despite the terms of the bill no one expected repayment of the loan, and before the year was out the severe drop in governmental income as a result of the depression created a deficit in the treasury. Earlier Calhoun had failed in an effort to induce the Senate to pass a bill providing for a similar disposal of the anticipated surplus of 1838. His zealous action in the whole matter belied his assertion two years later that "there was not a man in that chamber who was more opposed to distribution than he was. He resorted to it as a remedy rendered imperiously necessary by the existing state of things."[9]

If a surplus in the federal treasury was an evil, as the majority agreed, the logical procedure was to reduce the income from public lands which produced it. The administration would achieve this purpose by lowering land prices, while Clay's followers would maintain prices but accomplish the same result by adopting distribution of proceeds to the states as a permanent policy. Their mutual opposition blocked any legislation except the temporary distribution of the 1837 surplus. Benton and western congressmen pleaded in vain for the granting of "pre-emption" rights to actual settlers, who technically were squatters, and for "graduated" prices depending upon the amount of time land on the market had remained unsold. In his annual message of December, 1836, the President called attention to the relation of speculation in land to the current inflation, and advocated legislation of the type demanded by Benton's group.[10]

When such a bill was soon reported, Calhoun attacked it vehemently on the grounds that the ultimate result would benefit speculators rather than settlers; he openly charged that this was the President's secret intent. He offered instead an amendment ceding the lands to the states in which they were located, requiring them to return one third of the income from sales to the federal government and permitting them gradually to lower the price over a long period of years. Though he reiterated the disinterestedness of his motives, he was immediately attacked on all sides as seeking to increase his own popularity in the West. This was "the most splendid bribe," commented Senator James Buchanan of Pennsylvania, ever offered in Congress. The western states, said Benton, due to their rapid growth in the last decade, "in three years more ... could write their own terms, and lay them on the table of the Senate. They would be bid for, and bid deeply for, by every candidate for the presidency." Calhoun made his proposal in February, 1837, and it suggested that he was already thinking of breaking with the Whigs and returning to his earlier strategy of a southern-western alliance. His amendment, later introduced as an independent bill, was defeated in both instances, and of all the states along the Atlantic seaboard South Carolina alone voted in the affirmative.[11]

Despite the furor and the temporary strength of the opposition in the Senate, the administration controlled the House and Jackson emerged triumphant on the major issues of his second term as he had in the first. The Whigs failed to prevent the removal of deposits and to recharter the bank. When the Senate refused to confirm Taney's appointment to the treasury, the President later successfully named him chief justice of the Supreme Court. Early in 1837 the administration majority in the upper house voted to expunge from the journal the resolution of censure passed at a previous session. Before he retired, Jackson had obtained both the nomination and the election of Van Buren. While some legislation on lesser matters was blocked, the opposition won its only victory of any significance when Congress failed to pass a bill appropriating three million dollars to be used at the President's discretion in connection with his diplomatic dispute with France.

Jackson's conspicuous triumph in these matters was a serious political defeat for Calhoun as well as for the Whigs. But the strange sequel to this stage of the Carolinian's career was his reaffiliation with the Democrats in 1837. In September of that year, due to the outbreak of the panic, Van Buren called a special session of Congress to which he recommended the adoption of an independent treasury, thus divorcing the government from connection with all banks. Calhoun formally announced his support of the measure and at once broke his political friendship with the Whigs. "I am not of the same party with Webster and others," he wrote Duff Green in explanation. "I believe the sound portion of the country, if there be one, that is left, is to be found in the original Jackson party."[12]

His reasons for this sudden decision require a close examination of his political strategy during Jackson's second term and his leadership in defense of slavery when Congress began to debate the question of abolitionist petitions in 1836.

*　　　　*　　　　*

Although Calhoun ultimately arrived at a conscious policy of balance of power, such was not his immediate course in 1833, for he cut himself off from the Democrats by his almost petulant opposition to their legislative program and his bitter attacks upon Jackson and Van Buren. In subsequent years he freely expressed his scorn for the New Yorker, whom shortly before the election of 1836 he described, in contrast to the General, as not "of the race of the lion or the tiger; he belonged to a lower order, — the fox." And after Van Buren's victory, but while he was still presiding over the Senate as Vice-President, Calhoun told him openly from the floor, "if left to your own popularity, — without the active and direct influence of the President and the power and patronage of the Government, acting through a mock convention of the people, — instead of the highest, you would, in all probability, have been the lowest of the candidates."[13]

On the other hand, while he made common cause with the Whigs against the administration, he scrupulously maintained his formal independence of the "Nationals," as he continued to call them. On numerous occasions he reasserted this independence; he never attended any of their caucuses nor was he appointed a member of any standing senatorial committee. "My political convictions," he told the Senate more than once, "are with the small and denounced party which has voluntarily wholly retired from the party strifes of the day...and let me tell the Senator from Kentucky that, if the present struggle against Executive usurpation be successful, it will be owing to the success with which we, the nullifiers — I am not afraid of the word — maintained the rights of the States against the encroachments of the General Government at the last session." He sought vainly in 1834 to obtain the repeal of the Force Bill, and in a long speech defending his earlier stand in the nullification crisis he charged his new allies with the responsibility for the current situation. "I am the partisan of no class, nor, let me add, of either political party," he stated in another speech. "I am neither of the opposition nor administration."[14]

The Whigs seem to have regarded these protestations as the words of an artful politician playing hard to get, and they denounced him as a traitor when he broke with them over the independent treasury bill in 1837. But frequently Calhoun was not artful. Apparently he believed at the time that, by his devotion to his principles and his fight against executive tyranny and corruption, he would unite the whole South and much of the North under his leadership and that his state-rights party would become dominant. In 1834, when by the union of his followers with the Whigs the administration was outvoted on several issues in the Senate, he was full of hopes for the future.

"The overthrow of Jacksonism is certain" he wrote his brother-in-law early in that year, "and with it, Van Buren and his party.... We and our doctrines are daily growing in favour." And to his old friend Van Deventer he expressed even greater optimism: "You may put down the whole South as lost to the powers that be. I do not consider the question any longer to be the overthrow of the administration; but what is to come up in its place.... Our doctrines are spreading rapidly, and you must not be surprised to see them in the ascendant before two years.... As to myself, I never did, as far as I can judge, occupy a more elevated stand in the confidence of the intelligent and the virtuous. The clouds are beginning to break away and my motives and character begin to be understood. I speak freely to an old friend."[15]

In the same letter he clearly defined his attitude towards a potential alignment with the Whigs, an attitude which he consistently held until his return to the Democrats. "Of one thing you may rest assured," he informed Van Deventer, "that our party will firmly maintain its position. We shall make no choice of evils. We have had enough of that. Others may rally on us, but we rally on nothing but our doctrines.... Better — far better for us, that those in power should remain there against our consent, than that we shall put others there, who do not agree with us, with our consent."

Here Calhoun was referring to his sad experience of the past ten years, admitting that he realized the fundamental error in his previous tactics. In 1824 he had joined the opposition against Adams gratuitously and confidently, without demanding assurances as to the future. Having put the Jackson party in power, he found himself the leader of a minority wing of the coalition, unable to control its policy. As a consequence his section had to submit to injurious legislation, his personal ambitions were frustrated, and he himself was driven out of the party. The net result of his years of effort, it was now evident, had been the substitution of the more dangerous tyranny of Jackson for the milder tyranny of Adams.

In the 1830's, consequently, he was determined not to repeat this error. As long as his group remained a minority he would come to no terms with the Whigs; but he also expected it, in the rapidly changing political fortunes of the day, to become a majority. By his working alliance with the Whigs against Jackson he placed himself in a favorable position to absorb them at the proper moment. But neither of his expectations was fulfilled. Until 1836 the administration gained rather than lost power, and his state-rights group remained a minority. His only resort until a better day, therefore, was to use the balance of power which he controlled against both the major parties, and he continued his independence of the Whigs. At his direction South Carolina in 1836, as in 1832, refused her electoral votes to both national parties and instead threw them away on a nominal candidate. After the Democratic victory in 1836, despite Duff Green's pleadings, he withheld his support and that of his followers from a super-Whig coalition, though he was offered second place on the ticket for 1840.

In refusing, he was acting in accordance with his earlier reasoning: "We are in a minority of the opposition and would be sure to be voted down and be compelled to vote for Clay or Webster, or to violate the pledge implied in going into the convention. If we do the former, we would be merged in the national Republican party, and leave the whole states right ground open to be seized on by those in power; if the latter, we would be weakened, and disgraced in the eyes of the community."[16]

*   *   *

The development which caused Calhoun's strategy of the minority to crystalize, however, was the increasing activity of radical abolitionists in the thirties and the violent reaction it evoked in the South. Though it was recognized by everyone that the slavery question was involved in the controversy over the tariff and nullification, there was no extensive debate in Congress on the matter after the Missouri Compromise of 1820-21 until the year 1836. In that year the national legislature was forced to meet the twin problems of the dissemination in the South of abolitionist propaganda through the mails and of the procedure for handling abolitionist petitions in Congress.

Meanwhile public opinion in both sections had gradually undergone radical changes. In the North interest in colonization had waned, and the older philosophic opposition of the Quakers to slavery was bolstered by growing numbers of militant abolitionists, such as Garrison who started his fiery "Liberator" in 1831, demanding immediate and uncompensated emancipation. At the same time free-soil sentiment had increased among the general public, which was overwhelmingly nonabolitionist. In the South, with the great expansion of cotton into the interior and particularly after the Nat Turner insurrection of 1831, support of colonization virtually ceased. Many southerners by a natural process became ardent instead of apologetic defenders of their peculiar institution.

Southern indignation over the incendiary publications had been growing for several years before the congressional debates of 1836. In Charleston offensive mail had been seized from the post office and burned, without any effort by the postmaster general to prevent it or similar action elsewhere. A general demand arose in the South that postmasters throughout the nation refuse to forward such matter. Duff Green's *Telegraph*, which was published in Washington and was regarded as Calhoun's private political organ, incessantly called upon the South to unite in the face of a dangerous

181

crisis. It pled for a southern convention, demanded that the northern states suppress abolitionist societies, and warned the nation that the Union was in serious peril. It is noteworthy that its fiery language and its various proposals were later echoed by Calhoun on the floor of Congress, and that he expected an abolitionist attack in that body as early as 1833. In the summer of 1835 he gave the whole matter his careful attention, for he was certain that it would be brought up at the next session. His stand in 1836, therefore, was premeditated and his conclusions were positive. As he wrote Hammond some months later, "I have ever had but one opinion on the subject. Our fate, as a people is bound up in the question."[17]

The issue which at the moment presented itself was not the direct frontal attack upon slavery that shortly arose in the opposition to the annexation of Texas and in demands for the exclusion of slaves from the territories and the District of Columbia, but rather the peripheral matters of abolitionist propaganda and petitions. These equally involved the basic question of the liberty of the press and the right of petition. Nevertheless, Calhoun met the issue "at the frontier,"[18] as he called it, and boldly advanced what was to remain throughout his lifetime the position of southern extremists. In three eloquent speeches during the year before Van Buren's inauguration he clearly defined his attitude.

Jackson had proposed in his message of December, 1836, that a law be passed prohibiting under heavy penalties the circulation in the mail of publications designed to incite slave insurrection. Fearful of granting to the federal government the power of discretion in such a vital matter, Calhoun as chairman of a special committee submitted instead a bill, accompanied by a long report in which only one member out of four fully concurred, forbidding the receipt or delivery by postmasters of slavery publications addressed to post offices in states whose laws prohibited the circulation of such material. After much debate on the bill he accepted a milder substitute introduced by Senator Grundy of Tennessee, but this was defeated at its third reading. His net accomplishment was to force Van Buren, by contriving a tie at an earlier reading, to vote in the affirmative.[19]

In the same session both the House and the Senate discussed at length the proper handling of petitions requesting the abolition of slavery in the District and other legislation hostile to slavery. Each body finally adopted a procedure by which petitions were received but, in one way or another, immediately tabled. The House bill was called the "Gag" rule, against which Adams began his long fight that ended in success eight years later; the action of both houses was regarded by many in the North as an important southern victory over the cause of freedom. Actually the congressional decision was a defeat for Calhoun who, along with his colleague Hammond in the House, argued heatedly against reception on the grounds that it implied federal jurisdiction over slavery in the District and the territories, which he denied.

The right of petition, he insisted, was merely the right to present a petition. The Senate should take no action, not even that of a formal reception, on requests that members agreed were mischievous and that they had no intention of granting, particularly when the action requested was unconstitutional. What, he asked, would be their response to a request for a law denying the existence of the Deity? In the end he threatened to take no part in subsequent Senate proceedings if the reception bill should pass, but none of his southern colleagues supported him in such an attitude.[20]

*   *   *

The essence of Calhoun's speeches lay not in his arguments regarding the immediate measures, but in his clear analysis of the larger question of slavery and the Union.

> I hold that in the present state of civilization, where two races of different origin, and distinguished by color, and other physical differences, as well as intellectual, are brought together, the relation now existing in the slave-holding States between the two, is, instead of an evil, a good — a positive good.... There has never yet existed a wealthy and civilized society in which one portion of the community did not, in the point of fact, live on the labor of the other.... I fearlessly assert that the existing relation between the two races in the South, against which these blind fanatics are waging war, forms the most solid and durable foundation on which to rear free and stable political institutions.[21]

He pleaded with the nation to understand the South's uncompromising rejection of abolition:

> It is to us a vital question. It involves not only our liberty, but, what is greater (if to freemen anything can be), existence itself. The relation which now exists between the two races in the slave-holding States has existed for two centuries. It has grown with

183

our growth, and strengthened with our strength. It has entered into and modified all our institutions, civil and political. None other can be substituted. We will not, cannot permit it to be destroyed.[22]

If Congress even tacitly took jurisdiction over slavery at the moment, he saw in the future the disruption of the Union and war. Abolition sentiment in the North would grow and result in an attempt at emancipation which the South would resist by secession and by force. He feared for the Union, but he did not fear for the South, since her natural superiority left no doubt in his mind about her victory in a military struggle. "There would be to us one alternative — to triumph or perish as a people."[23]

The abolition movement was

no longer in the hands of quiet and peaceful, but I cannot add, harmless Quakers. It is now under the control of ferocious zealots, blinded by fanaticism, and, in pursuit of their object, regardless of the obligations of religion or morality. They are organized throughout every section of the non-slaveholding States; they have the disposition of almost unlimited funds, and are in possession of a powerful press, which, for the first time, is enlisted in the cause of abolition, and turned against the domestic institutions, and the peace and security of the South.[24]

Compromise and concession, therefore, he held to be fatal. Though he urged sane northerners, who were still in a large majority, to suppress the abolitionists as the price of Union,

it rests with ourselves to meet and repel them. I look not for aid to this Government, or to the other States ... no political party in those States will risk their ascendency for our safety. If we do not defend ourselves none will defend us; if we yield we will be more and more pressed as we recede; and if we submit we will be trampled under foot. . . . All we want is concert, to lay aside all party differences and unite with zeal and energy in repelling approaching dangers. Let there be concert of action, and we shall find ample means of security without resorting to secession or disunion. I speak with full knowledge and a thorough examination of the subject, and for one, see my way clearly.[25]

As in the case of his refusal to join the Whig coalition while his state-rights bloc remained a minority, his decision to meet the attack upon slavery "at the frontier" was the product of his bitter experience in recent years with the tariff. Both he and his state had voted for the tariff of 1816; when they began to fight protection a decade later as injurious to their section, their earlier stand proved embarrassing and they soon discovered that they had begun their fight too late. Since the slavery issue was even more dangerous to the preservation of the Union and to southern security, he logically concluded that it must be met immediately upon its formal presentation to Congress and must be opposed on the highest possible grounds.

In his autobiography written several years later Calhoun pictured himself in 1836 as a martyr valiantly fighting for a cause which he knew in advance to be hopeless. On the contrary, at the time he expected to be victorious, for shortly before the session he wrote in confidence that "I see my way clearly on the slave question and do not fear an entire triumph on our own conditions."[26] In this, as in many other expectations in his troubled career, he was mistaken. Many southerners refused to follow Calhoun's lead because they regarded his move, on its own merits, as premature and unwise. Equally devoted to slavery, they would reserve their weapons for a more vital issue. They correctly saw that he would appear to other sections to be taking the offensive and that he would alienate large portions of the northern public, not unfriendly to slavery, by seeming to attack the liberty of the press and the right of petition. They thought he exaggerated the danger of current abolitionist activity, and they saw the practical difficulties in the way of suppression of agitation by the northern states themselves.

Southern Whigs suspected him of seeking to make political capital of the situation, and they regarded the attack of equalitarian northern masses upon property as an equal if not greater danger. The proper defense, in both cases, was in their opinion a union of men of property; they did not wish a needless dispute over slavery to disrupt their conservative party in the process of formation. Here was a fundamental distinction between southern Whigs and Democrats which persisted until Calhoun's death.

*   *   *

The attack upon slavery and Jackson's approaching retirement turned Calhoun from his preoccupation with executive usurpation to a re-emphasis upon his original views as to the necessity of limiting federal power as the only sure means of attaining southern security. His drift in the direction of a stricter interpretation of the Constitution is noticeable in his stand on various measures in 1836. He began to consider all legislation, not merely on the basis of whether it hindered or benefited southern interests, but also with its effect upon the power of the states as a criterion. Thus he proposed to transfer public lands to the states, and in introducing his bill he gave as a primary reason his desire "to counteract the centralism, which was the great danger of this Government." Similarly he opposed a resolution for the purchase of Madison's manuscripts from his widow on the grounds that the power to do so had not been delegated to the national government. He also opposed acceptance in 1838 of the large gift from James Smithson, an Englishman, which was used to establish the famous scientific institution and museum.[27]

His failure to unite the South behind his extreme stand on slavery and the outcome of the election of 1836 left him the leader of a minority bloc. Van Buren had won the election, but southern Whigs had voted for Harrison or White; Clay by a trimming policy had won their confidence. For Calhoun's state-rights group to continue the alliance with the opposition exposed it to the danger of absorption; for the time being its only hope of exerting political influence was to play the balance of power. Since the national parties were evenly divided in the North, each might be forced to bid for the support of the abolitionist minority. To offset this tendency, therefore, Calhoun must make the power of his group count for the most with one or the other of the parties, and he closely examined their current trends with a view of their sentiments towards the related subjects of slavery and strict construction. Meanwhile, he did not in the least diminish his efforts for southern unity.

On both counts the Whigs were, by comparison, clearly deficient. Harrison had once expressed himself in favor of compensated emancipation, and White, though a strict constructionist in other matters, had voted for the Force Bill. A stronger tendency towards hostility to slavery existed among northern Whigs than among northern Democrats, and the former were definitely nationalist in their constitutional convictions. Calhoun trusted neither the northern Whigs nor Clay, despite the latter's avowed moderation at the moment. They made no secret of their desire to recharter the bank, and he fully expected them to attempt a restoration of the protective tariff when circumstances proved propitious. The whole program of the eastern industrial interests, which he was convinced the Whigs would attempt to enact if they returned to power, demanded a national concept of federal powers. Both the program and the concept were inimicable to slavery and to southern economy in its entirety.

Prominent Democrats, on the other hand, had expressed striking indications of friendliness for slavery and of emphasis upon the principle of limited national power. Van Buren had voted for the bill to eliminate abolition propaganda from the mails. In his inaugural address he repeated the declaration on slavery he had made during his campaign: "I must go into the Presidential chair the inflexible and uncompromising opponent of every attempt on the part of Congress to abolish slavery in the District of Columbia against the wishes of the slaveholding States, and also with a determination equally decided to resist the slightest interference with it in the States where it exists."[28] Possibly at his urging, Governor William L. Marcy of New York had declared that the legislature of that state had the power to prohibit abolition agitation by penal laws. In 1836 certain high Democratic journals were assuring southerners of their sympathy for the rights of minorities, admitting that the recent tendency towards consolidation had been excessive. In view of Calhoun's new sensitivity to the money power, his natural alliance — since the South was free from a conflict between capital and labor — was with the laboring masses of the North against a common enemy.

With Jackson passing from the national scene, the Carolinian began to view more critically his alliance with Clay. His earlier distrust of the "Nationals" became aggravated, and he recalled that his former party, except in matters of nullification and executive powers, had otherwise followed strict construction. On constitutional grounds the General had vetoed the bank and internal improvements bills, and for the same reason he had originally opposed distribution of the surplus. He had also supported the state of Georgia in her fight with the Supreme Court.

Calhoun was coming to a positive decision during the summer of 1837. When Van Buren in September recommended to the special session of Congress (called to deal with the panic) the establishment of an independent treasury, he ardently backed the proposal. At the same time he announced his break with the Whigs: "We part with our late allies in peace, and move forward — lag or onward who may — to secure the fruits of our long but successful struggle, under the old republican flag of 1798, which, though tattered and torn, has never yet been lowered, and, with the blessing of God, never shall with my consent."[29] This issue of the bank, which he had so recently favored, he now used to emphasize his renewed devotion to strict construction and to call attention to the fundamental conflict between southern and northeastern economic interests.

*　　　*　　　*

Shortly before this announcement, he had explained his reasoning in detail to members of his family. He wrote early in September to his daughter Anna Maria:

My position is one of great delicacy and will require consummate prudence with decision and boldness. . . . It puts me in a position much more congenial to my feelings, than that which I have occupied for the last few years. It was impossible for me to go with the leaders of the nationals. We disagreed on almost all points except resistance to Executive usurpation. We could not part on a point better for me, than the one on which we now separate. I stand now on my own bottom, with no influence acting on me but a rigid adherence to those great principles, for which I have made so many sacrifices.[30]

With his brother-in-law he was equally explicit:

Van Buren has been forced by his situation and the terror of Jackson to play directly into our hands and I am determined, that he shall not escape from us. We have a fair opportunity to break the last of our commercial shackles. I mean the control which the North through the use of Government credit acting through the banks, have [*sic*] exercised over our industry and commerce. How wonderful that the author of the Safety fund system and the favourite of New York (the State above all others the most benefitted by the Union of bank and state) should be forced by circumstances which he could not control, to give the fatal blow to his own offspring and supporters! Into what situation may not an artful but short-sighted politician be forced?[31]

The Whig Flirtation

All of Calhoun's actions during these years were attacked by contemporaries, both Whigs and Democrats, as solely designed to place him in the presidency. Even Ritchie, the prominent Virginia Democrat who edited the Richmond *Enquirer,* saw in the Carolinian's crusade against abolitionist activities only an attempt to win the South on a more popular issue than nullification. The Whigs never ceased to attack him for his desertion in 1837, which they attributed simply to the fact that he had concluded that Clay and Webster were too formidable rivals to his nomination by that party. Adams cynically referred to "Calhoun's bargain and sale of himself to Van Buren."[32]

Human motivation is often difficult to determine. Calhoun sought to take into account political realities, but his desire for the presidency was always a factor which, at least subconsciously, influenced his conduct. In this period his attainment of high office was certainly not consciously one of his immediate objectives, though he still regarded it as desirable and possible as a means to his fundamental ends. For a brief period he even toyed with the idea of retiring from politics; but he was afraid the South would be left without a national leader capable of protecting its interests, yet still devoted to the Union. His letters and speeches contain ample evidence that in his own mind he was not sacrificing his principles for personal ambition, and he vehemently denied the allegation. It is more plausible that here as earlier he was so convinced of the logic of his own analysis that he believed that the truth must soon be apparent to all honest men. Positive that preservation of the Union was possible only through southern security, and confident in his own wisdom, ability, and devotion to the public interest, he felt that by becoming President he could accomplish a permanent national salvation. This was rationalization, but not narrow, selfish ambition.

Nothing that he wrote is so pertinent to this point as his letter of July 27, 1837, to Duff Green, his devoted lieutenant who for years had been plugging for his nomination. Green had previously written him, urging that he join the Whigs and accept second place to Harrison on the ticket for 1840. The editor had also indulged in some frank but well-intended criticism of his chief, stating in particular that he overrated his own strength more than any other public man. Calhoun was "mortified," but not offended. He was sure, he replied to Green,

189

that if your letters would fall into the hands of those who are to come after us, they would infer from the topicks you urge on me to adopt the course you recommend, and the remarks with which you accompany them, that I was a vain, light headed, ill judging and ambitious man, ignorant alike of the nature of the times, and my own strength, and constantly leading myself and those who follow me, into false positions, and aiming constantly at the Presidency and destined constantly to be defeated. I know you do not and cannot so think of me. No one knows better than yourself, that in the heat of youthful years, I never sought, or desired the Presidency, but through a faithful discharge of my duty, and as an instrument of high usefulness and distinguished service.[33]

CHAPTER TWELVE

Balance of Power and a Pail of Water

WHEN Calhoun in 1837 announced his support of Van Buren's recommendation of an independent treasury, he merely led most of his minority following from an irregular position with the Whigs to an irregular position with the Democrats. For his support of the administration he demanded certain pledges in return, and not until he received some concrete assurance that they would be carried out did he formally rejoin his old party three years later. During these years he came to a positive decision as to the objectives and the political methods of the remaining thirteen years of his life.

These objectives were the preservation of the Union and the security of the South; his primary method in attaining these mutually supplementary ends was identification with and pressure upon the Democratic party. In his own mind he probably regarded his elevation to the presidency, as the candidate of that party, as a means rather than an end. At the same time he sought to develop, as corollary methods, the unification of the South, regardless of party, on a clear-cut legislative program in defense of slavery, and an alliance between the South and the West to insure the adoption of this program. In addition to these three practical methods, designed to obtain a congressional majority for those items of policy which he deemed essential, he constantly sought a permanent solution of the problem of liberty and union through national accept-

191

ance of a constitutional interpretation that would protect the minority against the legislative will of the majority.

In his choice and use of methods Calhoun was consciously opportunistic. The autobiography, written a few years later, is specific on this point:

> The great ends in his system of life, whether public or private, he has ever held to be fixed by reason and general rules; but the time and the mode of obtaining them he regarded as questions of expediency, to be determined by the circumstances under which he is called to act. . . . Seeing clearly his own ends, which have been long fixed by observation and reflection, he judges, with a rare sagacity, of the nearest practicable approach which can be made to them under the circumstances, and advances forward to the boundaries assigned by prudence without fear of the enemy, and halts when he has taken as much ground as he can occupy, without regard to the remonstrances of his followers, who take their counsels merely from zeal, and do not properly ascertain the limits upon human power, and the controlling force of events. . . . He uses time to control circumstances, and directs them both to his great object, which he is ever on the march sooner or later to attain. This it is which makes him the master-statesman of his age, and thus he has been able to accomplish so much with such inconsiderable means.[1]

Calhoun still firmly believed that it was possible to preserve the Union, and he honestly regarded preservation as his major objective. He did not desire southern independence, but his first allegiance was already to the South should the failure of his efforts compel him to choose between his section and his nation. He saw that the South might be driven to the necessity of secession, but he was completely sincere in stating that his efforts were directed towards its prevention rather than its encouragement. Replying in 1838 to his daughter's contention that peaceful separation was preferable to the current "state of indecision," he agreed that hers was

> a natural and common conclusion, but those, who make it, do not think of the difficulty involved in the word; how many bleeding pores must be taken up in passing a knife of separation through a body politick (in order to make two of one), which has been so long bound together by so many ties, political, social, and commercial. We cannot and ought not to live together as

we are at present, exposed to the continual attacks and assaults of the other portion of the Union; but we must act throughout on the defensive, resort to every probable means of arresting the evil, and only act, when all has been done, that can be, and when we shall stand justified before God and man in taking the final step. Any other course would fail in its object, and ruin those, who may attempt it. We must remember, it is the most difficult process in the world to make two people of one.[2]

Calhoun saw the southern dilemma of the 1830's clearly and met it in his own mind as a pragmatist rather than as a theorist. He selected the Democrats as the lesser evil and with reservations, and he was well aware of the danger of their equalitarianism. "The word democrat," he wrote to Rhett in 1838, "better applies to the North than the South, and as usually understood means those who are in favour of the government of the absolute numerical majority to which I am utterly opposed and the prevalence of which would destroy our system and destroy the South."* He never ceased in his effort to convert the party to his philosophy. But he was convinced that northern Democrats would be forced by the abolition issue to support the South. "The great point," he urged, "is to carry the war into the non slave holding states. . . . The resolutions [which he had introduced in 1838] will have a powerful tendency to bring the democratick party in these states into conflict with the abolition and consolidation parties."[3]

*   *   *

At the same time he fully appreciated the explosive potentialities of the social revolution which was occurring. Modern society "rushing to some new and untried condition" would soon face the central question of the distribution of wealth, "a question least explored, and the most important of any in the whole range of political economy."[4] Preoccupied with the fundamental question of liberty, and approaching the political problem from the viewpoint of the welfare and the rights of the minority, what he feared

*Calhoun to R. B. Rhett, Sept. 13, 1838. The reviewer of Francis Lieber's *Political Ethics* in the *Southern Quarterly Review* in 1847 expressed this sentiment more forcibly. He stated that he recalled the time when southern state-rights men insisted upon calling themselves "Republicans," and that they regarded the term "Democrat" as invidious. "It was never until the election of 1840, that decent persons could willingly stomach the name."

most in the Whigs was their nationalistic concept of government. Next, he feared the paternalistic program of finance capital which he was certain they would attempt to enact if they returned to power. Consequently he came to the earlier conclusion of John Taylor, high priest of Jeffersonianism, who had answered affirmatively the question, "whether the landed interest... had not better unite with the other popular interests, to strangle in its cradle any infant visibly resembling this terrible giant."[5] In seeing the vital conflict as one between landed capital and finance capital, he differed from the majority of men of property in the South. But when the Whigs did attempt the passage of their paternalistic program in the early 1840's, southerners in that party slowly began their trek to the Democrats.

The specific problem facing Calhoun was the protection of the South against the nonslave states, which were populous enough to control a sizable majority in the lower house of Congress. It was not merely his philosophic bent of mind which led him to express the conflict in the general terms of minorities and majorities, but in addition his belief that such general phraseology would protect him from the charge of special pleading for his section. He had concisely analyzed the problem during the nullification crisis, when he told the Senate that "the Government of the absolute majority, instead of the Government of the people, is but the Government of the strongest interests; and when not efficiently checked, is the most tyrannical and oppressive that can be devised." The proper solution was "to maintain the ascendancy of the constitution over the law-making majority."[6] The milk-and-water antidote of strict construction was not sufficient. "Everybody is for strict construction," he snorted, "Mr. Webster, Mr. Ritchie, and all."[7] The single remedy was to organize society on the basis of interests, not individuals, and by that organization give "to each part the right of self-protection."

The mechanism of this protection was the restoration of the states — which were economic as well as political units representing the conflicting interests of the nation — to their original power, and the strict limitation of the sphere of action of the general government. No measure was too insignificant for him to use for preaching the sovereignty of the states and the narrow limits of federal power. In 1837 he clashed with Senator Buchanan over the principle that "the will of a mere numerical majority is paramount to the authority of the law and constitution." He referred him to the constitution of South Carolina, which had provided an ideal compromise by giving the back country control of one house of the legislature and the tidewater the other. "Let me tell the Senator," was his parting shot, "it is a far more popular government than if it had been based on the simple principle of the numerical majority."[8]

Calhoun became so obsessed with this theme in the last decade of his life that he sometimes alienated audiences with his insistence. He reiterated the obvious fact that the equality of the states in the Senate proved that it was the intention of the framers of the Constitution to establish a check on the majority; in a cogent speech he defended Tyler's use of the veto power as in accordance with the same intention.[9] But the nation's rejection of nullification compelled him to seek some equally practical method by which the minority could exercise its veto power. Allegedly with this purpose he retired from the Senate in 1843 and began to write his two most famous treatises, one on government in general and the other on American government in particular, which he fondly hoped would convince the intelligent public.

In them he argued that liberty could only be preserved under a government by "concurrent" instead of absolute majorities. This necessitated "an organism as will furnish the ruled with the means of resisting successfully this tendency on the part of rulers to oppression and abuse. Power can only be resisted by power."[10] Parity between slave and free states in the Senate gave the South an effective veto power, but the loss of parity by the admission of California as a free state in 1850 (after Calhoun's death) did not convince a majority of southerners of the necessity of secession. He could find no adequate substitute for the veto power of the states upon federal legislation, though at the time of his death he was toying with the idea of a dual executive, one from the South and one from the North. In his last speech he referred to an amendment to the Constitution which he intended to propose, but he died before he could reveal its nature.

Calhoun's personal tragedy was that he failed to convince even the South by his logic. His reasoning, as many of his contemporaries pointed out, was too "metaphysical." Possibly the reaction of Senator William H. Roane of Virginia was typical. "There is no doubt," commented Roane, "that he entertains opinions heterodox, and far too *refined* for the American taste.... I cannot comprehend or assent to all this learned jargon about *minorities*. I have never thought that they had any other *Right* than that of freely, peaceably and *legally* converting *themselves* into a *majority* whenever they can."[11]

*   *   *

In this last period of his life, then, the practical steps which Calhoun took to align his southern minority with the majority were immediately more significant than the theorizing about government for which he is remembered. He dealt a body blow to the Whigs when he supported Van Buren on the independent treasury, for he led with him into alliance with the Democrats certain prominent leaders in the southern states. Chief among these were R. M. T. Hunter in Virginia, Dixon H. Lewis in Alabama, John A. Quitman in Mississippi, and men of second rank in other states. But he did not take his action until he had received definite commitments from Van Buren and other party leaders in regard to abolition and the tariff.[12]

Immediately he acted to compel the party leaders to carry out their commitments. In December, 1837, he introduced in the Senate six strongly worded resolutions defining the nature of the Union and the duties and powers of the government in regard to slavery. The first four stated that the purpose of the compact among the states had been to insure them against domestic as well as foreign insecurity; that they retained control over their domestic institutions and that intermeddling with these on any pretext was subversive of the Constitution and tended to destroy the Union; that the federal government was bound to protect such institutions; and that no change of feeling in other states in regard to slavery could justify their attacks upon it, which violated the solemn pledge of the states to protect each other. With a slight omission these four resolutions were finally adopted by large majorities.

His last two resolutions were more specific. They stated that abolition of slavery in the District of Columbia or in the territories would endanger slavery elsewhere; that the equality of rights and advantages among the states would be destroyed if Congress discriminated between them by refusing to annex territory or states on the grounds that the extension of slavery was sinful. The last, aimed at Texas, was withdrawn on the motion of his South Carolina colleague William C. Preston who had already introduced a resolution on annexation. The fifth was passed, but on the grounds of breaking faith with the states of Virginia and Maryland. Followers of both Van Buren and Clay voted in the affirmative. "One is a southern man," observed Calhoun, "relying on the North for support, and the other a northern man relying on the South. They of course dread all conflicting questions between the two Sections."[13]

But northern Democrats were more enthusiastic than northern Whigs, and the former soon gave more concrete evidence of their devotion to southern demands. In July the "Republican" members of Congress, in a long address to the nation, took the strong position on abolition and the tariff which Calhoun demanded. They stated that Congress had no power over slavery in the states and could not abolish it in the District as a means of injuring it in the states where it existed. The government should be administered economically and duties regulated so as to produce no surplus. Later in the year Charles G. Atherton, a New Hampshire Democrat, introduced in the House resolutions on slavery and on petitions in regard to it which incorporated Calhoun's demands of the previous year. Such petitions would "without any further action thereon, be laid upon the table, without being debated, printed, or referred."[14] In 1840 the House passed its "21st rule," which declared outright against reception of petitions asking the abolition of slavery or the domestic slave trade. And in their platform of 1840 the Democrats stated positively that the federal government had no power to interfere in the domestic institutions of the states.

Satisfied with these positive commitments, Calhoun formally resumed personal relations with the President and fully rejoined the party. After reading Van Buren's annual message in December, 1839, he called by appointment at the executive mansion with Senator Roane of Virginia, and he attended the presidential levee on New Year's Day. In the next election South Carolina gave the President her votes, though neither she nor her famous son were too chagrined at his defeat. Despite rumors of a bargain between the principals, Benton stated that he knew no pledge of any kind had been made as a condition of the reconciliation. It was not necessary, for the pledges had been made earlier.[15]

Calhoun's clever use of the balance of power at this time had its effect, as he intended, upon the Whigs. All the resolutions regarding slavery received a large affirmative vote from the northern Democrats and only a small negative vote from the southern Whigs.

This encouraged southerners to follow the Carolinian's lead over to the Democrats and forced southern Whigs to take a stronger stand in support of his program in defense of slavery. At the same time it exerted pressure upon northern Whigs to bid higher for southern votes, and indirectly led to the choice of Tyler as their vice-presidential nominee. When he later as President, upon Harrison's death, blocked Clay's nationalistic program and split the Whig party, it was evident that Calhoun's strategy had paid off handsomely.

It was this strategy also which forced Clay to commit himself positively on slavery in 1839 in an attempt to retain both southern and northern support. In a long speech he took a firm stand against immediate emancipation, for the presence of three million blacks among the populace made the continuation of their bondage necessary, in his opinion, to the preservation of the liberty of the white race. By agitation the abolitionists were defeating their own cause; their course would lead to disunion and civil war. The slaves were a tremendous economic investment, and the national government had no authority to prohibit the domestic slave trade. Slavery should not be abolished in the District because such action would constitute a breach of faith with Maryland and Virginia; Florida should be admitted with slavery in accordance with the treaty of 1819 with Spain and the terms of the Missouri Compromise. But, he admitted, he personally regarded the institution as the "one dark spot...on our political horizon." The only solution he had to suggest was the old proposal of colonization. Though Calhoun moderately praised this speech, it turned extremists in both sections against its author, and Clay's hedging on this question was a major factor in his failure to attain the coveted presidency.[16]

*　　　　*　　　　*

Little legislation of significance was passed during Van Buren's administration, but many of the old questions and the new one of Texas' application for admission to the Union were hotly debated. In this period Calhoun made a total of twenty-nine speeches in the Senate, but even with his support the independent treasury bill failed of enactment until July, 1840. All sorts of land bills were introduced, but none received the approval of both houses. The President favored a compromise between the various recommendations. Though the Whigs blocked the passage of such a bill,

Clay admitted that he could "not much longer defeat the combined action of the administration and the new States."[17] The Carolinian, anxious to cement a southern-western alliance, advocated the cession of the lands to the states. In 1840 he introduced a measure which included graduation, permanent pre-emption, and a return of 65 per cent of the gross receipts to the federal government.

Calhoun was much disturbed at this time with the approaching attempt of the Whigs to restore the protective tariff. For this reason he refused to vote for reduction of duties contrary to the terms of the 1833 compromise, realizing that the result would be to open the dike for legislation to raise rates. Similarly he fought the proposal for the assumption by the national government of the debts of those states that were bankrupt, since the resulting vacuum in the treasury would be used as an argument for raising the tariff to provide the essential revenue. Actually the government was at the time operating under a deficit, and as a consequence treasury notes had been issued in 1837.

In most of his speeches, however, he was plugging his familiar theme of the strict limitation of federal power. He even spoke against a bill to prevent the interference of certain federal officers in elections, on the grounds that by implication it questioned the exclusive authority of the states in the matter. On the same constitutional grounds he attacked the assumption of state debts and a bill to extend the Cumberland Road. In regard to his speech on the former subject, he wrote that "it is thought to be the most popular speech I ever delivered, and will receive a very wide circulation."[18]

His support of the independent treasury bill in 1837 involved him in two dramatic fights, one in South Carolina and another in the Senate with Clay and Webster. When he announced his approval of Van Buren's recommendation, he was opposed by his Carolina colleague, Senator William C. Preston, and all members of the state's House delegation except Francis W. Pickens. Even Pickens expected a defeat which would leave "Mr. Calhoun in a minority in our State," for ex-Governor Hamilton and most of the local newspapers were also against the "divorce" bill, as it was popularly known. But in a short while the powerful hold which Calhoun enjoyed over public opinion in South Carolina was evident. In a letter to a public meeting at Edgefield in November he explained the reasons for his action. He had selected this issue to break with the National Republicans, he stated, in spite of the fact that his continued alliance with them could overthrow the administration, because it was clear that such a "victory would enure, not to us, but exclusively to the benefit of our allies and their cause." The oracle had spoken, and when the legislature met the next month it passed resolutions fully supporting his stand.[19]

One resolution was included to save the face of Preston and the members of the House, stating that there was no intention "to imply any manner of censure upon other public servants of the State." A year later it was repealed and a new resolution substituted which asserted in strong language the opposite sentiment. Meanwhile when certain local papers had accused Calhoun of a "summerset," he replied with a heated defense of his consistency, which the legislature confirmed. In the summer of 1838 he refused to attend a barbecue at Columbia in honor of Preston, and he became engaged in a heated dispute with Congressman Waddy Thompson over the matter. "Preston and Thompson," he wrote, "have done much mischief — more than they can ever repair, if they were to live 100 years."[20]

But Preston found himself in such a minority that he resigned from the Senate in 1842, and Hamilton, though he remained on friendly terms with his former chief, moved at this time to Alabama. "The unanimity here is unnatural," concluded James L. Petigru. "Mr. Calhoun's triumph is too great for he has crushed his own lieutenants." In 1840 the legislature resolved "that this state has seen, with great satisfaction, the steady and consistent adherence of her senator, John C. Calhoun, to the well-known, avowed, and mature principles of the state, and they accord to him their deliberate and strong approval."[21]

Early in 1838, in the debate over the independent treasury bill, both Clay and Webster attacked Calhoun on the grounds of inconsistency and asserted that he had gone over to the Democrats to obtain personal political reward. His desertion of the Whigs had robbed them of certain victory; they were deliberately personal in their remarks, Clay much more so than Webster. His old rivals cited Calhoun's whole career as evidence, using in particular a passage in his Edgefield letter upon which it was easy to place a partisan interpretation. This "battle of the giants" is one of the most dramatic episodes in the history of the Senate; and Calhoun answered his attackers, who were as vulnerable as he to the charge of inconsistency, with telling sarcasm. Benton states that Calhoun was consciously imitating the style of Demosthenes in the "Oration on the Crown." These two speeches, one in reply to Clay and the other to Webster, are the liveliest and the most oratorical their author ever delivered.[22]

Webster accused him of being "sectional" and Clay characterized him as "metaphysical," eccentric, having too much of genius and too little common sense. In reply to the former Calhoun reviewed the New Englander's career prior to 1824 as the particularist spokesman for the eastern minority, but he reserved his sharpest shafts for the Kentuckian. "I cannot accuse him of possessing the powers of analysis and generalization, those higher faculties of the mind (called metaphysical by those who do not possess them).... The absence of those higher qualities of mind is conspicuous throughout the whole course of the Senator's public life.... We ever find him mounted on some popular and favorite measure, which he whips along, cheered by the shouts of the multitude, and never dismounts until he has ridden it down."[23] He answered the serious charges by copious quotations from his earlier speeches, and insisted that it was Clay and Webster, not he, who had changed positions on the bank between 1834 and 1837.

Calhoun's friends insisted he had ably vindicated himself, but the Whigs naturally thought otherwise. The net result was probably that more people than before were skeptical both of his consistency and the purity of his motives. His own protestations, in which he had indulged upon previous occasions, may have contributed to this end as much as the charges of his attackers. On the grounds of consistency all three were vulnerable; otherwise they would have long since been rejected by the electorate. And their "inconsistencies" over so long and hectic a period of public life might be regarded as proof of their intellectual stature.

*   *   *

At the beginning of 1840, and for a number of years thereafter, Calhoun looked to the future with optimism. Congress had completely accepted his recommendations as to the procedure for dealing with abolitionist petitions. Van Buren and the Democrats had committed themselves positively, it seemed, to his stand on the tariff and slavery, and he expected his own influence and that of the South to become dominant in that party. The Whig party

201

was destined to defeat and dissolution because it was "too heterogeneous to hold together under the shock of defeat." Undoubtedly he anticipated his nomination by his own party in the near future.

He expressed his confidence in two letters to his son Andrew, who had recently moved to Alabama. In the first he informed him that "the political prospect is good. I never was stronger; or stood on more solid ground." In the second he elaborated on this theme: "I certainly never had more control over measures, and I think public opinion is gradually coming around to our principles and policy. I keep one great object in view, to which I make every move subordinate: to expelling the whole system of federal consolidation measures, and to give the government a fresh start, in the state-rights direction."[24]

Though Calhoun expected a Democratic victory until the eve of the election, he regarded his position in the event of his party's defeat as almost as advantageous. The realism of his reasoning is revealed in his exchange of letters with his South Carolina friend Hammond on the subject of his use of the balance of power. Were Van Buren re-elected by a large majority, he contended, the New Yorker had made strong commitments to the southerners which he would then be in a position to carry out effectively. But should the President, in spite of the deterrent of the deficit in the treasury, "endeavour to govern on the spoil principles, the great body of the Whigs would be compelled to rally on us, with no small division of the administration party." Were the Whigs victorious, "the whole body of the administration party, with the discontented portion of the Whigs (it would be a large part) would join our Standard."[25]

The Whigs won, but the heterogeneous nature of their party and the death of Harrison shortly after the election soon produced a fatal split in their ranks. The southerners and westerners who had voted for Harrison had to be rewarded, and Tyler believed strongly in state rights and the principle of the Compromise Act of 1833. Arguing that the recent election was a mandate from the people for the American System, Clay attempted at once to get his full program enacted by the special session of Congress called by Harrison upon his inauguration in 1841. But these Whig measures were in part vetoed by Tyler, the Whig President, and in September all members of the cabinet resigned except Webster, who stuck to the President for two more years largely in hopes of capitalizing personally upon the situation at the expense of his old rival Clay. As Calhoun predicted, the Whigs found it "much more easy to gain the battle, than to reap its fruits."[26]

Once again the Carolinian, who recently had for the first time in a decade allied himself with the party in power, became the leader of the opposition when the Democrats were defeated in 1840. But this time he had with him the President of the United States. In the special session and the regular one which followed, Calhoun and the opposition fought hard for every inch of ground, but the Whigs had a congressional majority and it was upon the presidential veto that their program foundered. The independent treasury was repealed, but two bank bills which passed Congress were vetoed. To get his distribution bill passed, Clay had to couple it with a pre-emption bill to satisfy the West and, to suit the southerners, with a proviso that distribution would cease if tariff rates were raised. When a tariff bill repealing this proviso passed, it received a veto from the President, and upon the passage of the bill of 1842, which Tyler accepted because of the dire need for revenue, distribution ceased. Thus the net result of the Whig efforts was abolition of the independent treasury and an increase in the tariff.

Clay's attack upon what he charged was Tyler's illegal use of the veto power (Tyler was the first Vice-President to inherit the presidency) gave Calhoun an excellent opportunity to expound his thesis that the Constitution itself placed a check upon the unlimited power of the absolute majority. In a long speech he reasoned closely as to the electoral college, the Senate, the amending process, and the executive veto power, all of which were designed to protect the minority and to make governmental action in practice a matter of concurrent majorities.

The vote on the tariff bill, more highly protective than the measure of 1832 that had caused South Carolina to nullify, revealed a sectional pattern which cut sharply across party lines. It passed by the narrow margin of 104 to 103 in the House and 24 to 23 in the Senate. Both Democrats and Whigs in the two southern sections were almost solidly opposed, and the majority of Democrats from the Northwest sided with them. Democrats from the Middle Atlantic and the New England regions joined their Whig colleagues almost unanimously in the affirmative. Calhoun's efforts to unite the West and the southern Whigs behind his legislative program for southern defense had borne fruit.

203

Tyler hoped to receive the support of the Calhoun wing of Democrats, and his later zeal for the annexation of Texas suggests that he attempted to form a southern party to back his re-election. But the Senator from South Carolina refused to be cooperative. Instead, he maintained a strict independence and backed the President only on those measures he had previously advocated. He rejected the offer of the office of secretary of state "with a carte blanche as to the cabinet," an act which Rhett regarded as "one of the greatest blunders he ever committed."[27] At the same time he blocked a movement in South Carolina to nullify the tariff.

He did these things both because he had high hopes for the Democratic nomination in 1844 and because he thought that party could be won completely over to the southern position, despite the fact that Van Buren and his friends had voted for the recent tariff. (His decision was justified when the party under Polk restored the independent treasury and enacted the low tariff of 1846.) Since the Democrats were out of power in 1844, they needed his support more than ever, though by returning to the party he again became a rival of Van Buren for its leadership. In addition, as he had formerly deserted the Democrats for the Whigs and then the Whigs for the Democrats, he was simply in no position to risk a third shift in party affiliation. He saw also that Tyler would be forced to favor the program which he himself had already outlined.[28]

*   *   *

For some time Calhoun had been thinking of the Democratic nomination, but his first avowed reference to it appeared in a letter which he wrote to Hammond in September, 1841, from Georgia. The text is so indicative of the whole nature of his campaign that it must be quoted at length.

> Let me add in reference to myself. I found the prospect good both in Virginia and N. Carolina. I have no doubt, but that in both States I am by far the strongest. My friends in the latter state intend to make a movement, I understand, in my favor during the next session of the Legislature. If it should be done either there, or in this State [Georgia] my impression is, that it would be advisable to follow it up in our State. The state, I think, ought not to take a course, that would seem too forward, or too indifferent. It is a point, I rarely touch, in correspondence

or conversation. Apart from a sense of duty, and a desire to do all I can to carry the country and especially the South through their present difficulties I have no desire for the office.[29]

A month later he developed the same subject in letters to his brother-in-law James Edward Calhoun and to Armistead Burt, Carolina congressman: "Many of my friends think that the time has arrived when my name ought to be presented for the next presidency. It is my own impression, that, if it is ever intended, now is the time." He reasserted that he was responding only to the call of duty, and he emphasized the opportunity for a complete reform of the government. Such reform could be accomplished only through the executive. The selection of Van Buren would be fatal to this objective and, in fact, in his opinion only a southern man would seek to accomplish it.[30]

For the moment he agreed with his friends that an active canvass would be premature, but during 1842, as a result of his own efforts and those of a South Carolina steering committee under the direction of Franklin H. Elmore, careful plans were laid. Newspapers were selected throughout the Union, notably the Washington *Spectator* and the New York *Gazette*, and "spontaneous" demonstrations occurred in his behalf at various points. After long consultation he submitted, as did Clay, his resignation from the Senate, ostensibly to write a book on government. The legislature accepted it and formally nominated him for the presidency at the end of 1842. Calhoun was energetic in his own behalf. He wrote various letters to his friends suggesting in detail the copy which they might get in print about him. He visited Virginia, key state in the southern campaign, and to publicize himself outside the South he wrote or had written the anonymous biography published by Harper and Brothers the following year. This highly eulogistic pamphlet presented a full defense of his career against the charge of inconsistency, and it was extremely moderate in its tone towards Jackson. The support of the General was vital to the Democratic candidate, as the subsequent choice of Polk proved. A collection of Calhoun's speeches, omitting many of the early nationalistic ones which would have proved embarrassing, was published by Harper and Brothers to accompany the biography. When the omission was commented upon by his enemies, he denied all responsibility for its publication.[31]

Despite warnings from the more practical Duff Green, then traveling in Europe, Calhoun and his friends were full of confidence. "It seems to me Calhoun must be the man," wrote Hammond in the fall, "unless he kicks over the pail of water of which there is much danger."[32] The candidate himself repeated all the mistaken optimism of the campaign of 1822: Van Buren had no chance, New York and New England would go for him, the South was solid, and a majority of Congress was actively favorable.[33]

The Calhoun men faced a dilemma. If they relied solely on the nomination by the Democratic convention, their rivals might control that body or it might meet too early for the crucial issue of Texas to work in their favor. Through Secretary of State Abel P. Upshur they had received confidential information that Tyler would present a Texas annexation treaty to the Senate. In that case, even if they should fail to control the Democratic convention, they could form a third party and nominate Calhoun. By supporting annexation he might conceivably be elected in the House should no candidate receive a majority in the electoral college.

The fight within the party between the Calhoun and Van Buren forces centered on the convention procedure. The former insisted that each district should elect a delegate who could vote as he wished, instead of delegates on a general ticket being selected by local party conventions and the vote of a whole state cast as a unit. Actually this was a tacit recognition of the strength of the Van Buren machine. Calhoun argued that other methods would give control of the convention to the more populous nonslaveholding states to the exclusion of the South and in that way place control of the ballot box, the patronage, and the veto in the same hands.[34]

The later date for the convention advocated by Calhoun was gradually accepted, but the first sign of defeat appeared when a Virginia state convention in March, 1843, voted against him on the other points at issue. This convention resolved specifically that "any individual, however eminent, who refuses to abide [by the decision of the national convention] forfeits his claim to the confidence of the party."[35] Shortly thereafter Hunter and the Calhoun men in that state were defeated for re-election, and the previously noncommittal Ritchie came out openly for Van Buren. In September New York voted for Van Buren, and in December Alabama did likewise. The Democrats in the new Congress which met in the winter were three-to-one for Van Buren. By this time most of Calhoun's friends felt that he should withdraw rather than risk a defeat which would hurt his chances for 1848, but they still hoped that the appearance of the Texas issue might revive his candidacy before the election of 1844.

*   *   *

Hamilton wished to run Calhoun, not as a Democrat, but as a War Republican of 1812. Rhett and Virgil Maxcy, though despairing of a nomination by the Democratic convention, felt that Calhoun as an independent candidate still had a chance for election if he came out strongly on the questions of Texas and the tariff. With this in mind the hesitating candidate wrote strongly for annexation in a letter on December 25 to Thomas W. Gilmer, former governor of Virginia, not for publication but with permission to show it to his friends. Four days previously he had written another letter to the South Carolina Central Committee giving his reasons for withholding his name from the convention scheduled to meet in Baltimore. This letter, not intended for immediate publication, had been drafted after much discussion with his friends. At the suggestion of Duff Green and others he toned it down considerably by omitting, against his own judgment, an attack on the tariff and on Van Buren.[36]

As a result of this letter to the committee Calhoun's name was on January 27 omitted by the editor of the Charleston *Mercury* from the head of its columns where he had recently been running it as the *Mercury's* candidate for the Democratic nomination. A few days later his friends in the Virginia convention, thinking that he had retired from the race, withdrew Calhoun's name and accepted the nomination of Van Buren. Thus ended his canvass for the Democratic nomination, apparently to his dismay. In a letter to the *Mercury* he took the amazing position that he had not authorized the withdrawal. After a long and active campaign he insisted that he had not been an aspirant and therefore could not withdraw his name. His friends of the Central Committee, he argued, having in their possession his letter requesting that his name be withheld, should have decided either to continue their efforts, contrary to his expressed wish, or to withdraw his name from the convention and seek his nomination by some other method.[37] In this obtuse fashion Calhoun "kicked over the pail of water"; but the pail was empty, for it had become clear that Van Buren would defeat him in the convention.

At this point he grew bitter both about the presidency and about Van Buren, whom he charged with violating his solemn pledges on the tariff and abolition, "a case of political treachery almost without example." He urged his friends to forget him, to stand fast to their principles, and to refuse all support to the New Yorker until he had redeemed his earlier pledges. "I am too honest and patriotick to be the choice of anything like a majority," he wrote. "The great point for me, is *to preserve my character* in these corrupt and degenerate times."* Soon he rejoiced to Green, "I am now disentangled from the fraudulent game of President making, and hope never to have anything to do with it again."³⁸

A month before the Democratic convention met in May, both Clay and Van Buren by agreement came out in letters against the annexation of Texas on the grounds that it would lead to war with Mexico. This action stunned southern Democrats, many of whom swung over to Lewis Cass of Michigan. Jackson, who had already written a public letter supporting annexation, then urged James K. Polk to seek the nomination as a compromise candidate. Polk was assured privately by Van Buren men that he was the second choice of northern Democrats. When the convention met, Van Buren could not get the necessary two-thirds majority, or even obtain the repeal of this rule which had originally been passed for his benefit. Cass led on the fifth ballot, but shortly Polk was unanimously nominated and went on to victory over Clay in the election, with the slogan of reoccupation of Oregon and "reannexation" of Texas.

Thus annexation became the critical issue, but it rebounded to the benefit of Polk and not of Calhoun. Pickens wrote his chief from Baltimore that hundreds "say you ought to be the man, but they cannot get at you.... It does seem to me that the South ought to agree to push you."³⁹ The circumstances of his canvass for the nomination prove beyond the slightest doubt that he had a deep and burning ambition for the presidency, and present in bold relief the nature of his fatal complex. Though he was in part motivated by a sense of duty to his nation, ambition equally kept him in politics for forty years despite failing health and the desire to give full time to the management of his large plantation. The

*Italics added.

driving power of this ambition was apparent to most of his contemporaries.

Since neither Clay nor Webster succeeded in his quest for high office, it is probable that Calhoun never had a chance; but had it not been for the impediment of his own personality he might at least have been nominated by a major party once in his long career. It is noteworthy that the state of Virginia, and Ritchie in particular, refused him support because of his previous connection with nullification and because of the personal dislike of its leaders for him as an individual. Clay exclaimed after his defeat in 1844 that if there were two Henry Clays, one would get the other elected president. There were two Calhouns: one who schemed, dreamed, and worked for the presidency; and the other who not only denied the existence of a perfectly normal ambition, but who even refused to permit his friends to discuss with him practical methods of obtaining the office. Coyness in a candidate often has a definite value, but a man who most of the time refused to admit to himself or to his friends that he had ambition was doomed from the outset.

This trait of temperament was best described by Beverly Tucker, who disliked the Carolinian, in a letter to Hammond:

> Mr. Calhoun's misfortune is a fixed idea concerning the presidency.... In a sane moment he disclaimed it the other day, and sometimes in a lucid interval acts consistently and wisely. But let it be said of him in half a dozen papers "that he is winning golden opinions from all men — that no man stands so high in the respect of all men not of his own party," etc., etc., and presently the Rhetts and *id genus omne* proclaim that either the Whigs or the Democrats (no matter which) have a mind to drop their own candidate and take him. Then presently the frenzy begins to work.[40]

CHAPTER THIRTEEN

Rumors of War and War

THE Roaring Forties, which began inauspiciously during a depression so severe that Congress had to pass a national bankruptcy act, ended in the glory of the victory over Mexico, the Gold Rush of '49, and the admission of California into the Union as a state. The United States now became a Pacific as well as an Atlantic power. Undoubtedly the main event of the decade was the acquisition by the republic of its approximate continental limits. Texas entered the Union in 1845, Oregon was obtained by treaty the following year, and two years later Mexico was forced to cede the vast Southwest. England at last was completely defeated in her effort to confine the new nation she had borne.

Again the spirit of nationalism, popularly known as Manifest Destiny, was abroad in the land. It was perhaps only a lucky accident that prevented the annexation of all of Mexico in 1848, but the various filibustering attacks on the Caribbean islands and Central America in the next decade were by no means purely southern in motivation. Even in the South this nationalism was potent enough to defeat the secession movement of 1850; in the nation at large it accomplished the acceptance of the compromise of that year which saved the Union.

The rampant optimism of Americans at mid-century — their almost rash faith in their future — was also the product of another type of physical expansion. The first railroads were being constructed; the Deere plow and the McCormick reaper were rapidly extending a vast agricultural empire in the interior. More and bigger steamboats churned the inland waters, and along the many western rivers new and thriving towns arose. Older ports, like New York and New Orleans, increased greatly in size, wealth, and extent of their hinterland. Old factories grew larger and new ones sprang up at a rapid rate in the Northeast. Hordes of immigrants, notably Irish and German, poured in to provide the labor supply for farm and factory. With the repeal of the English Corn Laws insatiable markets in Europe beckoned, and the American merchant marine, proud of its fast new clippers, was second to none on the high seas. In ten years population increased one third, from seventeen million in 1840 to twenty-three million a decade later, and the immigrants still were coming.

Such rapid expansion was inevitably accompanied by growing pains, and beneath the surface the old forces initiated by the "Ferment of the 'Thirties" exerted telling strains upon the body social and the body politic. Men of property, staunch supporters of the Whig party, still feared the equalitarian democracy of the masses. With the acquisition of new territory the old debate over slavery and its relation to the political power of class and section took a more positive and concrete form. It is one of the paradoxes of the period that the Democrats, who executed the expansion and won a war, were twice defeated — in 1840 and again in 1848 — by the Whigs who opposed both. Expansion led directly to conflict. During the War with Mexico David Wilmot introduced his fatal proviso excluding slavery from the new territory. Churches were already splitting into northern and southern branches; the new struggle over slavery tended to embitter and unite the South in resistance. But the passage of the great compromise in 1850 exhibited the cogency of the force of nationalism among a majority of Americans in all the sections, and gave evidence of their confidence that destructive civil war could be and should be averted in the rapidly expanding nation.

Gradually new actors appeared upon the political stage. Just as Calhoun and his young War Hawks had replaced the older Revolutionary generation of statesmen, bringing in new ways and new ideas, their time now came to submit to the inexorable cosmic process. By 1850 new leaders like Seward and Douglas were pushing aside the statesmen of the Silver Age. But before their exit, the second generation of American statesmen played the leads in a final drama.

*   *   *

During middle age Calhoun continued to subordinate his personal life to his public career. In 1826 his family purchased the plantation in Pendleton District, South Carolina, near the mountains, which became known as Fort Hill. Actually it belonged to his mother-in-law, and he rented it until her death in 1836. Here he moved his family, here his ninth and last child was born in 1829, and here he spent most of his time when absent from Washington. Fort Hill had on an average seventy to eighty slaves, and in accordance with southern tradition its master devoted the little time he could spare from politics to the career of gentleman-farmer. He imported Bermuda grass, Siberian wheat, and blooded cattle from England, but necessarily he had to rely upon James Edward Calhoun, his brother-in-law, and Thomas G. Clemson, his son-in-law, for considerable aid in the management of so large a plantation.

Apparently he did not have too much confidence in the capacity of his wife for such direction, for he once wrote James Edward: "I have long since learned by sad experience, what it is to build in my absence. It would cost me twice as much.... I wish you could add your weight to mine to reconcile her to the course I suggest. I have written her fully on the subject."[1] He also acquired property in Alabama and Georgia, and when gold was discovered on the latter, there were prospects for a while that he might become a rich man. Actually most of his life he was under financial strain despite the land which he and his wife owned, and he died in debt. His difficulties resulted from a number of factors: the size of his family, his expenses in Washington, absentee management of his plantation, the drop in the price of cotton, and chiefly the debts of his sons which he indulgently assumed. But farming was his second love, though he wrote that he considered his absence "from my farm among my greatest sacrifices."[2] Few of his letters to his wife have been preserved, but because of his continued absence from home he corresponded frequently with members of his family. From these and from his letters to his friends and henchmen in South Carolina it is possible to obtain a more intimate insight into his personality.

212

Calhoun's letters dealt almost exclusively with politics, revealing the extent to which it was an obsession with him, and even those to members of the family were largely concerned with that subject. Apparently his daughter Anna Maria (later Mrs. Clemson) was his favorite, and she became the confidante of his later years to whom he revealed his lighter nature. In his letters to her he gave pen-pictures of President Harrison and Charles Dickens; in one he described at length the ironic fortune which placed R. M. T. Hunter of Virginia in the speaker's chair of the House. He told her how some of his southern friends had left his mess, not as alleged because of their rooms or the food, but because it was a "temperance Mess drinking neither Whiskey or wine. It suits me in that respect very well, for I have little relish for either except claret, and in the winter but little for that." He informed her in 1841 that the season was dull, but "I do not go to any parties at all, and can give you but little news of the gay world."³

Yet the dour Scots-Irishman was not straightlaced in all his views. He advised his daughter during a temporary illness to "avoid medicine, except the most simple kind, and rely on diet and proper exercise, with cheerfulness and amusement, and change of scene. ...You know how deeply I am impressed with the total neglect of health and constitution in the education of females, as well as in their mode of life. I regard it as one of the greatest calamities of the age. If not corrected, our whole race is destined to degenerate. The accomplishments acquired at school are nothing to be compared to the loss of a robust constitution and good health." And he commended her for sending her two sons to dancing school, "that is, if the master is a competent teacher. It is a desirable accomplishment, and an almost indispensable appendix to the social intercourse of the two sexes in early life, so necessary for the happiness and accomplishment of both."⁴

The public, in contrast to the private, personality of the man was unrelieved by any such lightness. His letters and speeches exhibit a colossal egotism, confirming the observation of many of his contemporaries. The autobiography is full of passages which prove the existence of a naïve vanity, particularly the one in which he referred to himself as "the master-statesman of his age" and praised his independence "of his followers, who take their counsels merely from zeal."⁵ The disappointments of later years only whetted this egotism and made it bitter.

John C. Calhoun

Calhoun's long career was littered with broken political and personal friendships, for he could never work long in harness with men prominent enough to share with him the center of the stage. Though he began his career in politics as Clay's trusted lieutenant, he quarreled with him later when they were rival aspirants for the presidency. During this period John Quincy Adams became his closest intimate, yet after their break in 1825 they remained forever enemies. Next, after years of political intimacy, he had his violent and never mended quarrel with Jackson. For a long while after his debate with Webster in the nullification crisis he scarcely spoke to the New Englander, and his expedient reconciliation with Clay in 1833 soon ended in a renewal of their personal enmity. Upon his return to the Democrats he patched up his differences with Benton, yet within a decade the Missourian was referring to him as John "Catiline" Calhoun. Shortly Benton denied the reference, avowing that he could not be "so unjust to the brave Roman conspirator as to compare the cowardly American plotter to him."[6]

President Polk, who sought to steer a middle course between the Van Buren and Calhoun factions of his party but never broke official relations with the southerner, privately attributed to him the basest motives. "Perfectly desperate in his aspirations to the Presidency," Polk recorded in his diary, the Carolinian pressed the sectional issue "as the only means of sustaining himself in his present fallen condition."[7] Varina Howell Davis, wife of the future president of the Confederacy who met Calhoun in Vicksburg on his way to the Memphis Convention in 1845, expressed a different opinion.*

Prejudiced because of her later fixation to the southern cause and also because Calhoun was to write her frequently during the remaining five years of his life, Mrs. Davis penned in her reminiscences the most nearly exact physical description of the southern leader and an estimate of his personality that contrasted with the evaluation of Polk:

*After this meeting Calhoun, according to Mrs. Davis, during the rest of his life wrote her long letters on government, all of which were later destroyed during the war. His handwriting, though neat, was almost undecipherable and upon one such occasion she returned a letter to him with the request that he translate it. "I know what I think on this subject," he replied, "but cannot decipher what I wrote." Mrs. Davis witnessed his last appearance in the Senate, of which she gives a touching description.

No dignity could be more supreme than Mr. Calhoun's. His voice was not musical; it was the voice of a professor of mathematics and suited his didactic discourse admirably. He made few gestures, but those nervous, gentlemanly hands seemed to point the way to empire. He always appealed to me rather as a moral and mental abstraction than a politician, and it was impossible, knowing him well, to associate him with mere personal ambition. His theories and his sense of duty alone dominated him.[8]

The record of his political relations with South Carolinians is similar. He forced his colleagues William C. Preston and Stephen D. Miller to resign from Congress. Governor Benjamin Perry of that state wrote in his *Reminiscences* that Calhoun "was absolute in South Carolina and all who sought promotion in the State had to follow him and swear by him. He thought for the State and crushed out all independence of thought in those below him." It is possible that Hamilton left the state for this reason, and Hammond grew bitter in his criticism in the 1840's. In 1846 Calhoun quarreled with Pickens, his most loyal follower, because he was alleged to have inspired an article critical of his chief's recent speech to the Memphis railroad convention on internal improvements. Pickens denied the allegation and apologized profusely, but he was excommunicated when Calhoun stated that it was impossible to "restore him to his former position."[9] The harsh comments of South Carolina radicals, whom Calhoun was forever restraining after the nullification crisis, can be discounted; but it is impossible to dismiss his high-handed treatment of his loyal lieutenants.

*   *   *

More valid, perhaps, than a reconstruction of the man from his letters are certain impressions of his southern associates who saw him in the flesh. With Calhoun in the presidency, said Senator Roane of Virginia, he would be in "constant terror, expecting from him some newfangled scheme or view." South Carolinian E. W. Johnston complained to Hammond that "I have been for the last three years, steadily cursing Calhoun.... We work on here and make a doctrine popular. Of a sudden, he comes forward, seizes it, spoils it with some vast nonsensical supplement of his own and ruins the impression which might have been made on the country by stitching the whole affair to his political kite-tail."[10]

Even the loyal four-hundred-pounder Senator Dixon H. Lewis of Alabama admitted that his idol was difficult. "Calhoun is now my principal associate," he confessed, "and he is too intelligent, too industrious, too intent on the struggle of politics to suit me except as an occasional companion. There is no *relaxation* in him." But a certain Judge Prioleau, a newcomer to Pendleton, was more direct when he stated that he never wanted to see his neighbor again: "I hate a man who makes me think so much ... and I hate a man who makes me feel my own inferiority." Beverly Tucker commented to Hammond on Calhoun's tactlessness: "A man of wonderful powers of mind and profound political knowledge, but no statesman.... How he might manage the affairs of a great nation I do not know, but he certainly is the most unskillful leader of a party that ever wielded a truncheon."[11]

But Hammond, his closest political intimate in South Carolina, was the most critical, partly because Calhoun would not support him for governor in 1840 and partly because the Senator defeated Hammond's attempt as governor in 1844 to start a movement to nullify the recent tariff. "He cannot bear contradiction," observed the governor. "He thinks any difference of opinion from him proves a man hostile, and is ready to open his batteries on him. Hence, again, his want of able friends. He drives off every man who has ability to think for himself." After Calhoun's death Hammond confided his final and considered estimate to his diary: "Pre-eminent as he was intellectually above all the men of this age as I believe, he was so wanting in judgment in the managing of men, was so unyielding and unpersuasive, that he could never consolidate sufficient power to accomplish anything great, of himself and in due season ... and jealousy of him — his towering genius and uncompromising temper, has had much effect in preventing the South from uniting to resist."[12]

It has been remarked that in view of his ineptitude for politics, Calhoun would have been much better suited for the fields of law or scholarship. Probably his strong ambition for political position would early have produced dissatisfaction with any other field of endeavor, but it is obvious that he had a powerful, inquiring, and in many ways an original mind. Actually, however, as an anonymous critic observed in the *Southern Literary Messenger,* he "was not a learned man, for he never had leisure for the details of scholarship. But he was an exceedingly well informed man.... He gleaned much information from talking with others." A close student of Aristotle's *Politics*, he often spoke of Machiavelli's *History of Florence*, and there was no writer of whom he was fonder than Edmund Burke.[13]

*   *   *

Shortly after Calhoun's name was withdrawn from the contest for the Democratic nomination, he was appointed secretary of state early in March to fill the vacancy created by the death of Upshur a few days before. One story has it that he was not the President's choice, for he had twice refused the office, and that his appointment in 1844 resulted from the bold action of Henry A. Wise of Virginia. Regarding him as the proper man for the job in the crisis at hand, and fearing both that he would probably refuse an offer made by Tyler and that Tyler would not voluntarily offer him the position, Wise asked George McDuffie to approach Calhoun. This gave McDuffie the impression that the President was about to send his name to the Senate. Then, unable to convince Tyler, who informed him that Calhoun was not the "man of my choice," Wise confessed his rash action and the amazed President surrendered in the matter.[14]

It is possible, however, that both Tyler and Calhoun regarded the Texas negotiations as above politics. The President must have known about the Wise-McDuffie dealings. He could have been trying to obtain Calhoun's support for his own nomination by the Democrats, since the Carolinian had already officially withdrawn his candidacy.

When Calhoun took over the Texas negotiations, the general outline of the treaty of annexation had already been agreed upon by Upshur and the Texas minister. The Carolinian was a logical choice for the position, not only because he had previously been in close contact with Upshur, but also because he had spoken frequently in the Senate in recent years on matters of foreign policy. He had indicated his support of annexation in the last of his slavery resolutions in 1837 and had worked out a realistic policy in regard to our relations with England. Though he demanded compensation for the slaves illegally freed in the "Enterprise" affair,* he realized

---

*There were several instances in this period in which American ships carrying slaves from one American port to another were forced into ports in offshore British islands, by weather or other adverse circumstances. There

the desirability of peace with England, and towards that end he supported the administration's Webster-Ashburton Treaty in a powerful speech in 1842, which led his South Carolina opponent Preston to exclaim that he had "covered himself with a mantle of glory."[15] Appreciating the value of Oregon and regarding the title of the United States to the area south of the 49th parallel as clear, he had urged a "wise and masterly inactivity" as the proper course, since increasing American migration was certain to obtain it in time.

Calhoun agreed with Tyler and Polk that England was seeking to prevent American expansion into California, Oregon, and Texas. In the four years since Texas had withdrawn its request for admission to the Union, Great Britain had intervened in the Southwest in a manner dangerous both to national interests and to those of the South. While Mexico had been unable to reconquer Texas, the new republic was bankrupt, and its expedition in 1841 to capture Santa Fe had failed. Desiring an independent Texas, both as a source of cotton and a market for her manufactured goods as well as a buffer to American expansion, England was exerting pressure upon Mexico to grant an armistice in return for a Texas agreement to emancipate its slaves. Compensation to the owners would be provided by funds advanced by the British.

Calhoun had been informed, through letters from Duff Green in Europe, of the activities of both British and American abolitionists in this matter.[16] The active interest of Foreign Secretary Aberdeen in the project aroused the fears of southerners over the menace of a free and independent Texas. Aberdeen advised Mexico to consent to the proposal and, in fact, in January, 1844, had secretly obtained the promise of France to join England in opposing annexation by the United States. At the time President Houston seemed to prefer the English to the Americans. As Tyler pointed out in his message of December, 1843, a weak Mexico and a weak Texas invited foreign interference dangerous to American interests.

Despite some hesitancy on the part of Texas, the real obstacle to the treaty was the opposition within the United States which

---

the slaves were freed by the authorities, on the grounds that England had abolished slavery in the empire in 1833. Both in the Senate, and as secretary of state, Calhoun insisted that such action violated international law and demanded full compensation for the slaveowners. (See his speech on the "Enterprise" case in *Works*, III, 462-87.) Finally England agreed to Settlement by an umpire, who in 1853 awarded damages to the various American slaveowners.

might induce the necessary minority of the Senate to reject it. Up-shur thought he had assured himself, through conversation with senators, that the treaty would receive the support of a two-thirds majority. Opposition had first been evident when John Q. Adams by a three weeks' filibuster in 1838 had defeated a resolution for annexation in the House. Almost immediately Texas withdrew the offer. Adams returned to the attack in the spring of 1843 when on the last day of the congressional session he issued a manifesto, signed by thirteen representatives, attacking annexation as a conspiracy of the "Slave Power" and asserting that its passage would be in effect a dissolution of the Union.

Opponents of annexation consisted of three groups: abolitionists and their fellow-travelers like Adams, who regarded abolition in an independent Texas as a step in the destruction of slavery in the southern states; northern capitalists who saw that the several states which might be created out of the territory would cast telling votes in the Senate against Clay's paternalistic program;* and those who feared that the honor of the nation would be compromised or that war with Mexico would result. It was on the last grounds that Clay and Van Buren both came out about the same time in April, 1844, against annexation, an action which indicated that they regarded northern sentiment against annexation stronger than southern sentiment for it. But many moderate southerners argued that slavery and cotton were as distinct American interests as New England shipping and should receive equal protection.

*   *   *

Calhoun quickly concluded negotiations and submitted the treaty to the Senate in the middle of April. In his letter to Governor Gilmer the previous December he had argued for annexation on the grounds of national security and of the market it would afford the northern and northwestern states. Now he replied in diplomatic correspondence to a letter in which the British Foreign Secretary had expressed a desire for abolition throughout the world with a spirited defense of annexation purely in the interests of slavery and slaveowners. The United States must annex Texas to resist the world movement for abolition, he argued; Negroes were

*This apprehension was soon justified when the Senate passed the low tariff of 1846 by a vote of 28 to 27, the two Texas senators voting in the affirmative.

worse off in areas where they had been emancipated than in those where they remained in bondage.[17]

Though his reply to Aberdeen was confidential and not intended for publication, it appeared shortly through some leak in Van Buren's New York *Evening Post*. On April 22 the treaty was defeated in the Senate by a vote of 35 to 16, and Tyler later blamed the defeat upon Calhoun for his narrow emphasis upon slavery. Surely the Secretary did not deliberately defeat his own treaty. Publication of his letter heightened the growing sectional bitterness which led to its rejection, but he cannot justly be accused of playing politics by means of arguments expressed in confidential diplomatic correspondence. Since Clay and Van Buren formally announced their opposition a few days after the completed treaty was submitted to the Senate, they were more responsible than the Secretary of State for its rejection.

Thus the annexation of Texas, on its own merit alone, was defeated. But when Polk coupled it with Oregon and thereby effected a southern-western alliance for a broader expansion program, he received in the election of 1844 what was assumed to be approval from the voters. At the end of February, despite opposition from Benton, Congress passed by a party vote a joint resolution to annex Texas, leaving it to the President to decide what further negotiations were necessary. Tyler signed the bill on March 1, but he preferred to leave the decision as to the ensuing procedure to Polk, as Congress probably intended.[18] The situation was urgent; Texas might still have accepted England's offer. Under Calhoun's prodding, however, the President offered annexation to Texas on the last day of his term. Polk, who previously had refused to cooperate in the matter, later accepted this action. In supporting the joint resolution, Calhoun clearly violated his principle of strict construction, for such procedure was merely an expedient means of nullifying the provision of the Constitution that two thirds of the Senate must ratify a treaty.

Calhoun also negotiated with British Minister Pakenham in regard to Oregon and rejected his offer of the 49th parallel as the boundary with the proviso that both nations be allowed free navigation of the Columbia River.[19] In masterly fashion he defended the American title to the whole Columbia valley, but his term expired before the matter got beyond the stage of diplomatic sparring.

Calhoun hoped to retain his office under the new administration in order to carry to completion negotiations in regard to both Texas and Oregon. Thus he was disappointed when Polk did not ask him to remain in the cabinet but instead offered him the mission to England. The new President probably preferred less eminent men in his cabinet, particularly men not bitten with the presidential bug. His more practical reason was his desire to unify his party by refuting the impression that it was excessively prosouthern and to regain the favor of Van Buren and his followers. A new cleavage within the party had arisen between the Benton and Calhoun factions, from both of whom Polk intended to maintain his independence.

"It was scarcely in the power of Mr. Polk to treat me badly," confided the retiring Secretary to his daughter. "I would consider it, at least, as much of a favor to him for me to remain in office under his administration, as he could to me, to invite me to remain." He was proud of his record, he told the Clemsons. In the face of numerous disadvantages "I have succeeded, by a bold unhesitating course, to secure Annexation, and leave a strong impression, both at home and abroad, in the short space of less than 11 months." He retired, he added, "with the good will of all, including the administration, and the regret, I may say, of almost the whole country, with no small censure on the administration, for not inviting me to continue."[20]

*　　　*　　　*

Before the election of 1844 Calhoun decided to support Polk, with a view both to his own nomination in 1848 and to the annexation of Texas. Most of his South Carolina followers accepted his decision, despite discontent with the tariff of 1842, the rejection of the Texas treaty, and the recent repeal of the gag rule by the House. But Rhett and a small minority, aided by the *Mercury*, persisted in an attempt at independent state action for a southern convention, contemporarily known as the Bluffton Movement. Eventually this movement was defeated in the legislature through Calhoun's influence. Certainly he recalled the isolated position of his state in 1833, and he realized that the Whigs would profit from a division in the Democratic ranks. Though his relations with Rhett were strained for a while, he made no attempt at revenge upon the rebel for his disobedience.

Previously disgruntled because Calhoun had not supported him for the governorship in 1840 for fear of reviving the Unionist-Nullifier cleavage, Hammond agreed with Rhett as to the desirability of state action. Having been elected governor in 1842, he was in a position of some influence during the crisis, and he confided to his diary his bitterness arising from the defeat of the movement. In his opinion Calhoun, tricked by the flattery of scheming northern Democrats, was

> deluded enough to believe that he can control and succeed him [Polk] and that if he was President he could cleanse the Augean Stable.... Mr. C. has fallen into it [the northern trap] again over head and ears and is straining every point to drag in the State and the South. He limits the forbearance of the State to *two years.* Why? Because he thinks two years will settle the question of his succession to the Presidency. If he is to be elected he will still oppose it [state action]. If he is not — he will be for doing any thing. What reckless sporting with the vital interests of the South and the honor of SoCa thus to place them and use them as entirely secondary and subsidiary to his elevation to the Presidency.

Hammond predicted that the movement would be bound to fail because

> the State will do nothing but what Mr. C. wishes now. There is only one hope. If Mr. Clay is elected President which is highly probable Calhoun may out of hatred to him attempt at once to make war on the Fed. Gov. and call up Nullification. He may still however wait until our Session has passed in the vain hope of seeing some straw on the surface at which he may catch. It is clear to me that in his ambition to be President he has forgotten or recklessly trampled on every thing else. Yet I paid $500 a year ago to advance him to that office.[21]

It is pertinent at this point to examine Calhoun's relation both to the growing antislavery movement in the North in the 1840's and to the defensive efforts of the South against it. Public sentiment in the North was both antisouthern and antislavery; though these movements were by no means identical, it is difficult to distinguish between them. But the increase in their intensity in this decade is evident from Adams' attack upon the annexation of Texas as a conspiracy of the "Slave Power," the rejection of Calhoun's treaty by the Senate, the introduction of the Wilmot Proviso in 1846 prohibiting slavery in any territory acquired from Mexico, and the successful bills of 1850 admitting California as a free state and abolishing the slave trade in the District of Columbia.

Abolitionist propaganda in the Northwest and the Northeast helped to convince the northern public that slavery was an evil and should not be extended into any new territory. But the North was won to free soil, not to abolition. The vast majority in that section were willing to accept the legal existence of slavery in the southern states and denied any intent to interfere with the institution in that area. In their effort to form a national political party, the Abolitionists met complete failure, the Liberty Party under James G. Birney receiving only 7,000 votes in 1840 and 62,000 four years later. Almost 300,000 votes were cast in 1848 for Van Buren and the Free Soil Party, but the size of this vote might be discounted on the grounds that it was determined more by personal loyalty to the New Yorker than zeal for free soil. Southerners regarded the whole movement as a dishonest and deliberate attack upon the institution of slavery and an underhand attempt to deprive the South of its political power.

Undoubtedly support for free soil, particularly as manifested shortly in the rise of the Republican party, was influenced by far more than a concern for the hard lot of the slave. Northern business interests opposed the extension of slavery, particularly with the vote of the Texas senators on the tariff of 1846 in mind, because slave states were almost certain to vote against the whole paternalistic program which they desired. Eastern laborers and western farmers planning to move farther west wanted neither Negroes nor aristocrats in their midst. The antipathy for slavery, into which many easily rationalized themselves, was a convenient and a popular slogan to cover up their more selfish objectives.

But southern hotheads who defended their peculiar institution by rash language and extreme arguments did much to increase northern aversion to slavery and slavocracy. As much as any southerner Calhoun was responsible for the growth of antisouthern sentiment in the North. Instead of waiting for a frontal attack upon slavery, as his saner fellow southerners urged, he struck out in the 1830's against the peripheral matters of petitions and the dissemination of abolitionist propaganda through the mails. This action gave Adams the necessary evidence to convince the South of opposition to freedom of speech and the right of petition.

At a time when popular sentiment in the North and West for equalitarian democracy was on the increase, Calhoun unflinchingly defended aristocracy and conservatism, attacked the will of the majority, and spoke disparagingly of the northern laborer. Instead of apologizing for slavery as a "necessary evil," he defended it without reservation as a "positive good," adding the far-fetched assertion that the bondage of the black man was the ideal base for the development of free institutions. His eloquent and extreme defense of slavery, designed in part to increase his popularity in the South, had a more significant effect in arousing adverse sentiment among the northern public.

No incident so well illustrates this point as a dramatic clash in 1848 between Calhoun and the new senator from Illinois, Stephen A. Douglas, then and always a spokesman for northern moderates. Calhoun and the Mississippian Henry S. Foote were incensed at some remarks of abolitionist John P. Hale of New Hampshire. The Carolinian, unusually moved, said that he would as soon argue with a maniac from bedlam as with Hale; Foote invited the latter to come to Mississippi where they would hang him to the tallest tree. Hale replied that if Foote came to New Hampshire he would receive a respectful hearing in every town in the state.

Douglas sought to bring his southern colleagues to their senses. He told them sarcastically that they had doubled the abolitionist vote in some few states that year. "It is the speeches of Southern men, representing Slave States, going to an extreme, breathing a fanaticism as wild as that of the Senator from New Hampshire, which creates Abolitionism in the North.... [Hale] is upheld at the North because he is the champion of Abolition; and you are upheld at the South, because you are the champion who meets him; so that it comes to this, that between those two Ultra parties, we of the North who belong to neither are thrust aside.... I believe, Sir, that in all this I have spoken the sentiment of every northern man who is not an Abolitionist." Still irked, Calhoun insisted that he was only defending "the Constitutional rights of the South"; Douglas's course was "at least as offensive as that of the Senator from New Hampshire."[22]

Then, having aroused this storm against the South, he was unable to unite his section in defense against its enemies in spite of his avowed efforts towards that end. Dislike of his austere personality and distrust of his ambition for the presidency, as Hammond observed, helped keep the South from uniting in this crucial moment when unity might have prevented the later impasse. Southerners who were not offended by his personality were unconvinced by his logic. Thus Calhoun not only retarded southern unity but also contributed to the defeat of the secession movement of 1850, which might well have resulted in the attainment of southern independence. The economic determinist would insist that a similar situation would have developed had there been no Calhoun; but it is an historical fact that he, the sincere champion of the South, was one agent of its undoing. And in his insistence upon absolute conformity with the axiom that slavery was a positive good, he inaugurated the closed-mind attitude that was to stultify his beloved South for a century.

Despite the failure of the Liberty and Free Soil parties in the forties, the pressure which they exerted upon the two major parties was out of all proportion to their numbers. Clay's alienation of the abolitionists had contributed to his defeat in 1844, and the Van Buren schism defeated Cass in 1848. Van Buren's break with the Democrats made that party more amenable to southern demands, but doubts as to its stability had already led Calhoun to seek an alliance with the West as an alternative to the continued alliance with the northern workingman. It was a Pennsylvania Democrat, David Wilmot, who introduced the fateful proviso which weakened the new alliance upon the eve of its initial victory.

*　　　*　　　*

In February, 1845, Calhoun suffered a severe attack of congestive fever which permanently impaired his health and led to his death five years later. As a result his voice gave out when he delivered his speech to the Memphis Convention in the fall. Upon his return to the Senate at the end of the year, he asked to be excused from serving as chairman of the importing Finance Committee because his voice was not strong enough for the constant speaking on the floor required by the office. For this reason he had earlier decided to remain in retirement should Polk not retain him in the cabinet. "His health was decaying," the Carolinian told the Pennsylvania manufacturer Francis Wharton in February, "and he was desirous also to finish a work he was then engaged in on political economy."[23]

But the opportunity to carry his program to success and the revival of his presidential ambitions soon caused him to reverse

225

his decision and return to the Senate. When he passed through Richmond in March a group of his Virginia friends gave him a dinner. Ritchie presided and led off with a complimentary toast "which was followed by three others, expressly naming me as the candidate for '48. The whole was unexpected to me. My friends there are intelligent, ardent and united." This ambition was whetted when he went to Memphis in the autumn by way of New Orleans and stopped in several cities en route.

"I was received everywhere," he wrote Clemson, whom he had induced Tyler to appoint as *chargé d'affaires* in Brussels, "in a manner sufficient to gratify the feelings of any, the most illustrious for talents and public services. All parties every where united without distinction, in a demonstration of respect, not exceed[ed] by that shown to Genl. Jackson in passing through the same places, and much greater than that extended to any other citizen." Within a year he was predicting that "the party will be defeated at the next election for President, unless, as my friends think, they should rally on me." And in July, 1847, he wrote Clemson that though Taylor would be the popular candidate in 1848 against the caucus nominees, "I think with you, that my position is the most eligible of all the publick men of the country. It is the only independent one; and I can see symptoms, that it begins to be felt."[24]

Calhoun was elected to the Senate by the Carolina legislature in November, 1845, to fill the place of Daniel E. Huger, who more than a year before had offered to resign for that purpose. "I am exceedingly averse to returning to public life," he confessed to his lieutenant Pickens, "and yet when I look at the momentous character of the present juncture, the great strength of our friends in Congress, if it could be brought to act in concert, the good it may possibly secure, and the calamities it might avert, and the utter *incompetency* of our two Senators...I do not see under all the circumstances, how I could decline the duty, if it shall be the desire of the Legislature and the State...."[25] The moment was pressing and propitious, and he returned to the Senate with specific objectives in mind: the successful conclusion of the Texas and Oregon matters, the prevention of war with England, the union of the South and the West, the reduction of the tariff, the defense of the South against the accelerated attack of the abolitionists, and his own elevation to the presidency.

Calhoun had withdrawn from the contest for the Democratic

nomination in 1843, in view of serious doubts as to his success, mainly to avoid ruining his chances for 1848. After the Democrats' victory in 1844 his hopes revived: Polk would be compelled to keep him in the department of state and his stand on Texas would insure his nomination. Assuming that there would be at least two other candidates, the election would be thrown into the House where the Whigs, with whom he had frequently flirted, would support him as the lesser of evils. Among the politically astute this strategy was generally recognized, and even his southern foes feared that it would be successful. D. I. McCord of South Carolina wrote Hammond that he presumed that Calhoun would be the next "president *of these United States....* Is this millstone to hang around our necks until we sink to the bottom never to rise? In God's name why not let the Democrats of the North have [Silas] Wright or anybody else, if they will concede our principles to us. 'Principles not men' should now be the watchword of the whole South; but the owner of this plantation will not have it so."[26]

Polk's failure to reappoint him did not dampen his enthusiasm, and for more than a year a Calhoun boom increased in intensity. He insisted upon taking up the old stand against a convention again, and to some friend, probably Crallé, he outlined his plan. A Virginia supporter with talent would write a pamphlet giving full grounds for opposition to a convention.

> On its appearance, the Southern papers should be out in motion to attract public attention to the subject.... When the publick mind in the South is sufficiently for it, then my friends if they should choose to present my name as the people's candidate in opposition to the Convention Candidate may do it with Success, provided they determine to nail the Colours to the mast.... We can only succeed by showing them, that I am the only man of the party who can be elected, which we can easily do if our Virginia friends choose to take the stand, early and firmly.[27]

The pamphlet for some reason never appeared, but the Calhoun movement grew apace. Then its candidate began, in his inimitable way, kicking over the pail of water. First, he broke with the administration over its Ten Regiment Bill and opposed the war with Mexico. Secondly, when Ritchie's Washington *Union* attacked him violently for this action, he took revenge by a resolution in the Senate excluding the *Union's* editor from a seat on the

Senate floor. Immediately an outcry against the Carolinian arose throughout the South, and even in the Richmond district a convention, which nominated a Calhounite, stated that it did not grant "any color of approval to the political course of the Hon. J. C. Calhoun, or any pledge to support him for the presidency."[28]

Shortly the introduction of the Wilmot Proviso gave him a last chance to recoup his fortunes. He turned his guns upon it and attacked its constitutionality in a series of resolutions in the Senate which received general and hearty support from the South. Then in the spring of 1847 he spoke to a huge meeting in Charleston, calling upon the South to meet the crisis by ending all party distinctions and uniting upon a southern candidate for the presidency. This maneuver failed because a majority of southerners saw, as Calhoun had seen when the Tallmadge amendment had been introduced back in 1820, that such a move would be futile and probably fatal. Zachary Taylor pointed out that if the South united behind one candidate, "the question as to who is to succeed Mr. Polk in 49 will be settled, the free States having the majority of voters."[29]

The novelist William Gilmore Simms elaborated upon the point in a letter to Hammond about Calhoun,[30] noting the

> remarkable contradiction between the constant and scornful denunciation of the presidential chair for the last 20 years by him and his followers, as an object of interest and importance, and the sudden change to a policy by which we are instructed (the Tariff and Int Imp being no longer available as pretexts) that the Presidency is *the* question – the interest paramount to all others. His scheme, as propounded at the Charleston meeting, means, if anything, that the South should organize a party for itself, all other interests merging in that of slavery, to the exclusion and defiance of the north . . . a proposition which at once forces a corresponding organization upon the North – a result which leaves us in rather worse condition than before. Any man with one idea so deeply fixed as to become with him a passion, must necessarily be demented, wherever that idea becomes the object of consideration.*

---

*Simms' statement might be compared with that of Martin Van Buren in his *Autobiography* to the effect that Jackson's "standing prophecy to me in regard to [Clay and Calhoun] was that the former would die a sot and the latter in a mad-house."

During 1847 the boom collapsed, and for the last time in his life Calhoun resigned himself to defeat. "All that remains for me," he confessed to Duff Green, "is to finish my course with consistency and propriety."[31]

*　　　*　　　*

At the very moment that the South Carolina legislature was voting to return him to the Senate in 1845, Calhoun was attending the Memphis Railroad Convention, over which he had been asked to preside. He went as a delegate from South Carolina along with Colonel James Gadsden, president of the South Carolina Railroad Company. This was more a western than a southern convention, with delegates from the entire Mississippi Valley. It presented Charleston with an opportunity to conclude arrangements for a railroad to the Mississippi, and the South with an opportunity to cement an alliance with the Northwest. For a decade Calhoun had been laying the ground for a western alliance, as is evident from his efforts in Congress for the cession of public lands to the states. In the same period he had been equally interested in the railroad building in his own state. He had fought with Hayne, first president of the Carolina Railroad Company; the proper terminal for the transsouthern road from Charleston, he insisted, should be the Tennessee and Mississippi rivers, not the Ohio, which Hayne and others preferred. Because of this dispute he had resigned from the board of directors in 1838, but he fully cooperated with Gadsden who was elected president after Hayne's death.[32]

While he probably did not foresee the broad scope of the convention's agenda, Calhoun surely realized in advance the political opportunity it presented to himself and to the South. In September Duff Green had advised him of the attitude of the northern Democrat E. A. Hannegan, delegate to the convention from Indiana. "The West will be united," Hannegan had told Green, "and will demand funds for the improvement of their harbours, rivers and the Cumberland road, and the graduation of the price of public land, and . . . if the South will give these to the West and the West will go with the South on the tariff." Gadsden had written Calhoun in the same vein: "Now is the time to meet our Western friends at Memphis — to set the ball in motion which must bring the Valley to the South; and make them feel as allies of the

Great Commercial and Agricultural interests — instead of the Tax gathering and monopolizing interests of the North."³³

Just as he had recently strayed from strict construction in the Texas joint resolution, Calhoun now gave his support, with reservations, to internal improvements at federal expense. In his key speech before the convention he referred to the valley as a great "Inland Sea." The time had arrived, he stated, when it should receive financial assistance from the government equal to that already appropriated for the Atlantic Coast, the Great Lakes, and the Gulf. Hedging on the constitutional question, he agreed with many of the nineteen resolutions passed by the convention. These called for the deepening of the Ohio and Mississippi rivers, the construction of levees, railroads, and canals, the improvement of harbors and aids to navigation, the location of foundries, armories, and dry docks in the West, and similar projects.³⁴

In his speech Calhoun was somewhat expansive. Later when he introduced the memorial of the convention in the Senate, it was referred to a special committee of which he was appointed chairman. The report of this committee, which he drew up, rejected some of the recommendations on constitutional grounds. It was a superb example of the logic-chopping at which he was a master. Congress had jurisdiction, not under the general welfare clause or national defense, but under its power to regulate interstate commerce. It could authorize specific projects only where the river passed through more than two states, and it could construct harbors only for shelter or naval stations, not for commercial purposes.

He rejected the ship canal from the Great Lakes to the Mississippi, but he urged that the national government grant alternate sections of lands for railroads and canals and that it reduce the duty on rails.³⁵ The specific legislation introduced by his committee was a bill setting up a three-man board of engineers to survey the main rivers of the Mississippi Valley in order to determine how navigation on them could be improved. Because of the split between Northwest and Southwest over the Wilmot Proviso, no legislation resulted. Even if Congress had responded favorably, Polk would probably have used the veto as he did on the rivers-and-harbors bill of 1846.

Consternation arose in South Carolina when the legislature received the first report of Calhoun's speech to the convention. Had it been received earlier, his election to the Senate might have been defeated. More accurate reports of his remarks prevented the passage of resolutions of disapproval which had been planned, but he was unable to carry the state with him in his new position. "It is indeed lamentable," commented the *Mercury*, "for more reasons than one that Mr. Calhoun had anything to do with the Memphis Convention." His action was generally regarded as a bid for the presidency, but he scorned the suggestion that he publicly deny any ambitions.[36] His enlightened opportunism in the matter contrasted with the narrow particularism of his state, and as a direct consequence Congress lowered the tariff in 1846.

*   *   *

The major issues of the Polk administration were the threatened war with England over Oregon and the war with Mexico, both of which found Calhoun leading the opposition. In his stand on the tariff he was supported by the President, although he earlier had doubts as to the soundness of the new executive on that matter. With assurance that England was about to repeal her Corn Laws and thus open her market to American wheat, Secretary of Treasury Robert J. Walker presented a careful report advocating significant tariff reductions. The bill of 1846, with the support of western Democrats, passed by a vote of 114 to 95 in the House and 28 to 27 in the Senate; only a single Whig vote in the House was cast in the affirmative. As Calhoun put it, the bill was "but the first step to a strictly revenue bill."[37] It abolished all specific duties and minimums and prepared the way for further reduction in 1857. But already the older questions of bank, land, and tariff were assuming secondary importance before the crucial issue of the exclusion of slavery from the territories.

Partly because Polk did not take Calhoun fully into his confidence, the Carolinian feared that the President by his actions regarding Oregon was exposing the nation to a war with both England and Mexico which might prove fatal. The two differed in that Polk's policy of "looking John Bull in the eye" involved the definite risk of war; the Senator believed the risk was unnecessary and dangerous. Actually Polk's strategy proved astute. Though he came out in his inaugural message for 54°40′, almost immediately he secretly offered England the 49th parallel as a compromise, which Pakenham rejected (the United States had made the same proposal several times before). But learning that Foreign Secretary

Aberdeen had condemned his minister's action and had expressed concern as to whether the United States would renew its offer, the President proceeded to apply constant pressure. First he asked Congress for authority to terminate the joint-occupation agreement, which was granted in the spring of 1846; then, when England in June proposed the 49th parallel as a compromise, he asked the Senate for its advice. Upon receiving that body's confirmation he ordered the signing of the treaty, thus cleverly avoiding the charge of inconsistency for his actions.

Calhoun was acutely disturbed by the danger of war with a powerful England. He successfully fought for an amendment to the notice of termination resolution allowing the President "at his discretion" to delay notice until a later date. Thus he felt he had prevented war by keeping open the door to compromise. On March 16, 1846, in the course of debate in the Senate Calhoun defined his position at length. He still believed in the efficacy of the "masterful inactivity" he had earlier advocated, and he refuted the charge that he was sacrificing Oregon for Texas. "In the case of Texas, time was against us; — in that of Oregon, time was with us; and hence the difference in my course of policy in reference to them."[38] But privately he saw that war with England over Oregon might lose the nation Texas in a war with Mexico. He feared war also because of the impetus it would give to centralization in government: "No one can realize the disasters which would follow the war, should there be one," he wrote his son Andrew. "I fear neither our liberty nor constitution would survive."[39]

For the same reason he opposed, to the great loss of his popularity in the South, the war with Mexico which broke out before the termination of the Oregon business. Polk's expansion program included Oregon, California, the Southwest, and the Rio Grande boundary for Texas. Hoping to obtain all of this southwestern territory by negotiation and purchase, he sent John Slidell to Mexico in the fall of 1845 with instructions to offer five million dollars for New Mexico or twenty million if California were included. In return for cession of the territory between the Nueces and the Rio Grande, which Texas claimed but to which Mexico's title was superior, Slidell was to offer assumption by the United States of unsettled claims against Mexico held by American citizens. When the Mexican government refused to receive Slidell, Polk may have decided to take the whole Southwest by force, for in January he ordered Taylor to move to the Rio Grande. Taylor advanced in March and a month later was attacked by the Mexicans. News of the attack was received in Washington on May 9, but Polk had already induced his cabinet the preceding day to support his decision to ask Congress for a declaration of war on the grounds of Slidell's rejection. This incident, however, enabled him to ask Congress instead to recognize a state of war, since Mexico had "shed American blood on American soil."

In midwinter Senator John M. Clayton of Delaware had informed the horrified Calhoun of Polk's provocative orders to Taylor. Clayton urged that some Democrat in Congress should inaugurate a movement to have the orders rescinded, but Calhoun could not act for fear of breaking with the President and thus endangering the more vital objective of peace with England. In May he sought in vain to delay a formal congressional declaration, and he refused to vote on the final question. In his opinion, war could have been easily avoided. The action taken by the President deliberately to provoke it was a clear violation of the Constitution; the executive had usurped the power of the legislative branch to declare war. "It was just as impossible for him to vote for the preamble," he indignantly informed the Senate, "as it was for him to plunge a dagger into his own heart, and more so."[40]

When hostilities started he advocated that the United States adopt a purely defensive strategy by holding a line in the extreme north of Mexico and merely repelling attacks upon it. Late in 1847 he introduced resolutions to this effect, but they never came to a vote. Particularly was he opposed to the movement to conquer and annex all of Mexico, and he spoke and voted against the administration's Ten Regiment Bill in the spring of 1848. But he realized the futility of opposition to the war. "Our people are like a young man of 18," he admitted, "full of health and vigour and disposed for adventure of any description, but without wisdom or experience to guide him, and I fear that we shall have the fate which usually befall such. While I admire the spirit, I regret to see it misdirected."[41]

He opposed the war, first, because he knew from his own early experience that rampant nationalism and expansion accelerated centralization. "Mexico is to us the forbidden fruit," he warned, "the penalty of eating it would be to subject our institutions to political death."[42] But his more practical reason was his desire to prevent the annexation of territory which might turn the balance in the

Senate against the South. Since Texas might be divided into as many as five states, the parity between slave and free states might be maintained if no more new territory than Oregon were annexed. Even before the Wilmot Proviso he saw that the conflict over the new area won by the war would lead to bitterness between the sections,[43] and he feared that the South would be the loser in the conflict. Waddy Thompson, the late minister to Mexico, had convinced him that the Mexican area was unsuited to slavery; territories in which slaves were unprofitable would enter the Union as free states.

In boldly taking this position he placed himself in a minority both in the Democratic party and in the South, for the Southwest and Northwest were eager for expansion. On this issue he joined the Whigs and New England against his former friends, thereby breaking his new alliance with the West and destroying any chances for the nomination in 1848. A Georgia correspondent of Howell Cobb reported that "Mr. Calhoun has killed himself about here as far as Democratic support goes. I have not heard the first Democrat sustain his course on the War bill."[44]

His followers were dismayed at his determined opposition to the war and the administration. Had he led his section into the conflict, wrote Dixon Lewis sadly to Crallé,

> all the politicians in the country could not have kept him from being President.... I told him I wished he had a little more of that "masterly inactivity" which would keep him from risking himself and his friends on occasions when all he had to do was to keep out of the traps and ambuscades set for him by his enemies. He reminds me of a great general, who wins great battles and then throws away his life in a street fracas. By his self-sacrificing course particularly over the Mexican War he has lost the presidency, and he has put himself in a position where not a friend he had out of Carolina could sustain him *and live.*[45]

CHAPTER FOURTEEN

Crisis Again

AS Calhoun feared, the war with Mexico produced another serious crisis between slave and free states, the outcome of which he did not live to see. In this critical period his balance of power strategy fell far short of his expectations. Early in the war, after initial victories on the tariff and the independent treasury, his new alliance with the West was broken largely because of western discontent at not getting the whole of Oregon. The rupture enabled northern antislavery forces to align some disgruntled westerners and some manufacturers offended by the recent reduction of the tariff in an antisouthern bloc. This political trend was evident when David Wilmot in August, 1846, introduced his bitterly fought proviso excluding slavery from any territory obtained from Mexico. In response to resolutions from eleven of the fifteen free-state legislatures, a northern majority in the House several times passed the proviso. Each time the southerners in the Senate blocked it.

"What is to come of all this," Calhoun wrote his daughter at the end of 1846, "time only can disclose. The present indication is, that the South will be united in opposition to the Scheme. If they regard their safety they must defeat it even if the union should be rent asunder.... I desire above all things to save the whole; but if that cannot be, to save the portion where Providence has cast my lot, at all events."[1]

In characteristic fashion he assumed a bold position on territories by introducing in the Senate a series of resolutions in February, 1847. Later to be accepted partially by the Supreme Court in the Dred Scott decision, at the moment they were not brought to a vote. Arguing from his state sovereignty and compact thesis, he asserted that the federal government held the territories in trust for the states, that its control under the Constitution applied only to public lands, and that Congress could not forbid any citizen of a state to take his property, recognized and protected by the Constitution, into the area. Under this interpretation the Missouri Compromise had violated the Constitution. But neither could the people of a territory, despite the new popular sovereignty theory soon to be advanced by Lewis Cass of Michigan, deny a slaveholder his rights. Not until a territory entered the Union as a sovereign state could it decide the question for itself; a republican form of government was the only restriction Congress could place on its admittance.

In an accompanying speech he made his position clear. Were the South excluded from the territories, there would in time be twelve more free states than slave, leaving it entirely at the mercy of the North. Such destruction of the balance between the sections would lead to "revolution, anarchy, and civil war." But a remedy lay in the Constitution: "Ours is a Federal Constitution, of which the States are parties, and they — the 'States United' — own jointly the territories."

> I may speak as an individual member of that section of the Union. There is my family and connections; there I drew my first breath; there are all my hopes. I am a Southern man and a slaveholder — a kind and merciful one, I trust — and none the worse for being a slaveholder. I say, for one, I would rather meet any extremity upon earth than give up one inch of our equality — one inch of what belongs to us as members of this great republic.[2]

In a Charleston mass meeting the following month he elaborated upon his analysis of the situation. The exigencies of contemporary politics had produced the attack upon slavery. Northern politicians cared little about slavery, but since their section was more populous and since the major parties were so evenly divided there, they had increasingly appealed for the support of the 5 per cent who were abolitionists. In defense the South should unite and exert an even stronger pressure upon the national parties. Southerners had only to defend their rights as spiritedly as their enemies attacked them:

> Henceforward, let all party distinctions among us cease, so long as this aggression on our rights and honor shall continue.... But far be it from us to desire to be forced on our own resources for protection. Our object is to preserve the Union of these States, if it can be done consistently with our rights, safety, and perfect equality with other members of the Union. On this we have a right to insist. Less we cannot take.[3]

The rapid settlement of the Far West, particularly after the gold rush of 1849, made the organization of formal government essential in that area; but the two houses of Congress were deadlocked by the dispute over slavery in the territories. Four different solutions had been proposed. At the two extremes were the total exclusion stipulated in the Wilmot Proviso and the total inclusion demanded by Calhoun. Possible compromises were the extension of the 36°30′ line to the Pacific or popular sovereignty (letting the territorial legislatures decide the question for themselves). Most southerners favored, with President Polk, the extension of the Missouri Compromise line as a practical measure, but even extension would not ensure slave states if slaves were not taken into the region. Popular sovereignty, should slavery prove unprofitable in the new area, would result eventually in a free state majority.

The fight in Congress developed heat in the summer of 1848 over the bill to organize the territory of Oregon. When the House passed a bill prohibiting slavery in the territory, the Senate answered with a substitute called the "Clayton Compromise." Actually it was drawn up by a committee of two members of each party from each house under the chairmanship of John M. Clayton, a Delaware Whig. It proposed the organization of Oregon without slavery, but with a grant to its territorial legislature of power to act in the matter, and the organization of California and New Mexico without the grant to their legislatures of power over slavery, thus leaving the decision in these territories to the courts. The Senate passed a bill to this effect, but the House rejected it. Polk stated that Calhoun, anticipating its passage, sought from him a pledge that only southern men would be appointed to territorial judgeships, and that the Senator also at first opposed the right of appeal from territorial courts to the Supreme Court.

The Senate Committee on Territories sought to water down the House bill by adding a phrase that slavery was excluded because Oregon was north of the 30°36′ parallel. Thereupon Calhoun announced that he would vote both against the original bill because it assumed that Congress had power to legislate on slavery in the territories, and against the revised bill because it gave the South no assurance in regard to California and New Mexico.[4] To preserve the Union, however, he might accept a compromise were one sincerely offered by the North. At this point Douglas proposed an amendment extending the Missouri Compromise line to the Pacific. Calhoun voted for the amendment and against the bill, but both of them passed the Senate by a considerable majority. When the House rejected this second compromise, its original bill was finally accepted by the upper house. After long hesitation President Polk decided against a veto.

*   *   *

In his final speech on the Oregon bill Calhoun called upon all senators for broad action to save the nation. He was convinced, he said, that "the Union and the institutions of the country are in imminent danger." The issue was deeper than the Wilmot Proviso; it involved an honest recognition of all the rights of the South under the Constitution. The extension of the Missouri Compromise line, "even if it should put at rest the Proviso, would not stop abolitionism, or prevent it from accomplishing its end." Through the action of private citizens, and even of state laws, the North had encouraged the theft of southern property in slaves. It had permitted the formation of societies which were attacking southern slaveowners and institutions and which were seeking to incite a slave insurrection. Even if the Proviso were defeated, the growing demand that slavery be abolished in the District of Columbia and in national forts and navy yards was equally serious.

Again Calhoun called upon the South to defy this aggression, which if unchecked would end in compulsory emancipation: "Nothing short of the united and fixed determination of the South to maintain her rights at every hazard, can stop it." He demanded that the North suppress antislavery agitation:

> Notwithstanding we have so much less to fear from disunion, we are profoundly anxious to preserve the Union, if it can be done consistently with our liberty and safety. It is for you to

say by your acts, whether it can be preserved on these conditions or not. I say by your acts; for we have been too often deceived to rely on your promises or pledges. The only proof we can accept, is for you to desist from your agitation and assaults on our rights, and to respect the compromise of the constitution. Until this is done... we are bound by the highest obligation of duty to ourselves and our posterity, to continue our resistance... and to adopt whatever measures may be necessary to make it successful.[5]

Already he was planning to call a southern convention, but he postponed the move until after the presidential election. According to Hammond, Calhoun "furiously" opposed the nomination of Lewis Cass by the Democrats. He stated privately, asserted Foote, that he would "prefer the election of *any respectable southern planter* whatever to any man of *northern birth and residence.*" Surely Zachary Taylor was his personal preference, but he could hardly have risked a return to the Whigs. He abandoned the idea of a movement for the Whig candidate in South Carolina, the Georgia Whig Robert Toombs charged, only because he "found all the upper part of the State strongly against him."[6]

Shortly after Taylor's victory the House passed a bill for the abolition of the slave trade in the District of Columbia by a vote of 98 to 88 on December 21. Two days later in response to a call from Foote of Mississippi and Hunter of Virginia, 69 of the 118 southerners in Congress met in the Senate chamber. At this meeting a special committee of fifteen was appointed to prepare an address to the people of the South. This larger committee selected a subcommittee of five, with Calhoun as chairman, to draft the address.

At the various meetings of these committees and the larger southern caucus held the next month, southern Whigs attended largely to defeat the whole movement. At the outset they failed by a vote of 8 to 7 to pass a motion that it was inexpedient to issue any address, and gradually they absented themselves from the sessions. For that reason they were unable to substitute a milder address for the one written by Calhoun, but they did force him to consent to several modifications and to change the title to an "Address to the People of the United States." Never did more than 88 southern congressmen attend the sessions, and only 48 signed the final version, of whom 46 were Democrats.

Restating his recent speeches, Calhoun's address called upon southerners to unite in a demand that attacks upon slavery cease. Unless abolition agitation were immediately checked, the address predicted, the ultimate result would be not merely emancipation but the acquisition by the Negroes of the right to vote and to hold office. The blacks would then unite politically with the North and hold southern whites in permanent subjection.[7]

Toombs claimed that the Whigs had defeated Calhoun's main objective (Toombs himself a year later would threaten secession unless the South obtained concessions on slavery in return for the admission of California):

> We have . . . foiled Calhoun in his miserable attempt to form a southern party. . . . I told him that the Union of the South was neither possible nor desirable until we were ready to dissolve the Union, — that we certainly did not intend to advise the people now to look anywhere else than to their own government for the prevention of apprehended evils, — that we did not expect an administration which we had brought into power would do any act or permit any act to be done which it would become necessary for our safety to rebel at . . . and that we intended to stand by the government until it committed an overt act of aggression upon our rights, which neither we nor the country ever expected.[8]

Thus the Whigs rejected Calhoun's attempt at southern unanimity. (After his death the southern public as a whole would repudiate the Nashville Convention when Congress passed the Compromise of 1850.) Though they disliked him personally and feared that he was seeking to strengthen the Democratic party at their expense, they fought his proposal upon more fundamental grounds. Even after the admission of California as a free state, most of them continued to believe that southern rights and interests were sufficiently secure. Many of them would remain in the Union regardless of restrictions that might be imposed upon slavery. "Patriotism should prompt the North to abstain from urging the proviso," argued the Mobile *Advertiser*, "and, if the proviso be adopted, patriotism should prompt the South to cling still to the Union." Denying any affection for the proviso, the New Orleans *Bee* announced that "the South will have none of Mr. Calhoun's desperate remedies."[9] But the Senator from South Carolina persisted in his efforts for a southern convention, and in October, 1849, Mississippi issued a call to her sister states for a meeting in Nashville the following summer.

*   *   *

Calhoun's intentions in the last year of his life must be determined from his speeches in the Senate, his letters and private conversations, and his two works on government which were published posthumously. Clearly his strategy was still opportunistic, for on the very eve of his death in March, 1850, he denied that he had ever advocated secession.[10] Since he was obviously seeking to exert pressure on the North and to arouse the South, however, his words cannot be taken at face value. Upon occasion both his emotions and the clarity of his thinking were affected by his illness.

Intellectually Calhoun, a conservative, was closer to the Whigs, but the exigencies of politics had made him a Democrat. In the 1820's he had joined what Van Buren called the alliance between "the planters of the South and the plain Republicans of the North." After an enforced isolation in the next decade, he returned to this alliance; but his return was both skeptical and tentative. Foreseeing as early as 1844 that "a split between us and the northern democracy is inevitable,"[11] he turned for a brief period to the plain republicans of the West. This stratagem also ended in failure, and at the end of his life he was working for a rapprochement with the northern commercial interests whom he had joined in the fight against Jackson.

Ever since the nullification crisis, in fact, Calhoun had consciously kept the door open for an alliance either with the West or with the conservatives of the Northeast. Early in the 1830's he had predicted the inevitability of the class struggle in the increasingly capitalistic society of the United States:*

> As the community becomes more populous, wealthy, refined and highly civilized, the difference between the rich and the poor will become more strongly marked; and the number of the ignorant and dependent greater in proportion to the rest of the com-

*Richard N. Current presents a provocative but somewhat exaggerated Marxian interpretation of Calhoun's position in an article in the *Antioch Review* (Summer, 1943), entitled "John C. Calhoun, Philosopher of Reaction." Richard Hofstadter (*American Political Tradition*, New York, 1948) argues that Calhoun correctly analyzed the direction of social evolution, but misjudged its velocity.

munity. With the increase of this difference, the tendency to conflict between them will become stronger; and, as the poor and dependent become more numerous... there will be... no want of leaders among the wealthy and ambitious, to excite and direct them in their efforts to obtain the control.

He was amazed that northern conservatives had not at once realized the value of nullification as a defense against such a development. Since the "wealthy and talented of the North" would be the first victims of a mass uprising, "the intelligence of the North must see this, but whether in time to save themselves and the institutions of the country God only knows."[12]

In this regard a significant passage from his second speech on the Oregon bill in the summer of 1848 should be quoted:

> I aim not at change or revolution. My object is to preserve. I am thoroughly conservative in my politics. I wish to maintain things as I found them established. I am satisfied with them, and am of the opinion that they cannot be changed for the better. I hold it to be difficult to get a good government, and still more difficult to preserve it, and as I believe a good government to be the greatest of earthly blessings, I would be adverse to the overthrow of ours, even if I thought it greatly inferior to what I do, in the hope of establishing a better. Thus thinking, my sincere desire is to preserve the Union.[13]*

His contemporary comments in letters to his family expressed strong disapproval of the revolutions of 1848 in Europe. He rejoiced at the failure of the Chartists in England: "Had they been successful, it would have been long — very long, before order and authority would be restored." He had hope for Germany because her internal circumstances were similar to those of the United States, but France was "not prepared to become a Republick." In his opinion "what is called the progress party, both in this country and in Europe, have not advanced beyond Dorrism [a radical movement for manhood suffrage in Rhode Island in the 1840's]; that is, the right of a mere majority to overturn law and constitution at its will and pleasure." He voted with the minority against a resolution congratulating the French upon their establishment of the Second Republic.[14]

*He had expressed the same idea even more forcefully a decade earlier in his speech (1837) on the Michigan bill (*Works*, II, 614 ff.).

At the same time he openly refuted the Declaration of Independence and Jefferson by denying the "prevalent opinion that all men are born free and equal" and the related concept of a "state of nature." Men were certainly not equal at birth or later, for they were born subject to the authority of their parents, the state, and the institutions of society. A state of nature was "purely hypothetical. It never did, nor can exist; as it is inconsistent with the preservation and perpetuation of the race. . . . His [man's] natural state is the social and political."[15]

The fear of northern conservatives at the European revolutions in 1848 made his new strategy timely. What he offered them, in return for their concession to southern demands on slavery, was the political support of the South against their own growing proletariat. There could be no doubt about the certainty of this support, since no conflict existed in the South between capital and labor — the latter being Negro slaves. Calhoun could not openly propose such a bargain, but he was clearly hinting at it in his Oregon speech when he urged, as a reason for northern acceptance of slavery, the fact that "from the conservative nature of the institution, it would prevent that conflict between labor and capital, which must ever exist in populous and crowded communities, where wages are the regulator between them." An independent South would be secure from revolution, but the North "would, with the increase of its population and wealth, be subject to all the agitation and conflicts growing out of the divisions of . . . capital and labor, of which already there are so many and so serious." Earlier he had expressed the same idea when he stated that the "blessing of [slavery] extends beyond the limits of the South. It makes that section the balancer of the system; the great conservative power, which prevents other portions, less fortunately constituted, from rushing into conflict."[16]

Probably the event which induced Calhoun to attempt a southern convention was the success of the Free Soil party in 1848 under his old enemy Van Buren. That party, which polled almost 300,000 votes, was unmistakably antislavery and antisouthern — a purely sectional party. He sought to meet this threat by calling for a showdown. He was for the Union, he told a Kentucky friend, "but if that could not be preserved, he was for taking care of the South." Despite the strong southern Whig opposition, he went ahead with his convention move "to present with an unbroken front to the North the alternative of dissolving the partnership or of ceasing . . .

to disregard the stipulations of the Constitution in our favor."[17] If the South must soon choose between union and disunion, a convention "would give us the great advantage of enjoying the conscious feeling of having done all we could to save it, and thereby free us from all responsibility in reference to it, while it would afford the most efficient means of united and prompt action." Yet his words here must be discounted, for he had to persuade the South first in order to frighten the North. When he died he had not made a final decision himself, nor had he launched a movement directed irrevocably at secession.

Actually Calhoun's tactics in his last year were a combination of force and persuasion. A formal convention of the southern states would convince the North of the southerners' determination to insist upon their rights; the threat of secession would influence it to yield to southern demands. In his Senate speeches he reminded northern business interests of their tremendous economic stake in the southern market, which a southern confederacy could severely restrict by a tariff on imports from the United States. And in case they hoped to prevent secession by coercion, he advanced various arguments to prove that the South possessed sufficient military strength to achieve its independence. "It is not for us who are assailed," he asserted, "but for those who assail us, to count the value of the Union." At the same time, employing the gentler method of persuasion, he made a feverish effort to complete his two works on government. In them he insisted that the South was asking not for new concessions, but merely for the observation of her constitutional rights. It was her simple request that the federal republic established by the states in 1789 be restored to its pristine form.[18]

As free-soil sentiment increased in the North, Calhoun at times lost confidence in both the Whigs and the Democrats. "The prospect is as things now stand," he wrote in 1849, "that before four years have elapsed, the Union will be divided into two great hostile sectional parties."[19] Yet he was not foolishly seeking to form an exclusively southern party, but a new party which would include a united South and sufficient northerners to constitute a majority in the nation. Such was the identical purpose of the Constitutional Union party established by southern Whigs in 1860.

*　　　*　　　*

In both the *Disquisition on Government* and the *Discourse on the Constitution and Government of the United States,* therefore, Calhoun was writing mainly to convince a northern audience. As in his earlier Exposition, he selected his premises from his conclusions, but his arguments are regarded as the ablest defense ever made of the state sovereignty and strict construction interpretation of the Constitution. Possessing an acute historical sense and aware of the dynamics of social evolution, he was also putting on record his studied conclusions in regard to the nature of government and politics. In the first volume he discussed the historical evolution of government in general, based on a comparative study of specific instances such as the Roman Empire, Poland, and England. In a second and longer volume he examined the evolution of American government in the light of these postulates.*

Government, argued Calhoun, is essential to the preservation of society because man's individual feelings are stronger than his social. It must therefore be given the power of coercion. But since laws are administered by men, both under a popular and a monarchical government this power tends to be abused. To reduce the abuse of power, constitutions are established, defining its limits and providing means for checking its abuse. "Power can only be resisted by power — and tendency by tendency," he argued. "Those who exercise power and those subject to its exercise, — the rulers and the ruled, — stand in antagonistic relations to each other. The same constitution of our nature which leads rulers to oppress the ruled, — regardless of the object for which government is ordained, — will with equal strength lead the ruled to resist, when possessed of the means of making peaceable and effective resistance."[20]

The means of such resistance (this was his fundamental premise) can be provided only by a constitutional recognition of the principle of the concurrent rather than the absolute majority. Each major interest in a nation — and he ignored the difficult question of how such major interests would be determined — must be given the power of vetoing legislation. Earlier he had illustrated this point by citing a community consisting of twenty-four members, divided into a major interest of thirteen and a minor interest of eleven.

*For the application of Calhoun's theory to a current issue, see Mitchell Franklin, "The Roman Origin and the American Justification of the Tribunitial or Veto Power in the Charter of the United Nations," *Tulane Law Review,* XXII (Oct., 1947), 24-61.

Under an absolute numerical majority system the thirteen members of the major group could pass any law they desired; but under a concurrent system the approval of a majority of each group would be required — i.e., a minimum of seven votes from the larger group and of six from the smaller.

In support of his panacea he argued that

> the concurrent majority tends to unite the most opposite and conflicting interests, and to blend the whole into one common attachment to the country. By giving to each interest, or portion, the power of self-protection, all strife and struggle between them for ascendancy is prevented. . . . Under the combined influence of these causes, the interest of each would be merged in the common interest of the whole; and thus, the community would become a unit, by becoming a common centre of attachment of all its parts. And hence, instead of faction, strife, and struggle for party ascendancy, there would be patriotism, nationality, harmony, and a struggle only for supremacy in promoting to common good of the whole.[21]

Obviously Calhoun regarded the North and the South as the two major interests in the United States, but he expressed his idea in terms of the majority and the minority. Were the minority not given power to protect itself, it would become disaffected and weaken the nation, as New England had done during the War of 1812. It might even attempt to disrupt the nation, as the South would do in 1861. Not only did justice and the preservation of individual and regional liberty require the acceptance of the concurrent principle, but it was equally essential to permanent national strength. And in practice the rule of the absolute majority often became the rule of a numerical minority — the majority group within the majority party.

In the *Discourse* Calhoun argued that the federal republic created in 1787-1789 had gradually been perverted into a consolidated democracy. For the concurrent principle, intentionally written into the fundamental law by the framers of the Constitution, had been substituted government by the absolute numerical majority. Only in the House, according to that document, did the absolute majority prevail; in the Senate, in the executive, in the judiciary, and in the amending process, the minority had been given power equal to the majority.

He listed various acts and developments which had destroyed

the *federal* structure of the government: the section in the Judiciary Act of 1789 permitting appeals from state to federal courts; the act of 1791 establishing the Bank of the United States; the Alien and Sedition Acts; the War of 1812; the Missouri Compromise; the Tariff of 1828; the Force Bill of 1833; the spoils system and the growth of executive power; the usurpation of the power of judicial review by the Supreme Court and its broad construction of the Constitution; the control of the presidency by the same majority which dominated the House; and the corruption of political parties arising from patronage. As a consequence a northern majority organized in a sectional party could dominate all branches of the national government. Unless the whole development were reversed, monarchy or disunion in his opinion were inevitable.

As a solution he proposed the repeal of certain acts, particularly the 25th section of the Judiciary Act of 1789, the Force Bill, and "all acts by which the money power is carried beyond its constitutional limits." The powers of the states must be restored and the "executive department must be rigidly restricted within its assigned limits." But the mere restoration of the government to its original form would not be enough, since the means of preventing diseases "are not usually sufficient to *remedy* them." Some organic means must be found to re-establish the equilibrium between North and South; he suggested as a possibility the creation of a dual executive, one elected by each section and each having an independent veto power. More enthusiastically, he cited his own state of South Carolina as a model, where the tidewater minority had been given control of the upper house of the legislature and the upcountry majority control of the lower. Even in the latter, however, property owners were given disproportionate representation in that half the members were allotted on the basis of white population and the other half on the basis of taxes paid. Could Calhoun have been hinting that the wealthy be given an extra vote?

One political scientist has analyzed the successive positions adopted by the South as a conscious minority.[22] These, he concludes, were the principle of local self-government, which ended with the Missouri Compromise of 1820; of the concurrent voice, which ended with the admission of California in 1850; of constitutional guarantees, upon which it relied from 1850 to 1860; and of southern independence, which it attempted in 1861. As a corollary a fifth should be added — the threat of secession which the South used so effectively in the decade before the Civil War.

Though Calhoun died in 1850, he was the intellectual father of all five of these principles. While defending one position, he was constantly forced, by his acute realization of the South's minority status, to prepare the next line of defense should retreat become necessary. Inevitably both his strategy and his tactics were opportunistic. On the record he disagreed with most of his southern colleagues in 1850 in refusing to accept constitutional guarantees, which he regarded as mere verbal assurances that would later be broken, in the place of the concurrent voice. Should California be admitted as a free state, he proposed to restore the concurrent principle by a constitutional amendment. Were the amendment rejected, one logical alternative was secession.

But it cannot be stated that Calhoun favored independence if southern equality were lost in the Senate; in fact, he specifically denied it. With his penchant for taking the highest ground, and in view of his willingness to accept an extension of the Missouri line at a time when he was vigorously defending the right of slaveholders to migrate to all territories, he was probably attempting to obtain stronger constitutional guarantees than otherwise would have been granted. Death took him before he indicated what would have been the minimum terms he would have accepted rather than disrupt the Union.

*   *   *

During the month of January, 1849, when he was fighting for the adoption of his address by the southern caucus, Calhoun fainted three times in the lobby of the Senate. While he made light of these attacks to his daughter, apparently he realized that his death was near. On one of these occasions he told Rhett, who hurried to him, that his career was almost over and that the battle must be carried on by "you younger men." In the winter he suffered a severe attack of bronchitis which affected his heart. Though his condition improved in the spring and the summer, which he spent at Fort Hill, his friends sought to dissuade him from returning to the Senate. In fact, both Rhett and Hammond were making discreet inquiries in South Carolina about the expected vacancy. But the old warrior insisted that he must "renew his labors in defense of the Constitution and the preservation of the Union," and when

Congress convened in December he was in his seat.[23] He moved to a mess closer to Capitol Hill and resumed personal relations with Clay, from whom he had been estranged for years. At once he attacked President Taylor's message in January recommending the admission of California under the free-state constitution drawn up by its residents.

Once again, as in 1841, the victorious Whigs were split, with Clay and a group of southern insurgents under Toombs leading the fight against the new President. Secretly Taylor had sent word to California and New Mexico that he would support their admission regardless of the provisions on slavery in their constitutions. Later when Toombs and Stephens threatened secession unless the South were granted concessions, he angrily told them that he would not hesitate to use the army to preserve the Union. Southern Whig insurgents were willing to admit California as a free state, but demanded certain compensations on slavery in return. Actually they had come to an unofficial agreement with northern Democrats on the terms of compromise, which Douglas as chairman of the Senate Committee on Territories was planning to introduce as separate measures. Instead, at the end of January Clay proposed eight resolutions, most of which a special Senate committee grouped in an "Omnibus Bill." But President Taylor and the vast majority of northern Whigs opposed it; after several months of debate, despite the eloquent speeches of Clay and Webster for it, the Senate rejected the Omnibus.*

Before the end of January Calhoun's condition took such a turn for the worst that he could no longer participate actively in debate. In his speech for his compromise Clay begged both sections to make concessions to save the Union. He told the North that the Wilmot Proviso was unnecessary because nature had permanently excluded slavery from the territories, and that it should accept a federal fugitive slave law in compliance with the Constitution. Calhoun was anxious to reply, but lacked the strength. Finally he consented to have his answer read by his colleague, Senator Andrew P. But-

---

*After the death of Taylor and Calhoun, Douglas and the Democrats put essentially the same terms of compromise through both houses in a series of separate bills. Clay's proposals had offered the North the admission of California as a free state and the abolition of the slave trade (not slavery) in the District; the South a strict federal fugitive slave law, the organization of the territories of Utah and New Mexico without restriction on slavery, and noninterference with the domestic slave trade.

ler; but because of poor eyesight Butler passed it on to a younger messmate, James M. Mason of Virginia. Emaciated and wrapped in flannels, the author gesticulated to emphasize his points as Mason on March 4 read the words he had written. According to Mrs. Davis, his friends feared he would die on the floor.

His arguments were a condensed version of the works on government which he was still in the process of revising. "I have, Senators," he began, "believed from the first that the agitation of the subject of slavery would, if not prevented by some timely and effective measure, end in disunion." He repeated the various wrongs the South had endured, but he placed his major emphasis upon the fact that she no longer possessed adequate power to protect herself. Already heavily outnumbered in the House and in the electoral college, with the admission of more free states in the next decade the South would probably be outnumbered in the Senate by ten votes. It was "a great mistake to suppose that disunion can be effected by a single blow [for] the cords which bound these States together in one common Union, are far too numerous and powerful for that"; but the cords were already breaking. Three of the main Protestant denominations were in the process of schism into northern and southern branches, and a similar split was imminent in the two national political parties.

The North must therefore assure the South that her runaway slaves would be returned; stop all agitation against slavery by private citizens; allow the South an equal share in the public domain; and consent to an amendment restoring the original equilibrium between the sections. "If you, who represent the stronger portion," he concluded, "cannot agree to settle...on the broad principle of justice and duty, say so; and let the States we both represent agree to separate and depart in peace. If you are unwilling we should part in peace, tell us so, and we shall know what to do, when you reduce the question to submission or resistance."[24]

Thus Calhoun formally demanded complete surrender by the North on all issues, as he had done earlier in 1833 in his speeches against the Force Bill. Most of all he insisted upon what Hammond called an "equality of power" for the South, both by the rejection of California and an amendment to the Constitution. It is significant, therefore, that his fellow southern Democrat Foote the next day attacked his proposals on this very point. The Mississippian had supported the southern caucus, but all along he had favored the admission of California. He had even urged Calhoun, since admission was inevitable, to come out for it and thereby win the sympathy of the new state for the South. He argued spiritedly that most southerners disagreed with Calhoun, that no amendment was necessary, that Calhoun's remarks had encouraged disunion sentiment, and that the disputed questions could be settled honorably within ten days.[25] Obviously Foote had become an ardent supporter of Clay's compromise; a year later his state would confirm his stand by electing him governor over Jefferson Davis. Calhoun arrived in the midst of the Mississippian's remarks and pronounced them a personal affront. A dramatic scene followed with the Senate so strongly in sympathy with the dying man that even his enemy Benton called Foote a coward.

In his rebuttal the Carolinian insisted that an amendment *was* necessary for southern security. As for the charge that he condemned the whole North as hostile to the South, he answered that "there were three divisions of sentiment in the North on the subject. The first (and it constitutes but a small portion) believes the institution of slavery immoral; — a larger portion believe it to be criminal; — and all believe it to be a blot on our national escutcheon. ... Whenever it comes to a question, all parties would join in fighting against the South." But later in his remarks he protested that "if I am judged by my acts, I trust I shall be found as firm a friend of the Union as any man within it."[26]

After Webster's eloquent plea for the compromise on March 7, the two men chatted of their long friendship and their past arguments about the Constitution. "I have no desire to do it now," said Calhoun, and Webster replied that he had "quite as little."[27] They had discussed their respective speeches in several long conferences before their delivery, and there can be no doubt that they were collaborating to produce an acceptable compromise which would save the Union.* The Carolinian was also present several

---

*When James Hamilton asked Calhoun what he should do if Webster succeeded in an adjustment, the Senator replied "nominate him for President. ...I will not only not allow my name to be used against him, but will regard it as a sacred duty to support him." The respect was mutual, for Webster told his future biographer Peter Harvey that Calhoun was the greatest man he had ever met. Waddy Thompson to Webster, Mar. 2, 1850, Webster MSS, Library of Congress; Henry S. Foote, *A Casket of Reminiscences* (Washington, 1872), 43-44; Peter Harvey, *Reminiscences and Anecdotes of Daniel Webster* (Boston, 1877), 219-20.

days later when Seward made his "higher law" attack on the compromise and on slavery. He listened intently and chided Webster for his attempts to heckle the New Yorker, but at the conclusion of Seward's speech, the southerner was heard to say that Seward was "no gentleman." Shortly he told Foote, "the honorable Senator from New York justifies the Northern treachery. I am not the man to hold social intercourse with such as these."[28]

Calhoun appeared in the Senate for the last time on March 13. On that day he debated with Foote and Cass about his earlier speech, and he angrily denied that he had advocated disunion should California be admitted. In this last month of his life he had numerous talks with his fellow southerners, in particular with Rhett, Toombs, and Mason. Clearly he was torn between his desire to save the Union and his growing fear that it could not be preserved if the South was to avoid catastrophe. "Nothing short of the terms I propose," he wrote Clemson, "can settle it finally and permanently. Indeed, it is difficult to see how two peoples so different and hostile can exist together."[29] Once with amazing exactness he predicted to Mason the sequel to the crisis:

> The Union is doomed to dissolution, there is no mistaking the signs. I am satisfied in my judgment even were the questions which now agitate Congress settled to the satisfaction and the concurrence of the Southern States, it would not avert, or materially delay, the catastrophe. I fix its probable occurrence within twelve years or three Presidential terms. You and others of your age, will probably live to see it; I shall not. The mode by which it will be is not so clear; it may be brought about in a manner that none now foresee. But the probability is it will explode in a Presidential election.[30]

Rhett and Morehead of Kentucky both stated that Calhoun prepared a paper contending that secession was the only salvation for the South, and that he even outlined the specific course for South Carolina should she be abandoned by the rest of the South as she had been in 1832. Upon one occasion, in Elijah fashion, he passed on his mantle to Toombs.[31] Against all of this must be placed his open protests to Foote and Cass in the Senate. To the end he hoped against hope that the Union would somehow be miraculously saved; he could not, though logic demanded it, bring himself to initiate a move to disrupt it. "If I had my health and strength to devote one more hour to my country in the Senate," he told his friends the night before he died on March 30, "I could do more than in my whole life."[32]

In considering Calhoun's actions in these last months, it must be borne in mind that it was his predetermined strategy to exert all sorts of pressure upon the North in order to obtain the maximum concessions possible. To do so he must make the South appear to northerners in dead earnest about seceding were the terms of compromise not satisfactory. Otherwise his frequently expressed pessimism as to the prospects of compromise and his unjustified optimism about southern unity would suggest that his primary objective was secession and independence. His pessimism, voiced publicly and privately, served the dual purpose of increasing southern sentiment for the Nashville Convention and of impressing the northern public with the necessity of yielding on the disputed issues as the price of union. Such a course was in keeping with the back-handed tactics of his long political career, particularly in the nullification crisis, and it was confirmed by certain of his statements *after* his speech against compromise.

*   *   *

The South was definitely the loser in the compromise which passed Congress in the fall of 1850. Parity between slave and free states in the Senate ended with the admission of California, depriving the South of the only sure means of vetoing acts of the lower house. Both the basic principles of the Missouri Compromise were abrogated, for the 36°30′ line was not extended to the Pacific. Decision on slavery in the new territories of Utah and New Mexico was left to their legislatures or to the territorial courts, with the right of appeal to the Supreme Court. Nevertheless, southerners repudiated the Nashville Convention and in their state elections of that year voted positively for the compromise and for union. The large majority accepted its terms in good faith.

It should not be overlooked, however, that southern ultras used Calhoun's tactics of the threat of secession with greater success after 1850. The surrender of the northern wing of the Democratic party to southern demands in the next decade disrupted the party and led directly to Lincoln's election. The South won victory after victory on vital sectional issues — the Gadsden Purchase, the Ostend Manifesto, the repeal of the Missouri Compromise, the Dred Scott decision, the tariff reduction of 1857, and Buchanan's veto of the homestead bill in 1859. In disgust anti-Nebraska Democrats helped form the Republican party in 1854, and subsequent southern "aggression" drove increasing numbers of northern farmers, laborers, and businessmen into a new coalition whose union was symbolized by the "Chicago Bargain" at the Republican convention in 1860.

Certainly the War for Southern Independence resulted from such an involved chain of causations that it is absurd to place the major responsibility upon any one man. Had Calhoun not lived, the course of both North and South might have been somewhat different, but it is doubtful that the conflict between those who lived with slavery and those who did not would have been minimized. His tragedy, like that of Cassandra, was that he prophesied and pled to a people who would not hear him; but his failure, like that of Hamlet, was in large part determined by his own personality.

There can be no question of the sincerity of his devotion to the Union. But like Robert E. Lee, to whom history has been far kinder, he put his allegiance to the South ahead of it. The final judgment of the man must take into account this fundamental conflict in loyalties with which he wrestled for so long. "There, indeed, is my only regret at going," he told Rhett shortly before his death. "The South! The poor South!" But for half a century the estimate popularly held by more than half the nation would be the remark overheard by Walt Whitman in a conversation between two Union soldiers a few weeks after Appomatox. The true monuments to Calhoun, said one soldier, were the wasted farms, the broken railroads, the ruined shops, and the gaunt chimneys scattered over the Confederacy.

Appendix

I FOLLOW Gaillard Hunt and William M. Meigs in regarding the *Life of John C. Calhoun, presenting a condensed history of political events from 1811 to 1834* (published anonymously by Harpers in 1843 but currently attributed to Robert M. T. Hunter) as essentially a political autobiography. Hunt's brief article on the subject in the *American Historical Review*, XIII (1908), 311-12, cited a letter from Robert B. Rhett to Calhoun's editor, Richard K. Crallé, October 25, 1854, to this effect:

"There is but one thing written by Mr. Calhoun that you ought not to publish as his — and that is — 'his life.' He wished me to Father it — but I told him that it was impossible for me directly or indirectly to allow any one to understand that I was the author of a publication which I had not written. Hunter and I read it over together in my house at Georgetown. He inserted about a page and a half, and became the putative author; and it has done more to lift him to his present position than anything else in public life."

Hunt came to the conclusion that the "page and a half" inserted by Hunter were the most eulogistic passages; but fully half of the *Life* is eulogistic. Yet such evidence is not necessary to convict Calhoun of an inordinate vanity; his other works and speeches do that.

The *Life* of 1843 was the fourth such sketch of Calhoun which had appeared. The first, printed in the *Philadelphia Franklin Gazette* in 1822, was thought to have been the work of his friend George M. Dallas. An anonymous pamphlet, *Measures Not Men*, published a year later in New York and supposedly edited by his friend General Joseph G. Swift, was practically a reprint of the *Gazette* sketch. The third appeared in Duff Green's *Telegraph* in the spring of 1831, supposedly written by Virgil Maxcy. Each was simply an expansion of the previous sketch, as was the *Life* of 1843.

The significant facts are: (1) the sketches always appeared when Calhoun was actively in a campaign for the presidency or for nomination; (2) they were anonymous; (3) their authorship was attributed to one of his intimate friends.

Wiltse, who always gives Calhoun every benefit of the doubt and insists in every instance upon the most favorable interpretation of his hero, rejects the Rhett statement. In an appendix to his first volume (amplified in the third) he argues that "the most that can be said is that the *Life* is an 'official' biography, prepared under Calhoun's eye and perhaps in part by his hand; but it is not in any legitimate sense of the word an autobiography."

Calhoun's clerk Scoville, Wiltse believes, did the first part; Calhoun's daughter Anna Clemson the second; and then Hunter revised the whole. He admits that Calhoun was quite capable of self-adulation, that he might have written the expansion in the *Life* of the period from 1831 to 1843, but he does not believe so.

Rhett's statement can be discounted somewhat, on the grounds of possible jealousy of Calhoun and Hunter; but historians, it seems to me, must accept it more or less at face value. What motive did he have to malign his dead friend and to fabricate a bold-faced lie? Would he not be closer to the truth than a scholar, honest but prejudiced, investigating the matter a century later?

Wiltse's arguments can be refuted. He cites Calhoun's statements about the authorship, but surely the latter, if he did write it, would not have admitted it. He points out differences in style to Calhoun's other writing, but once again, if he wrote it, Calhoun would have tried to change his style. He says Calhoun would never have misspelled the name of his friend Cheves (Cheeves), but Calhoun was frequently guilty of errors in spelling.

My own belief is that Calhoun wrote the major part of all the sketches. Even Wiltse admits that he furnished the material for the *Life* and approved the final product. Surely the *Life* is more his own work than present day articles of politicos, composed by ghost-writers but written in the first person.

Wiltse's main point is that Calhoun would have thought it improper to have written his own biography, just as he thought it improper to take the stump in his own behalf. This is the very heart of the matter. Calhoun could not make speeches in his own behalf because *people would know* he was seeking the presidency; he could write a eulogistic biography of himself, with the collaboration of his closest friends upon whose silence he could count, because *people would not know*. This was in keeping with the complex which kept his right hand from knowing what his left hand was doing; with the methods of indirection he frequently used from the beginning of his long career; with his insistence both to himself and his friends that *everything* he did was morally and logically right.

I believe Calhoun was so convinced in his own mind that by becoming President he could permanently save both the South and the Union that he would not have hesitated to use any means or method which he thought would contribute to that end.

Notes

CHAPTER ONE

1. *Life of John C. Calhoun* (New York, 1843), p. 6. See Appendix. Hereafter cited as "Autobiography."
2. *South Carolina Gazette*, Feb. 23, 1760, quoted in A. S. Salley, "The Calhoun Family in America," *South Carolina Historical and Genealogical Magazine*, VII (1906), 81-98, 153-69.
3. The third source for the history of the Calhoun family and John Calhoun's early years is "Account of Calhoun's Early Life, Abridged from the Manuscript of Col. W. Pinkney Starke," *Annual Report of the American Historical Association, 1899*, II, 65-89. A southern gentleman of the old school writing in a flowery manner about a local hero, Starke is a biased amateur, but he includes statements from members of the Calhoun family which might be accepted, with reservations, as primary sources. Calhoun's autobiography is quite brief on his early life. Of these three accounts, Salley's is by far the most reliable.
4. Autobiography, pp. 5-7.
5. Quoted in Salley, "The Calhoun Family," p. 90.
6. Autobiography, p. 5.
7. Starke, "Early Life," p. 74.
8. Calhoun to Mrs. Calhoun, April 13, 1806, Oct. 1, 1807, May 8, 1811. Unless otherwise stated, all Calhoun letters cited are to be found in J. Franklin Jameson (ed.), "Correspondence of John C. Calhoun," *Annual Report of the American Historical Association, 1899*, vol. II. See also Mary Bates, "Private life of Calhoun," *International Magazine* (Charleston), IV (1852), 173-80.
9. Autobiography, pp. 6-7. Starke gives a slightly different version of the incident.
10. Starke, *Early Life*, p. 80. The quotation in the autobiography is similar in language and in tone.
11. Walter Miller, "Calhoun as a Lawyer and a Statesman," *The Green Bag*, XL (1899), 201-2.
12. Calhoun to Mrs. Calhoun, Aug. 29, 1804; Autobiography, p. 6.

CHAPTER TWO

1. Calhoun to Noble, Oct. 15, 1804.
2. John B. O'Neall, *Bench and Bar of South Carolina* (Charleston, 1859), II, 207, and Starke are corrected on this by Charles M. Wiltse, *John C. Calhoun, Nationalist* (Indianapolis, 1944), Chap. 2, 8n.
3. Calhoun to Mrs. Calhoun, Sept. 26, 1805, July 3, Sept. 11, Dec. 22, 1806, Jan. 30, 1810, May 23, 1811.
4. *Ibid.*, Aug. 12, 1805, Jan. 19, 1806.
5. *Ibid.*, Aug. 12, Sept. 19, 1805.
6. Autobiography, p. 6.
7. *Congressional Debates*, XIII, Part I, 301-2.
8. Calhoun to Pickens, Nov. 24, 1805.
9. *Ibid.*
10. Calhoun to Mrs. Calhoun, Aug. 12, 1805.
11. *Ibid.*, March 3, April 13, 1806.
12. Starke, *Early Life*, pp. 85-88; O'Neall, *Bench and Bar*, II, 284.
13. Calhoun to Mrs. Calhoun, April 6, 1809.

14. *Ibid.*, July 18, 1810; Autobiography, p. 6.

15. Calhoun to Mrs. Calhoun, Sept. 7, 1810.

16. *Ibid.*, April 6, June 23, 1809.

17. *Ibid.*, June 25, Oct. 1, 1809, Jan. 20, June 12, 1810.

18. Starke, *Early Life*, p. 88.

19. Calhoun to Mrs. Calhoun, Oct. 1, 1809, June 12, Sept. 13, Sept. 28, 1810.

20. *Ibid.*, July 18, 1809.

21. William E. Barton, *The Paternity of Abraham Lincoln* (New York, 1920), p. 266.

22. Autobiography, p. 12.

23. *Ibid.*

24. *Ibid.*, p. 7.

25. *Ibid.*, p. 8; Calhoun to Mrs. Calhoun, July 18, Sept. 28, 1810; Starke, *Early Life*, p. 88.

26. Calhoun to Mrs. Calhoun, May 8, Dec. 21, 1811.

CHAPTER THREE

1. *Writings of George Washington*, ed. John C. Fitzpatrick (Washington, 1931-40), XXXIV, 401.

2. For a summary of the economic factors see Warren H. Goodman, "Origins of the War of 1812," *Mississippi Valley Historical Review*, XXVIII (Sept., 1941), 171 ff.

3. Bernard Mayo, *Henry Clay* (Boston, 1937) and Henry Adams' multivolume classic, *History of the United States of America during the Administrations of Thomas Jefferson and James Madison* (9 vols., New York, 1889-1890), give full accounts of the party conflicts.

4. Harriet Martineau, *Retrospect of Western Travel* (London, 1838), I, 243.

5. Gaillard Hunt, *John C. Calhoun* (Philadelphia, 1908), pp. 19-20.

6. Autobiography, p. 12.

7. St. Julien Ravenel (Mrs.), *Life and Times of William Lowndes of South Carolina* (New York, 1901), pp. 84-86.

8. *Ibid.*

9. Calhoun to Mrs. Calhoun, Dec. 21, 1811.

10. Quoted in Mayo, *Clay*, p. 474.

11. *Ibid.*, p. 518n.

12. *Works of John C. Calhoun*, ed. Richard K. Crallé (New York, 1854-57), II, 5-7. Hereafter cited as Calhoun, *Works*.

13. Quoted in Mayo, *Clay*, p. 508.

14. Calhoun to James McBride, April 18, 1812, McBride MSS, Library of Congress.

15. William Lowndes, "Commonplace Notebook," quoted in Mayo, *Clay*, p. 522.

16. *Dictionary of American Biography* (New York, 1929), III, 412.

17. *Annals of Congress*, 12 Congress, 1 Session, Part II, 1397.

18. William Reed to Timothy Pickering, Feb. 18, 1812, quoted in Mayo, *Clay*, p. 446.

19. *Memoirs of John Quincy Adams*, ed. C. F. Adams (12 vols.; Philadelphia, 1874-77), V, 361.

20. Calhoun, *Works*, II, 27-30.

21. *Ibid.*, 49-51.

22. *Ibid.*, 52-54.

23. *Ibid.*, 87-90.

24. *Ibid.*, 115-16.

25. Autobiography, p. 23; William M. Meigs, *Life of John C. Calhoun* (New York, 1917), I, 216.

26. *Annals of Congress*, 14 Congress, 2 Session, 621; Autobiography, pp. 23-24

27. Calhoun, *Works*, II, 37.

28. *Ibid.*, 41-42.

29. *Annals of Congress*, 13 Congress, 2 Session, 1983-84, 1989-90; Autobiography, p. 13.

30. Calhoun, *Works*, III, 126.

31. *Ibid.*, 102 ff.; Autobiography, pp. 16-17.

32. George T. Curtis, *Life of Daniel Webster* (New York, 1870), I, 143.

33. Autobiography, p. 18.

34. *Ibid.*, pp. 13-14.

35. Curtis, *Webster*, I, 126.

36. Autobiography, pp. 12-13.

37. *Annals of Congress*, 13 Congress, 3 Session, 469.

38. *Ibid.*, 13 Congress, 2 Session, 1983.

39. Calhoun, *Works*, II, 133.

CHAPTER FOUR

1. Calhoun to Mrs. Calhoun, Dec. 21, 1811; to Floride Calhoun, Feb. 7, 1814; Meigs, *Calhoun*, II, 81.

2. Calhoun to Mrs. Calhoun, Dec. 21, 1811; to Floride Calhoun, Feb. 7, 1814.

3. Calhoun to Mrs. Calhoun, April 9, 1815.

4. *Ibid.*, Nov. 23, 1812.

5. Autobiography, p. 23; *Charleston Courier*, Feb. 10, 1816, quoted in Meigs, *Calhoun*, I, 199; John S. Jenkins, *Life of Calhoun* (Auburn, N. Y., 1850), p. 64.

6. *Annals of Congress*, 14 Congress, 1 Session, 1183; Autobiography, p. 23.

7. Adams, *Memoirs*, V, 10.

8. Undated letter of Mills in *Proceedings of the Massachusetts Historical Society*, XIX (1881-82), 37-38.

9. March 15, 1814, quoted in Theodore D. Jervey, *Robert Y. Hayne and His Times* (New York, 1909), p. 51.

10. Calhoun, *Works*, II, 136 ff.; *Annals of Congress*, 14 Congress, 1 Session, 728-29.

11. Calhoun, *Works*, II, 142.

12. *Ibid.*, 191.

13. *Ibid.*, 152.

14. *Ibid.*, 173.

15. *Ibid.*, 172-73.

16. *Ibid.*, 190.

17. *Ibid.*, 153-62, 325.

18. *Ibid.*, 206.

19. Calhoun to Virgil Maxcy, June 11, 1823, Maxcy-Markoe Papers, Library of Congress.

20. James A. Hamilton, *Reminiscences* (New York, 1869), p. 62.

21. Calhoun, *Works*, II, 192-94.

22. *Ibid.*, I, 359, 371.

23. *Congressional Debates*, XIII, Part I, 866.

24. Calhoun, *Works*, II, 148-49.

25. *Ibid.*, III, 67.

CHAPTER FIVE

1. Autobiography, p. 28.

2. *Ibid.*, pp. 24-25.

3. *Ibid.*, p. 27. Calhoun's official reports as Secretary of War are in *Works*, vol. V.

4. Ravenel, *Lowndes*, p. 187; *Niles' Weekly Register*, Mar. 27, 1824, quoted in Hermann Von Holst, *Life of John C. Calhoun* (Boston, 1882), p. 41; William E. Dodd, *Statesmen of the Old South* (New York, 1927), p. 109.

5. "Report to the House of Representatives," Dec. 18, 1818, Calhoun, *Works*, V, 8 ff.

6. Adams, *Memoirs*, IV, 36.

7. *American State Papers, Military Affairs*, I, 689.

8. Richard K. Stenberg, "Jackson's Rhea Letter Hoax," *Journal of Southern History*, II (1936), 490-96.

9. Adams, *Memoirs*, IV, 108 ff.; Calhoun to Jackson, May 29, 1830.

10. Adams, *Memoirs*, V, 128.

11. *Ibid.*

12. *Ibid.*, IV, 530-31; V, 5-12.

13. Calhoun to Tait, Oct. 26, 1820, Oct. 21, 1821, "Letters from Calhoun to Charles Tait," *Gulf States Historical Magazine*, I (1902), 98-104.

14. Calhoun to Garnet, July 3, 1824.

15. Adams, *Memoirs*, V, 309.

16. Jenkins, *Calhoun*, p. 150.

17. Taylor to James Monroe, April 29, 1823, "Letters of John Taylor of Caroline, Virginia," *John P. Branch Historical Papers* (Richmond, 1901-16), II (1905-08), 348-53.

CHAPTER SIX

1. Calhoun to John E. Calhoun, Jan. 16, 1822.

2. Meigs, *Calhoun*, II, 102; Hunt, *Calhoun*, p. 38.

3. Bates, "Calhoun," pp. 173-80.

4. Adams, *Memoirs*, V, 434-35.

5. Thomas H. Benton, *Thirty*

Years' View (2 vols., New York, 1854-56), I, 34-36.

6. Undated letter of Mills.

7. *Southern Literary Messenger,* XVI (1850), 376-79; Henry A. Wise, *Seven Decades of the Union* (Philadelphia, 1872), p. 75.

8. Story to Mason, *Memoirs and Correspondence of Jeremiah Mason* (Cambridge, Mass., 1873), pp. 264-65; Martin Van Buren, "Autobiography," *Annual Report of the American Historical Association, 1918,* II, 116; Henry Adams, *Albert Gallatin* (Philadelphia, 1880), p. 599.

9. Adams, *Memoirs,* IV, 477; V, 327, 333-34.

10. Ravenel, *Lowndes,* p. 226; Jervey, *Hayne,* pp. 125-28.

11. Ravenel, *Lowndes,* pp. 26 ff.; Adams, *Memoirs,* V, 466-70; Autobiography, p. 28.

12. Calhoun to Maxcy, Dec. 31, 1821, Maxcy-Markoe Papers.

13. Adams, *Memoirs,* V, 477-78.

14. Calhoun to Maxcy, March 12, 13, 1822, Maxcy-Markoe Papers.

15. Adams, *Memoirs,* VI, 233-34, 241-42.

16. Calhoun to James E. Calhoun, Jan. 30, 1824.

17. McLean to Edward Everett, Aug. 8, 1828, *Massachusetts Historical Society Proceedings,* 3rd Series (1907), I, 364n.

18. Green to Edwards, Dec. 10, 1823, *Edwards Papers,* ed., C. B. Washburne (Chicago, 1884), pp. 212-15.

19. Calhoun to Maxcy, Feb. 27, 1824, Maxcy-Markoe Papers; Margaret B. Smith, *First Forty Years of Washington Society* (New York, 1906), p. 164.

20. Calhoun to Swift, *The Memoirs of General Joseph G. Swift* (Worcester, 1890), pp. 294-95.

21. Calhoun, *Works,* II, 217.

CHAPTER SEVEN

1. Benton, *Thirty Years' View,* I, 95-97.

2. Frederic Bancroft, *Calhoun and the South Carolina Nullification Movement* (Baltimore, 1928), p. 21.

3. David F. Houston, *A Critical Study of Nullification in South Carolina* (Cambridge, Mass., 1896), p. 67.

4. Jervey, *Hayne,* pp. 188, 193.

5. *Ibid.,* p. 176.

6. Hunt, *Calhoun,* p. 118.

7. *Niles' Weekly Register,* XXVIII (1825), 267.

8. *Congressional Globe,* 28 Congress, 1 Session, Appendix, p. 747.

9. Calhoun, *Works,* III, 49-50.

10. *Niles' Weekly Register,* XXXIII (1827), 28.

11. Robert J. Turnbull, *The Crisis,* quoted in Meigs, *Calhoun,* I, 359.

12. Calhoun to James E. Calhoun, Aug. 26, 1827.

13. *Ibid.,* May 4, 1828.

14. Calhoun to Monroe, July 10, 1827.

15. Calhoun to James E. Calhoun, Aug. 26, 1827.

16. Calhoun to Yancey, July 16, 1828, *Sprunt Historical Publications,* X, No. 2, 75-76.

CHAPTER EIGHT

1. Calhoun to Swift, Feb. 19, 1826, in Swift, *Memoirs,* p. 300.

2. Calhoun to Jackson, June 4, 1826, *Jackson Correspondence,* ed. John S. Bassett, 7 vols. (Washington, 1926-35), III, 304-05.

3. Jackson to Calhoun, July 26, 1826, *ibid.,* 307-08.

4. Calhoun to Swift, Dec. 11, 1825, in Swift, *Memoirs,* p. 300.

5. *Congressional Debates,* II, Part I, 572.

6. Glyndon G. Van Deusen, *The Life of Henry Clay* (Boston, 1937), pp. 222-23.

7. Hugh A. Garland, *Life of John Randolph* (New York, 1881), II, 265; Ben P. Poore, *Perley's Reminiscences of Sixty Years in the National Metropolis* (New York, 1886), I, 64.

8. Van Buren to Benjamin F. But-

ler, Dec. 12, 1826, Van Buren Papers, Library of Congress.

9. Calhoun to Monroe, Feb. 30 [*sic*], Dec. 22, 1827, March 7, July 10, 1828; Calhoun, *Works*, VI, 349 ff.; Meigs, *Calhoun*, I, 400.

10. Calhoun to Jackson, July 10, 1828, *Jackson Correspondence*, III, 413-15.

11. *Charleston Courier*, July 18, 1828, quoted in Meigs, *Calhoun*, I, 373.

12. *Niles' Weekly Register*, XXXV (1828-29), 202; Houston, *Nullification*, pp. 72-74.

13. Autobiography, p. 35.

14. Calhoun to Maxcy, Sept. 10, 1830, Maxcy-Markoe Papers.

15. Jervey, *Hayne*, p. 290.

16. Bancroft, *Calhoun*, p. 48.

17. *Ibid.*, p. 38 ff.; Autobiography, p. 36; Calhoun, *Works*, VI, 1-59.

18. Calhoun, *Works*, VI, 57.

19. Bancroft, *Calhoun*, p. 88.

20. Calhoun to Maxcy, Sept. 10, 1830, Maxcy-Markoe Papers.

21. Augustus C. Buell, *A History of Andrew Jackson* (New York, 1904), II, 204.

22. James A. Hamilton, *Reminiscences*, 100-01; Calhoun, *Works*, VI, 443.

23. David Campbell to his wife, May 28, June 3, 1829, quoted in Marquis James, *Andrew Jackson, Portrait of a President* (Indianapolis, 1937), p. 210.

24. Adams, *Memoirs*, VIII, 185; Calhoun, *Works*, VI, 439.

25. James A. Parton, *Life of Andrew Jackson* (New York, 1860), II, 299.

26. Jackson to Overton, Dec. 31, 1829, *Jackson Correspondence*, IV, 108.

27. The full correspondence on the background of the quarrel with Jackson, which Calhoun later released, appears in *Works*, VI, 349 ff. For different versions, see James, *Jackson*, 236 ff.; Meigs, *Calhoun*, I, 399 ff.; Wiltse, *Calhoun*, II, 76 ff.

When Calhoun published his pamphlet on the issue, Jackson prepared a reply which James A. Hamilton dissuaded him from publishing. A large portion of it is in Benton, *Thirty Years' View*, I, 167-80.

28. See Major Lewis' narrative in Parton, *Jackson*, II, 310-30.

29. Wiltse, *Calhoun*, II, 71; Meigs, *Calhoun*, I, 398.

30. Meigs, *Calhoun*, I, 310.

31. *Jackson Correspondence*, IV, 108; Jervey, *Hayne*, p. 280.

32. James, *Jackson*, p. 268.

33. *Ibid.*, 269-70.

34. *Ibid.*, 274-75.

35. Benton, *Thirty Years' View*, I, 215-19.

36. James, *Jackson*, p. 296.

CHAPTER NINE

1. Calhoun, *Works*, VI, 45, 151 ff.

2. Bancroft, *Calhoun*, pp. 71-74, 93-96; Madison to Edward Everett, Aug. 28, 1831; to C. E. Haynes, Aug. 27, 1832, *Writings of James Madison*, ed. Gaillard Hunt (New York, 1910), IX, 383 ff., 482 ff.

3. Calhoun, *Works*, VI, 46.

4. Henry D. Capers, *Life and Times of G. C. Memminger* (Richmond, Va., 1893), p. 47.

5. "Letters on the Nullification Movement in South Carolina," *American Historical Review*, VI (1901), 744.

6. James D. Richardson (ed.), *Messages and Papers of the Presidents* (Washington, 1900), II, 556.

7. Meigs, *Calhoun*, I, 392.

8. Bancroft, *Calhoun*, p. 91 ff.

9. *The John Branch Historical Papers*, Randolph Macon College, III, 207-09.

10. *Ibid.*

11. Calhoun to Hammond, Jan. 15, 1831.

12. Adams, *Memoirs*, VIII, 237; Meigs, *Calhoun*, I, 422-23; F. W. Moore (ed.), "Calhoun as Seen by his Political Friends: Letters of

Green, Lewis, and Crallé, 1831-1848," *Publications of the Southern History Association,* VII (1903), 167.

13. Calhoun to Samuel L. Gouverneur, March 30, 1830; to Christopher Van Deventer, May 12, 1830.

14. Adams, *Memoirs,* VIII, 195.

15. *Ibid.,* 333; Calhoun to Van Deventer, May 25, 1831; Hammond's memorandum of a conversation with Calhoun, Dec. 4, 1831, in "Calhoun Correspondence," p. 305.

16. This and the following quotations from Hammond's account of the conversation are printed in the *American Historical Review,* VI (1901), 741 ff., along with numerous letters which the leading Nullifiers exchanged with each other.

17. Hamilton to Hammond, June 16, 1831, *ibid.,* 747.

18. Calhoun to Ingham, June 16, 1831.

19. *Publications of the Southern History Association,* VII, 169.

20. Calhoun, *Works,* VI, 61.

21. Rhett to Crallé, Oct. 25, 1854, in G. Hunt, "Robert Barnwell Rhett on the Biography of Calhoun, 1854," *American Historical Review,* XIII (1908), 311.

22. McLean to Gouverneur, Sept. 25, 1831, in Meigs, *Calhoun,* I, 361.

CHAPTER TEN

1. Adams, *Memoirs,* VIII, 446.

2. *National Intelligencer,* July 31, 1832, quoted in Meigs, *Calhoun,* I, 441.

3. Bancroft, *Calhoun,* p. 131. See also *State Papers on Nullification* (published by the state of Massachusetts, Boston, 1834) for the replies of other states in particular.

4. Bancroft, *Calhoun,* p. 125.

5. *Ibid.,* p. 141.

6. Calhoun, *Works,* VI, 95.

7. *Ibid.,* p. 131.

8. Calhoun to Crallé, May (n.d.), 1832.

9. Calhoun to J. E. Calhoun, Dec. 25, 1831.

10. *National Intelligencer,* June 7, 1831, quoted in Meigs, *Calhoun,* I, 432.

11. Calhoun, *Works,* VI, 172.

12. Bancroft, *Calhoun,* pp. 142 ff.

13. Richardson, *Messages and Papers,* II, 640 ff.

14. James, *Jackson,* pp. 316 ff.

15. Jackson to Poinsett, Jan. 24, 1833, *Jackson Correspondence,* V, 11.

16. James, *Jackson,* p. 319; Autobiography, p. 44.

17. Calhoun, *Works,* II, 229.

18. *Ibid.,* 262-63; *Congressional Debates,* 1832-33, p. 238.

19. Bancroft, *Calhoun,* p. 165.

20. Meigs, *Calhoun,* II, 24.

21. Calvin Colton, *Life and Times of Henry Clay* (New York, 1846), II, 258. Colton goes into details on the tariff of 1832.

22. Autobiography, pp. 48-49; Meigs, *Calhoun,* II, 30; Bancroft, *Calhoun,* p. 168.

23. Bancroft, *Calhoun,* p. 170.

24. *Ibid.,* p. 172; Calhoun to Van Deventer, March 24, 1833.

25. Bancroft, *Calhoun,* pp. 184-85.

CHAPTER ELEVEN

1. Calhoun, *Works,* II, 335-37.

2. *Congressional Debates,* XI, Part I, 249.

3. See his speeches, Jan. 13, 1834, on the removal of public deposits (*Works,* II, 309 ff.); and Feb., 1834, on removals from office (*Works,* II, 426 ff.).

4. *Ibid.,* 336, 370.

5. *Ibid.,* 336, 364.

6. *Ibid.,* 371 ff.

7. *Ibid.,* 446 ff.

8. Calhoun to James E. Calhoun, Sept. 2, Dec. 9, 1836; to J. A. Williams, Oct. 17, 1835; F. J. Turner, *The United States, 1830-1850* (New York, 1935), pp. 176, 536.

9. *Congressional Globe,* 25 Congress, 3 Session, 31.

10. Turner, *United States,* p. 445.

11. *Ibid.,* pp. 448-49; Calhoun, *Works,* II, 634 ff.

12. Calhoun to Green, July 27, 1837.

13. *Congressional Debates*, XII, Part I, 555; Calhoun, *Works*, II, 608.

14. Calhoun, *Works*, II, 339, 349; *Congressional Debates*, X, Part I, 206.

15. Calhoun to James E. Calhoun, Feb. 8, 1834; to Van Deventer, Jan. 25, 1834.

16. Calhoun to Green, June 26, 1837.

17. Calhoun to Pickens, Jan. 4, 1834; to Green, Aug. 30, 1835; to Hammond, Feb. 18, 1837; Calhoun, *Works*, II, 510 ff.

18. Calhoun, *Works*, II, 484, 636-37.

19. Turner, *United States*, pp. 432 ff.

20. Calhoun, *Works*, II, 465 ff., 509 ff.

21. *Ibid.*, 631-32.

22. *Ibid.*, 488.

23. *Ibid.*, 449.

24. *Ibid.*, 530-31.

25. *Ibid.*, 632-33.

26. Calhoun to James E. Calhoun, Sept. 23, 1835.

27. Calhoun, *Works*, II, 637, III, 36-43; Meigs, *Calhoun*, II, 182.

28. Richardson, *Messages and Papers*, III, 318.

29. Calhoun, *Works*, III, 92.

30. Calhoun to Anna Maria Calhoun, Sept. 8, 1827.

31. Calhoun to James E. Calhoun, Sept. 7, 1837.

32. Adams, *Memoirs*, IX, 398.

33. Calhoun to Green, July 27, 1837.

CHAPTER TWELVE

1. Autobiography, pp. 52-53.

2. Calhoun to Anna Maria Calhoun, Jan. 25, 1838.

3. Calhoun to James E. Calhoun, Jan. 8, 1838.

4. Calhoun to Hamilton, Feb. 15, 1837.

5. John Taylor, *An Inquiry into the Principles and Policy of the Government of the United States* (Fredericksburg, Va., 1814), pp. 551-52.

6. Calhoun, *Works*, II, 251-55.

7. Calhoun to Green, Sept. 20, 1834.

8. Calhoun, *Works*, II, 613.

9. *Ibid.*, IV, 74 ff.

10. *Ibid.*, I, 12.

11. Roane to Van Buren, Sept. 11, 1843, Van Buren Papers.

12. Calhoun to McDuffie, Dec. 4, 1843; to Hunter, Feb. 1, 1844.

13. Calhoun, *Works*, III, 140-41; Calhoun to Burt, Jan. 24, 1838.

14. Turner, *United States*, pp. 467-68.

15. Calhoun to James E. Calhoun, Feb. 1, 1840; Benton, *Thirty Years' View*, II, 120.

16. Van Deusen, *Clay*, pp. 311 ff.; Turner, *United States*, pp. 469-70.

17. Turner, *United States*, p. 476.

18. Calhoun to James E. Calhoun, Feb. 13, 1840.

19. Meigs, *Calhoun*, II, 197-200.

20. *Ibid.*, 211-12; Calhoun to James E. Calhoun, April 28, 1838.

21. Petigru to H. S. Legaré, Dec. 17, 1837, quoted in Meigs, *Calhoun*, II, 201; Hunt, *Calhoun*, p. 244.

22. Calhoun, *Works*, III, 244 ff., 279 ff.; Benton, *Thirty Years' View*, II, 98.

23. Calhoun, *Works*, III, 274.

24. Calhoun to A. P. Calhoun, Dec. 7, 1838, June 8, 1840.

25. Calhoun to Hammond, Feb. 23, 1840.

26. Calhoun to Nicholson, Dec. 18, 1841.

27. Calhoun, *Works*, V, 414; G. Hunt, "Rhett on the Biography of Calhoun," *American Historical Review*, XIII (1908), 311.

28. Calhoun to A. P. Calhoun, Sept. 12, 1841.

29. Calhoun to Hammond, Sept. 24, 1841.

30. Calhoun to James E. Calhoun, Nov. 1, 1841; to Burt, Nov. 28, 1841.

31. *Niles' Weekly Register*, XLIV (1833), 382-83.

32. Hammond Diary, Sept. 11, 1842, Hammond Papers, Library of Congress.

33. See particularly his letter to his

son-in-law, Thomas G. Clemson, April 3, 1842.

34. Calhoun, *Works*, VI, 239 ff., 255 ff.

35. Charles H. Ambler, "Virginia and the Presidential Succession, 1840-44," *Turner Essays in American History* (New York, 1910) pp. 165-203.

36. Rhett to Calhoun, Oct. 16, Dec. 8, 1843; Maxcy to Calhoun, Dec. 3, 1842; Hamilton to Calhoun, Nov. 21, 1843 (all in "Calhoun Correspondence"); Calhoun to Gilmer, Dec. 25, 1843; to Green, Feb. 10, 1844; Calhoun, *Works*, VI, 239-54; Benton, *Thirty Years' View*, II, 581-90.

37. Calhoun to Green, Feb. 10, 1844.

38. *Ibid.*; Calhoun to James E. Calhoun, Feb. 7, Feb. 14, 1844.

39. Pickens to Calhoun, May 28, 1844, "Calhoun Correspondence."

40. Tucker to Hammond, Mar. 13, 1847, Hammond Papers.

CHAPTER THIRTEEN

1. Calhoun to James E. Calhoun, April 21, 1838.

2. Calhoun to John E. Calhoun, Sept. 27, 1821.

3. Calhoun to Anna Maria Calhoun (Mrs. Thomas G. Clemson), Dec. 18, 1840, Jan. 3, Feb. 17, 1841.

4. *Ibid.*, May 30, 1840, Jan. 3, 1841.

5. Autobiography, pp. 52-53.

6. William M. Meigs, *Life of Thomas Hart Benton* (Philadelphia, 1904), pp. 300, 496-97.

7. *The Diary of James K. Polk* (Chicago, 1910), II, 458; see also p. 371.

8. Varina H. Davis, *Jefferson Davis* (New York, 1890), I, 210-11.

9. Benjamin F. Perry, *Reminiscences*, p. 49; Calhoun to Mrs. Clemson, June 11, 1846; to James E. Calhoun, Oct. 29, 1846.

10. Ambler, *Turner Essays*, p. 189; Meigs, *Calhoun*, II, 119.

11. Lewis to Crallé, March 20, 1840, *Publications of the Southern History Association*, VII (1903), 355; Charles

G. Pinckney, "John C. Calhoun from a Southern Standpoint," *Lippincott's Magazine*, LXII (1898), 84; Tucker to Hammond, March 13, 1847, Hammond Papers.

12. Hammond Diary, quoted in Meigs, *Calhoun*, II, 120 ff.

13. "A Few Thoughts on the Death of John C. Calhoun," *Southern Literary Messenger*, XVI (1850), 376 ff.

14. Wise, *Seven Decades of the Union*, pp 220-25.

15. *Proceedings on the Death and Funeral Ceremonies of John C. Calhoun* (Columbia, 1850), p. 43.

16. Green to Calhoun, Aug. 2, 1842, Sept. 2, Sept. 29, 1843.

17. Calhoun, *Works*, V, 340-47.

18. Tyler to Calhoun, Oct. 7, 1845.

19. Calhoun, *Works*, V, 419 ff.

20. Calhoun to Mrs. Clemson, March 11, May 22, 1845.

21. Hammond Diary, Oct. 25, 1844.

22. *Congressional Globe*, 30 Congress, 1 Session, Appendix, 506-07.

23. *Ibid.*, 29 Congress, 1 Session, 153; "Calhoun Correspondence," p. 644.

24. Calhoun to Clemson, March 23, Dec. 13, 1845, July 24, 1847; to Mrs. Clemson, Nov. 21, 1846.

25. Calhoun to Pickens, Sept. 23, 1845, "Letters from John C. Calhoun to Francis W. Pickens," *South Carolina Historical and Genealogical Magazine*, VII (1906), 12 ff.

26. Joseph G. Rayback, "The Presidential Ambitions of John C. Calhoun, 1844-1848," *Journal of Southern History*, XIV (1948), 331 ff.; McCord to Hammond, Dec. 12, 1844, Hammond Papers.

27. Calhoun to [?], May 16, 1845, C. H. Ambler, ed., "Hunter Correspondence," *Annual Report of the American Historical Association, 1916*, II, 78.

28. Rayback, "Presidential Ambitions of Calhoun," *Journal of Southern History*, XIV (1948), 339.

29. *Ibid.*, 348-49, quoting Taylor to John J. Crittenden, Nov. 1, 1847.

30. Simms to Hammond, Mar. (n.d.), 1847, Hammond Papers.

31. Calhoun to Green, June 10, 1847.

32. Calhoun to Hayne, Nov. 17, 1838.

33. Green to Calhoun, Sept. 24, 1845; Gadsden to Calhoun, Oct. 9, 1845.

34. Calhoun, *Works*, VI, 273 ff.; Gerald M. Capers, *Biography of a Rivertown* (Chapel Hill, 1939), pp. 85-88.

35. Calhoun, *Works*, V, 246 ff.

36. *Charleston Mercury*, Dec. 5, 1845, quoted in Meigs, *Calhoun*, II, 370; Calhoun to James E. Calhoun, Jan. 16, 1846.

37. Calhoun to Clemson, July 30, 1846.

38. Calhoun, *Works*, IV, 286, 288.

39. Calhoun to A. P. Calhoun, Jan. 16, 1846.

40. Meigs, *Calhoun*, II, 382; Calhoun, *Works*, IV, 338, 378 ff.; *Congressional Globe*, 29 Congress, 1 Session, 782, 85.

41. Calhoun's speeches on the war are in *Works*, IV, 303-425.

42. *Ibid.*, 308.

43. *Ibid.*, 323.

44. William H. Hull to Cobb, May 22, 1846, Ulrich B. Phillips, ed., "Correspondence of Toombs, Stephens, and Cobb," *Annual Report of the American Historical Association, 1911*, II, 79.

45. Moore, "Calhoun as Seen by his Political Friends," *Publications of the Southern History Association*, VII (1903), 425; Hunt, *Calhoun*, 289. I have quoted Hunt's version of this letter.

CHAPTER FOURTEEN

1. Calhoun to Mrs. Clemson, Dec. 27, 1846.

2. Calhoun, *Works*, IV, 339 ff.

3. *Ibid.*, 394-95.

4. *Ibid.*, 513 ff.

5. *Ibid.*, 529-30, 534-35.

6. Henry S. Foote, *War of the Rebellion* (New York, 1866), p. 90; Hammond to William G. Simms, Sept. 7, 1848, Hammond Papers; Toombs to J. J. Crittenden, Sept. 27, 1848, in Phillips, "Toombs Correspondence," *Annual Report of the American Historical Association, 1911*, II, 127-28.

7. Calhoun, *Works*, VI, 285 ff.

8. Toombs to Crittenden, Sept. 27, 1848.

9. Quoted in A. C. Cole, *The Whig Party in the South* (Washington, 1913), pp. 138-42, 194.

10. *Congressional Globe*, 31 Congress, 1 Session, 518-20.

11. Calhoun to James E. Calhoun, Feb. 7, 1844.

12. Calhoun, *Works*, II, 487, 632; Calhoun to Green, Aug. 30, 1835.

13. Calhoun, *Works*, IV, 531-32.

14. Calhoun to T. G. Clemson, Mar. 22, April 13, May 13, May 26, 1848; to Mrs. Clemson, Mar. 7, April 28, June 23, 1848; to James E. Calhoun, April 13, 1848; *Works*, IV, 450; Charles M. Wiltse, "A Critical Southerner: John C. Calhoun on the Revolutions of 1848," *Journal of Southern History*, XV (1949), 299-310.

15. Calhoun, *Works*, I, 57-59; IV, 507-08.

16. *Ibid.*, III, 180, IV, 533.

17. Calhoun to John H. Means, April 13, 1849; Meigs, *Calhoun*, II, 428.

18. Calhoun, *Works*, IV, 532-34.

19. Calhoun to Means, April 13, 1849.

20. Calhoun, *Works*, I, 12.

21. *Ibid.*, I, 48-49, II, 247-49.

22. Jesse T. Carpenter, *The South as a Conscious Minority* (New York, 1930).

23. Hammond to Simms, Oct. 12, 1849, Hammond Papers; Meigs, *Calhoun*, II, 441.

24. Calhoun, *Works*, IV, 542 ff.

25. *Ibid.*, 576; *Congressional Globe*, 31 Congress, 1 Session, 461-64.

26. Calhoun, *Works*, IV, 576-77.

27. *Congressional Globe*, 31 Congress, 1 Session, 478-79, 483-84.

28. *Ibid.*, 518-20; Meigs, *Calhoun*, II, 458-59.

29. Calhoun to Clemson, Mar. 10, 1850.

30. Virginia Mason, *The Public Life and Diplomatic Correspondence of James Murray Mason* (Roanoke, Va., 1903), pp. 72-73.

31. Rhett to R. K. Crallé in Hunt,

"Rhett on the Biography of Calhoun," *American Historical Review*, XIII (1908), 312; Charles S. Morehead to John J. Crittenden, March 31, 1850, in Anna M. B. Coleman, *Life of John J. Crittenden* (Philadelphia, 1871), I, 353; Ulrich B. Phillips, *Life of Robert Toombs* (New York, 1913), p. 79.

32. *Proceedings on the Death and Funeral Ceremonies of John C. Calhoun* (Columbia, 1850), p. 101.

Bibliographical Note

THIS is intended to be a brief critical bibliography listing only published works dealing specifically with Calhoun. Other works cited are identified in the notes.

CALHOUN'S WORKS AND LETTERS

Works of John C. Calhoun, Richard K. Crallé, ed. 6 vols. New York, 1854-57. Vol. I includes his two essays on government, II-IV his speeches, and V and VI his reports and public letters.

Speeches of John C. Calhoun. New York, 1843.

Life of John C. Calhoun. New York, 1843. (See Appendix.)

Measures Not Men. New York, 1823. (See Appendix.)

"Correspondence of John C. Calhoun," J. Franklin Jameson, ed., *Annual Report of the American Historical Association, 1899,* Vol. II. Washington, 1900.

"Correspondence Addressed to John C. Calhoun, 1837-1849," Chauncey S. Boucher and Robert P. Brooks, eds., *Annual Report of the American Historical Association, 1929.* Washington, 1931.

"John C. Calhoun and the Presidential Campaign of 1824: Some Unpublished Calhoun Letters," Thomas R. Hay, ed., *American Historical Review,* XI, (1934-35), 82-96, 287-300.

"Letters from John C. Calhoun to Charles Tait," *Gulf States Historical Magazine,* I (1902), 92-104.

"Correspondence of Calhoun, McDuffie, and Charles Fisher, relative to the Presidential Campaign of 1824," *North Carolina Historical Review,* VII (Oct., 1930), 477-504.

A projected 15-volume edition of *The Papers of John C. Calhoun* is being prepared at the University of South Carolina. The first volume, edited by the late Robert L. Meriwether and covering the period 1801-17, was published in 1959 by the University of South Carolina Press.

BIOGRAPHIES

Coit, Margaret, *John C. Calhoun: American Portrait.* Boston, 1950.

Hunt, Gaillard, *John C. Calhoun.* Philadelphia, 1908.

Jenkins, John S., *Life of John C. Calhoun.* Auburn, 1850.

Meigs, William M., *Life of John C. Calhoun,* 2 vols. New York, 1917.

Pinckney, Gustavus M., *Life of John C. Calhoun.* Charleston, 1903.

Stryon, Arthur, *The Cast-Iron Man: John C. Calhoun and American Democracy.* New York, 1935.

Von Holst, Hermann E., *John C. Calhoun.* American Statesmen Series. Boston, 1882.

Bibliographical Note

Wiltse, Charles M., *John C. Calhoun, Nationalist, 1782-1828.* Indianapolis, 1944
John C. Calhoun, Nullifier, 1829-1839. Indianapolis, 1949
John C. Calhoun, Sectionalist, 1839-1850. Indianapolis, 1951.

SHORTER SKETCHES

Bates, Mary, "Private Life of Calhoun," *International Magazine*, IV (Charleston, 1852) 173-80.

Bancroft, Frederic, *Calhoun and the South Carolina Nullification Movement.* Baltimore, 1928.

Current, Richard N., "John C. Calhoun, Philosopher of Reaction," *Antioch Review*, III (1943), 223-34.

Dodd, William E., *Statesmen of the Old South*, 91-167. New York, 1911.

Hofstadter, Richard, *The American Political Tradition*, 67-92. New York, 1949.

Johnson, Gerald W., *America's Silver Age.* New York, 1939.

Pinckney, Charles C., "John C. Calhoun from a Southern Standpoint," *Lippincott's Monthly Magazine*, LXII (July, 1898), 81-90.

Stephenson, Nathaniel W., "Calhoun, 1812 and After," *American Historical Review*, XXXI (July, 1926), 701-707.

Trent, William P., *Southern Statesmen of the Old Regime.* New York, 1897.

ARTICLES AND OTHER WORKS

Anderson, John M., ed., *Calhoun: Basic Document.* State College, Pa., 1952.

Capers, Gerald M., "A Reconsideration of Calhoun's Transition from Nationalism to Nullification," *Journal of Southern History*, XIV (Feb., 1948), 34-48.

Hay, Thomas R., "John C. Calhoun and the Presidential Campaign of 1824," *North Carolina Historical Review*, XII (Jan., 1935), 20-44.

Moore, Frederick W., ed., "Calhoun as Seen by his Political Friends," *Publications of the Southern History Association*, VII (1903), 159-69, 269-91, 353-62, 419-26.

Rayback, Joseph G., "The Presidential Ambitions of John C. Calhoun, 1844-1848," *Journal of Southern History*, XIV (Aug., 1948), 331-56.

Salley, Alexander S., Jr., "The Calhoun Family of South Carolina," *South Carolina Historical and Genealogical Magazine*, VII (1906), 81-98, 153-69.

Spain, August O., *The Political Theory of John C. Calhoun.* New York, 1951.

Starke, W. Pinkney, "Account of Calhoun's Early Life," *Annual Report of the American Historical Association*, 1898, II, 65-89.

Stenberg, Richard K., "A Note on the Calhoun-Jackson Break of 1830-1831," *Tyler's Quarterly and Historical Magazine*, XXI (Oct., 1939), 65-69.

Wiltse, Charles M., "A Critical Southerner: John C. Calhoun on the Revolutions of 1848," *Journal of Southern History*, XV (Aug., 1949), 299-310.

"Letters on the Nullification Movement in South Carolina, 1830-34," *American Historical Review*, VI (Oct., 1902), 736-65, VII (Oct., 1903), 92-119.

Proceedings on the Death and Funeral Ceremonies of John C. Calhoun. Columbia, S. C., 1850.

Index

Index

tion, 1841-1843, 204-208; his plantation and private life, 212-213; relations with his political associates, 213-215; impressions of his southern associates, 215-216; his intellectual interests, 216-217; appointed Secretary of State by Tyler, 217; negotiations on Texas and Oregon, 217-220; supports Polk in 1844 and blocks Bluffton Movement in S. C., 221-222; increases antisouthern sentiment in North but fails to unite South, 222-225; clashes with Douglas in Senate, 224; returns to Senate, 1845, 225-226; failing health, 225, 241, 248, 250; campaign for Democratic nomination in 1846, 227-229; presides over Memphis Railroad Convention in 1845 and forms alliance with West, 229-231; supports internal improvements, 230; efforts to prevent war with England and Mexico, 231-233; opposed to war with Mexico, 233-234; resolutions on slavery in territories, 236; calls for southern unity against Wilmot Proviso, 236-237, 240; calls conference of southern congressmen and writes its address, 1849, 239; demands that North stop all attacks on slavery, 238, 240; his strategy in crisis of 1850, 241-244, 247-248, 250-253; seeks alliance with northern conservatives, 241-243, 247; his political conservatism, 241-242; his disapproval of republican movements of 1848 in Europe, 242-243; summary of his *Disquisition on Government* and his *Discourse on the Constitution and Government of the United States*, 245-247; his speech against the Compromise and demands on the North, 250-251; denies that he favored secession 251, 252; predicts civil war within a decade, 252; death, 253, 254

Calhoun, John E., brother-in-law of JCC, 75

Calhoun, Martha, mother of JCC, 5-6, 8, 13

Calhoun, Patrick, father of JCC, 3-6

Calhoun, Patrick, brother of JCC, 19

Calhoun, William, bother of JCC, 6, 9

California, 218, 223, 232-253 *passim*

Canada, 27-43 *passim*, 48, 65, 66

Cass, Lewis, 208, 225, 236, 239, 252

Charleston *Courier*, 45-46, 142

Charleston *Mercury*, 117, 207, 231

Cheves, Langdon, 23, 29, 34, 35, 39, 42, 43, 58, 60

Clay, Henry, 10, 41, 42, 73, 122, 181, 197, 202-205, 220, 249: leads War Hawks in 1812, 29-34; reverses original Republicanism with "American System," 35, 47, 58, 92, 99; opposes Monroe administration, 61, 62; relations with JCC, 67, 148, 161-163, 179, 187, 189, 199, 200-201, 214, 249; presidential candidate in 1824, 68, 76-90 *passim;* in 1832, 143, 144, 147, 149-151; in 1844, 208, 209, 219, 222, 225; Secretary of State, 89, 90, 103, 110, 112, 114; bill for distribution of land proceeds to states, 150, 164, 176, 203; compromise of 1883, 161-163; leads Whig opposition to Jackson, 169-173 *passim*

Clayton, John M., 233, 237

Clemson, Thomas G., 212, 221, 226, 252

Clinton, De Witt, 23, 76, 87, 110

Coit, Margaret, v, 13n, 77n

Compromise of 1850, 223, 240, 249-253

Concurrent majority, 195, 225-246

Constitution, U. S.: JCC's early broad interpretation of, 55-58; frame of national government under, 95-96; Marshall's interpretation of, 96; Virginia and Kentucky Resolutions, 97, 134n; amendments to, proposed by Hartford Convention, 98; "South Carolina Exposition," 118, 130-135; Webster's debates with Hayne, 139-140, and JCC on, 159-160; Jackson's stand on, 126, 136-137, 157; JCC's theory of territories under, 236; JCC's written views on, 245-247. *See also* Nationalism; Nullification; State rights; Supreme Court

Cooper, Thomas, 81, 101, 103, 106

Crallé, Richard, 154, 227, 234, 255

Crawford, William: Secretary of Treasury, 61-68 *passim;* campaign for presidency, 70, 72, 76-90 *passim;*

Index

Tucker, Beverly, 104n, 209, 216
Turnbull, Robert, 106, 163
Tyler, John, 161, 171, 198: presidency of, 202-204, 217-220, 226; distrusts JCC, 217, 220

Unionist party in S. C., 116, 117, 121, 136-156 *passim*, 163, 165
Upshur, Abel P., 206, 217

Van Buren, Martin, 81, 143, 182, 214, 220, 221: works for Jackson's election, 90, 110, 111; relations with JCC, 103, 105, 114, 122, 124, 142, 162, 172, 178, 189; stand on tariff, 105-106, 121, 204; influence on Jackson, 123-126, 157-158; presidency of, 170, 171, 176, 177, 186-202 *passim;* later candidacy, 205-208, 223, 225, 243
Van Deventer, Christopher, 63, 86n, 142, 179, 180
Verplanck bill, 157-162 *passim*
Virginia and Kentucky Resolutions, 97, 99, 108, 116, 132-133, 139, 140, 146

Waddell, Moses, JCC's brother-in-law, school of, 6, 9
Webster, Daniel, 10, 51, 78, 81, 100, 104, 162, 171, 173, 178, 181, 189, 194, 202, 209, 249: Federalist congressman, 36, 38, 53, 54, 60, 97; debate with Hayne, 121, 126, 137, 139-140; debate with JCC, 159-160; relations with JCC, 200-201, 214, 251-252
Whig party: origin, 162, 169-171; in 1830's, 177-201 *passim;* split under Tyler, 202-204; in 1840's, 221-249 *passim*
White, Hugh L., 122, 170, 171, 186
Williams, David R., 42, 60
Wilmot Proviso, 211, 223-240 *passim,* 249
Wiltse, Charles M., v, 13n, 255, 256
Wirt, William, 81, 147
Wise, Henry A., 81, 217

Yale College, 1, 2, 9-15 *passim,* 23

275